The Causes of the American Revolution

PROBLEMS IN AMERICAN CIVILIZATION

Under the editorial direction of

Edwin C. Rozwenc

Amherst College

The Causes of the American Revolution

Third Edition

Edited and with an introduction by

John C. Wahlke

University of Iowa

D. C. HEATH AND COMPANY

Lexington, Massachusetts Toronto London

Published simultaneously in Canada.

Printed in the United States of America.

International Standard Book Number: 0-669-82685-5

Library of Congress Catalog Card Number: 73-7044

CONTENTS

IV IDEOLOGICAL ASPECTS OF THE REVOLUTIONARY MOVEMENT

V INTERPRETATION OF HISTORICAL REALITY: IDEAS, MOTIVES, INTERESTS

INTRODUCTION

Not so very long ago Americans were taught that the American Revolution came about solely and simply because all colonists hated tyranny and loved freedom; because all colonists resented a foreign government's denying their right to share in governing themselves; and because all colonists, therefore, rising in heroic resistance to the government which oppressed them, determined to make America an independent nation founded on the principles of political liberty and equality. The persistence of such a simple, black-and-white picture of the revolutionary struggle is reflected in the widely held belief that the chief point at issue between colonies and mother country was the rightness or wrongness of the principle that "taxation without representation is tyranny."

Historical research and analyses by scholars of the past two generations, however, have made it impossible to believe quite so surely that the Revolution was no more, and no less, than a conflict produced by verbal disagreements between a people united in the cause of freedom and a regime which refused to accept freedom as the necessary basis of all governments. The reappraisal of the colonial and revolutionary era, begun by such scholars as Charles M. Andrews, George Louis Beer, Herbert Levi Osgood, and others has made it clear that to see selfless devotion of the patriots to political ideals as the sole cause of the Revolution might well be a national tradition, but it is hardly sound history. Significant facts which today seem obvious—for example, the extreme tardiness of the patriot leaders in formulating the demand for independence, or the apparent lack of unity among the colonists concerning what they wanted, why they wanted it, and how they proposed to get it—were long overlooked by the traditional explanations of why the revolutionists fought. Beginning in the 1890s, historians directed their attention more closely to the revolutionary use of the political ideals of freedom and equality, independence and self-government; they carefully considered the influence of economic interests, the accidental conjunctures of men and events, and the personal ambitions and prejudices of revolutionary leaders or members of Parliament; they looked more closely into the everyday attitudes and activities of working men, poor farmers, and other hitherto neglected "lesser folk," as well as the historic actions and pronouncements of historically preeminent figures; and they sought to establish more precisely the actual, as well as the abstract, logical connections between each step in the conflict. As a result, it is generally recognized today that to understand why the Revolution was fought, one must do more than cite at face value the familiar political slogans and catchwords. The historian must consider the actions and the motives of diverse individuals, groups, sections, and classes; and he must be aware of the relationship of the British-American conflict to British imperial problems in general and to larger problems of world affairs. There is no longer any doubt that the causes of the American Revolution were complex and deep-seated.

Despite general agreement that the question, "What caused the American Revolution?" has no simple and easy answer, historians are still far from agreeing about the relative merits of different answers. Now, more than ever, their works present an array of diverse, often contradictory and conflicting interpretations, from which the student of the problem, like other interested citizens, must somehow choose or construct his own answer. The readings in this volume present some of the most cogent of these interpretations, interpretations which not only elucidate the arguments for and against particular hypotheses, but which point out and sharpen the issues involved in the choice among them.

One critical point of comparison in considering the arguments of any author is the causal importance he attributes to revolutionary ideas and ideals. It is possible to classify almost all interpretations into two general categories on the basis of this one point. One group de-emphasizes the differences of political and constitutional ideas between the colonies and England. This group asserts that such conflicts of opinion are simply a by-product of some more basic economic or social factor or maintains that the disagreements, though genuine enough, could readily have been overcome in the absence of other, more serious conflicts. Those holding this general viewpoint say, in effect, that what the colonists said and wrote about the rights of British citizens and the rights of men does not, by itself, tell us why the Revolution came about. On the other hand, there are writers who admit the complexity of causes of the Revolution but insist that colonial ideas about democratic self-government were a direct and important cause—the political ideas of the revolutionists cannot be satisfactorily explained in terms of the revolutionists' material interests nor by some "inner logic" of the events themselves operating independently of colonists' motivating ideals.

Historians' disagreement about the causes of the American Revolution involve much more, however, than a difference in historical philosophy between "materialists" and "idealists." There are crucial disagreements about matters of fact as well as about the interpretations to be put upon the facts; and there are disagreements about the values and standards by which historians should choose and evaluate facts and about the meaning of such terms as "explanation" and "understanding." All these issues are amply illustrated in the readings which follow. The last two readings in this book, by Page Smith and Gordon S. Wood, discuss the trends and issues of historical interpretation from the perspective of historians.

The reader will be much better able to follow and comprehend the arguments there, however, if he first grapples with some of the major components of the problem piece by piece, as it were. The first four sections of the book focus on four major aspects of the problem. But these sections do not merely present four discrete discussions of analytically distinct components of the general question. In certain respects, they parallel the evolution of historical treatment of the Revolution; in other respects, they tend also to deal with different stages in the revolutionary process itself. Reflection upon the interrelationships among the materials presented in the different sections of the book, therefore, will not only illuminate the problems of historiography and historical interpretation. It will also afford insight into the evolutionary and dialectical processes through which the originally vague feelings and stirrings of colonial discontent, seemingly so modest and restricted in scope, developed ultimately into intensely felt, eloquently articulated ideas and violent actions of the utmost historical moment.

The first group of readings deals with what is perhaps the most familiar assault on the traditional, simplistic picture of the revolutionary process, which had been given classic statement in George Bancroft's ten-volume *History of the United States* (Boston, 1834–1874). This is the so-called "economic interpretation," a general name given to a number of related but by no means identical explanations, all sharing one common, central conclusion: that it was the conflicts between colonial and British economic interests—mercantile, industrial, and landed—which led to the Revolutionary War, and that the economic motivations generating those conflicts were the basic driving forces underlying other, more superficial conflicts of political ideas and ideals. The selection by Louis M. Hacker offers the clearest possible statement of the viewpoint:

> *The struggle was not over high-sounding political and constitutional concepts; over the power of taxation or even, in the final analysis, over natural rights. It was over colonial manufacturing, wild lands and furs, sugar, wine, tea, and currency, all of which meant, simply, the survival or collapse of English mercantile capitalism within the imperial-colonial framework of the mercantilist system.*

The "high-sounding political and constitutional concepts" in question are discussed at some length in the third and fourth sections of this volume. The second selection here, by Oliver M. Dickerson, confronts the economic interpretation on a somewhat different plane by questioning the factual correctness of its premises. It is Dickerson's contention that the mercantile system in general, and the Navigation Acts in particular, did not have the deleterious effects on the American colonial economy alleged by Hacker and other economic interpreters. According to analysts of Dickerson's persuasion, the conflicts of economic interest between colonial tradesmen and manufacturers and their British rivals and competitors were by no means as severe as claimed; they could not, therefore, have played the major causal role in the movement toward independence attributed to them by the economic interpretation.

Investigation of such issues led historians to delve deep into the data of economic life in colonial times, to discover and marshall significant new facts about those times, and to produce new insights into the character and course of colonial economic development and its relationship to the course of political events. Despite continuing controversy about its overall validity and continuing doubts about the justifiability of some of its premises, the economic interpretation has unquestionably added an important new dimension to Americans' understanding of their Revolution.

Other historians around the turn of the century, not persuaded that economic interpretations satisfactorily explained why the Revolution came about, but equally concerned to push beyond stereotypical generalizations of the Bancroft sort, were also moved to inspect more closely the details of pre-Revolutionary history. To a number of these writers it seemed that, whatever the facts about economic and related conflict earlier in the colonial period, the decade or two immediately preceding the outbreak of open hostilities was crucial. They contended that the course of events leading from that point to the war itself was not preordained or deterministically dictated by some economic or other underlying force. It was, in fact, shaped by the specific political decisions taken during this period by governments and politicians on both sides of the Atlantic. Some writers placed particular emphasis on what they saw as stupidity, folly, and irresponsibility on the part of George III and his court, who were seen as surmounting the principled opposition of Parliamentary Whigs and forcing decisions which violated rights and interests dear not just to American colonists but to British liberals as well. Others, like Sir Lewis Namier, while disputing the exemplary role imputed to Whig politicians and liberal political principles by this kind of "Whig interpretation of the Revolution," evaluated the role of George III much more kindly and attributed much more free play to idiosyncratic personal whims, ambitions, and passions of the politicians involved. They nonetheless agreed with the "Whig interpreters" in assigning crucial importance to the political decisions of the decade or two before the Declaration of Independence.

The second group of readings in this book deals with the most important of these decisions and addresses the general issue: To what extent was the outbreak of hostilities between colonies and mother country the product of "policy blunders" in British government? To what extent, that is, were events shaped and guided by British failures to predict accurately the colonists' responses to the policy decisions of British government, particularly decisions dealing with problems tangential to or transcending the direct and immediate concerns of American colonists alone, however much Americans might feel their interests threatened by those decisions? More specifically, on what did those crucial political decisions, those alleged "errors" or "blunders" in British policy making, turn? It is the contention of Lawrence Henry Gipson, the first author represented in this section, that the key factor in the sequence of events was the attempt of British policy makers to cope with the world struggle for Empire. Gipson maintains that decisions taken in 1763, following one important round in the imperial wars with France (fought in part on the American continent, remember), inevitably generated irreconcilable conflicts with the American colonists who were called upon to bear the burden of maintaining the British Empire. Bernhard Knollenberg, in the second selection, however, sees decisions in the period 1759–1765, not merely the explicitly imperial decisions of 1763, as crucial. In both accounts, the key actors are British politicians and government officials. The colonists play little part in the British decision-making processes; they enter the picture primarily through reactions to the decisions made for them and about them in Britain.

While Gipson and Knollenberg are by no means agreed about the relative importance of various British policy decisions or in their accounts of the political factors and forces underlying them, they both diverge in similar fashion from the economic interpretations of Hacker and others. Their acounts of the political facts surrounding the workings of the British imperial system in the critical decades just before the Revolution make it clear that key British decisions were by no means simple reflections or reflexes of British economic interests. Significant conflicts of interest among Englishmen, significant contests of political will in which contending British politicians risked their political careers, as well as political controversy between king, Parliament, and political groups in England lay behind the British decisions which came to antagonize many American colonists. All this, however, does not necessarily prove that economic factors were irrelevant or unimportant. Rather, it emphasizes the necessity of examining them in the context of actual political events and ongoing social processes. The readings in this section therefore not only focus the reader's attention on a different period of revolutionary development, chronologically speaking. They also add one more dimension to his perceptions of events.

The third and fourth sections of this volume reflect concerns which are closely related to, but by no means identical with or even directly supportive of, the position of strictly economic interpreters of the causes of the American Revolution. But the selections included here recognize and take into account much more directly the complexities and intricacies of both British and colonial politics, including the fact that political issues, political cleavages, and political alliances varied considerably from one colony to another and from one period to another. Whereas selections in the first two sections dealt primarily with the evolution and elaboration of British policies affecting the colonies and with presumably unified or monolithic colonial reactions to overall British policy, those in the next two sections deal primarily with divisions of interest, opinion, and aim among the American colonists themselves.

Both sections are relevant to another basic general issue on which there is considerable division of opinion, namely, the extent to which the American Revolution was not one integral line of development, but two overlapping and mutually interacting social processes. The thesis that America's was a "dual revolution" was stated early and effectively by Carl Becker, in his important work, *The History of Political Parties in the Province of New York, 1760–1776* (Madison, Wis., 1909, pp. 5, 22):

> *The American Revolution was the result of two general movements; the contest for home-rule and independence, and the democratization of American politics and society. Of these movements, the latter was fundamental; it began before the contest for home-rule, and was not completed until after the achievement of independence. . . . The first [question] was whether essential colonial rights should be maintained; the second was by whom and by what methods they should be maintained. The first was the question of home-rule; the second was the question, if we may so put it, of who should rule at home.*

The first of these two groups of readings (section 3 of this volume) presents three selections examining the role of different social groups in the pre-Revolutionary period, and the character and extent of conflict among them. Carl Becker's brilliant recreation of the period through the eyes of Jeremiah Wynkoop and his father-in-law, Nicholas Van Schoickendinck, describes how issues separating colonists from the mother country often mingled with and cut across issues which divided the colonists themselves. James Truslow Adams argues, in the second selection here, that economic and social-class divisions between American merchants and radicals led to disagreement about goals and tactics in opposition to British colonial policies, with the merchants and more conservative classes allowing the radicals to propagandize and agitate against Britain but not supporting the radicals' growing claims for internal democracy in the colonies. The first selection by Jesse Lemisch emphasizes these divisions even more strongly, stressing the vital importance of the radicalism of the "lower" classes, exemplified here by the merchant seamen, in the activities leading ultimately to insurrection. Both Adams and Lemisch paint a picture of much sharper social-class conflict in pre-Revolutionary America than does Becker. All three accounts, though in varying degrees, resemble the economic interpretation presented earlier in that they identify conflicts of material interest as the dynamic of the movement toward revolution. But their interpretation is in each case somewhat more sociologically complex, in that social-class interest is implicitly recognized to involve more than the simple reflection of an individual's economic position or status. All three selections show how the various classes and sectional groupings in pre-Revolutionary America constituted distinctively different "subcultures." All demonstrate that social conflict among these groups, while intimately bound up with economic conflicts of interest, was not simply identical with the economic-interest cleavages, nor was it just another name for direct opposition between strictly economic interests.

The fourth group of readings deals with the ideological aspects of the "dual revolution" issue and brings us back to fundamental questions about the role of political and constitutional ideas in the processes leading up to the Revolution. The questions here concern the relationship of conflicts between radical proponents of democracy and defenders of a more aristocratic social and political order, on the one hand, to ideological arguments for and against political independence from England, on the other. Clinton Rossiter asserts that the colonists, virtually unanimous in their growing opposition to British rule, manifested a basically conservative "American consensus," eventually and reluctantly accepting political freedom from England as the only effective way to maintain rights long recognized and protected in the colonies. Elisha P. Douglass, however, in the second article of this section, sees, not ideological consensus, but ideological conflict during the same period. The dynamic force, according to his interpretation, is not the conservative desire to preserve long-established, universally accepted political values and ideals, but the persistent demand for recognition of new, more democratic values on the part of new groups in society. Bernard Bailyn, the third author represented here, shares certain views with Douglass and Rossiter and, at the same time, diverges in important respects from each. Agreeing with Rossiter that the revolutionary ideology was thoroughly grounded in eighteenth-century ideas, many of which were widely accepted long before the Revolution, Bailyn differs from him in finding colonial ideals to be essentially dynamic and innovative in their consequences, rather than "conservative" in Rossiter's sense. On the other hand, Bailyn does not support the contention that the Revolution was "democratic" in aim or intentions.

Rossiter, Douglass, and Bailyn all plainly believe that colonial ideas and ideals, whether properly labeled "conservative," "democratic," "radical," or whatever, did play some sort of autonomous part in the revolutionary movement. All three, therefore, conflict sharply with a major premise of the economic interpretation and, to some extent, with implicit assumptions of the social-conflict hypotheses discussed in the preceding group of readings. The concluding selection of the fourth group of readings presents a viewpoint much more congenial to these interpretations. Here, Jesse Lemisch stresses the ideology of the radical and democratic working classes as the true "revolutionary" ideology, emphasizing the ideological differences between major social groups in the colonies and thereby tying ideological aspects of the revolutionary movement much more closely to economic and social class interests than any of the other three authors of this section.

As previously mentioned, the final two readings in this volume provide an overview of the major issues and interpretations found in the historical literature. The selection by Page Smith defends the cogency and accuracy of the explanation of the American Revolution offered by David Ramsay, a contemporary of the Revolution. Smith reviews all the issues presented in this volume and presents Ramsay's views of them. He also offers a summary of the rise and fall of the various schools of thought concerning the causes of the American Revolution from Ramsay's time to the present. The final selection, by Gordon S. Wood, reviews much the same ground, but from a different perspective. In disagreeing at all important points with Ramsay's views (and therefore with Smith's), Wood not only helps clarify and sharpen the points at issue but also reminds us of the importance and the difficulty of distinguishing rhetoric from reality, not in the events of the Revolution alone, but in the works of historians as well.

The major problems presented in this volume, then, are problems of broad historical interpretation: the relative significance of political ideas and economic interests; the interrelationships between American aspirations for political independence and American demands for political and social equality; the relative contributions of different social groups and different types of political leaders at different stages of pre-Revolutionary history; the relationships between British domestic politics and British imperial policy decisions; and the relationship of both of these to domestic political controversies in America and colonial policy-responses to British decisions. To deal with such problems, however, the reader must face a number of essentially factual subsidiary questions upon which there is disagreement at many points.

One such question concerns the nature of British colonial policy after 1763. Did the British government change its policy at that time, thus producing grievances which would not have arisen otherwise, or did it maintain an established mercantilist policy which intensified old grievances? Related to this is the question: To what extent were the colonists themselves aware of specifically economic grievances, and to what extent did they express them? What grievances did the colonists have, if not primarily economic ones?

Another critical group of questions concerns the role of different social groups in the colonies. What grievances and what political ideas did artisans and small farmers have in common with merchants, or frontiersmen with city-dwellers, and where did the interests and ideas of such groups diverge? To what extent did farmers of Virginia, the Carolinas, New England, and elsewhere suffer common ills and express common grievances? To what extent did they take similar actions in similar circumstances? Is it possible to determine, in crucial revolutionary events, which actions were the work of merchants, which the work of workingman radicals, and which the result of their joint efforts?

Yet another set of important questions concerns the precise character, as well as the role, of political ideas and ideals. How closely did the values and goals ultimately cited by rebellious colonists as the cause or the justification of their fight coincide with the values and goals of colonists in more peaceful times, generations earlier? To what extent did the colonists think of themselves as British citizens being denied settled British rights, and to what extent had they, perhaps unwittingly, come to think of themselves as members of some different community, distinct from and now set upon by hostile people in distant (and now, suddenly, foreign) England? To what extent were the incidents and events leading up to Revolution an expression of indigenous radicals' efforts to wrest rights and political power as effectively and forcefully from "establishment" Americans as from aristocratic and royal English oppressors? To what extent did "establishment" Americans share the political goals and ideals of their more fiery radical countrymen.

Only on the basis of his answers to such questions as these will the reader be able to decide whether he thinks the Revolution came about because of the devotion of some or all colonists to political and constitutional ideals, because the economic interests of some or all colonists could be served, in the long run, only by political separation from England, or for still some other reason.

It need hardly be said that the formulation of an intelligent opinion about the problems raised here should yield something much more valuable than mere intellectual exercise. A study of the causes of the American Revolution, since it demands that the function of democratic ideals in the founding of the American nation be examined, necessarily demands further questioning of the function of those same ideals in our own time. An understanding of the relationship of the ideas of 1776 to the economic and social situation of the revolutionary period will contribute to understanding the utility of those ideas in resolving ideological and interest conflicts within the American community today. And an understanding of the relationship of the interests and ideals of 1776 to the constitution of the eighteenth-century British Empire will certainly offer some basis for deciding what should be America's role in the twenty-first-century world community of nations.

I BRITISH MERCANTILISM AND COLONIAL CAPITALISM

Louis M. Hacker

ECONOMIC AND SOCIAL ORIGINS OF THE AMERICAN REVOLUTION

In The Triumph of American Capitalism *(1940), the best known of his many books and articles, Louis M. Hacker set forth an economic interpretation of American history. His chapters on the American Revolution, parts of which are here reprinted, stress the importance of economic interests and interest groups in the events that led to the outbreak of hostilities in April 1775. Professor Hacker taught economics at Columbia University.*

The Pressures on Colonial Mercantile Capitalism

Colonial Commerce. In a functioning imperial economy, the capitalist relationships between mother country and colonies as a rule lead to a colonial unfavorable balance of payments. The colonies buy the goods and services of the mother country and are encouraged to develop those raw materials the home capitalists require. In this they are aided by the investment of the mother country's balances and by new capital. Thus, in the southern colonies, tobacco largely was being produced to furnish returns for the English goods and services the plantation lords required; but, because the exchange left England with a favorable balance, by the 1770s its capitalists had more than £4 million invested in southern planting operations. To meet the charges on this debt, southern planters were compelled constantly to expand their agricultural operations and to engage in the subsidiary activities of land speculation and the fur trade.

The northern colonies were less fortunately placed. The northern colonies directly produced little of those staples necessary to the maintenance of the English economy: the grains, provisions, and work animals of New England, New York, and Pennsylvania could not be permitted to enter England lest they disorganize the home commercial agricultural industry; and the fishing catches of the New England fishing fleets competed with the English fishery industry operating in the North Sea and off the Newfoundland banks. The

From *The Triumph of American Capitalism* by Louis M. Hacker, pp. 145–170. Copyright 1940 by Simon and Schuster, Inc. Reprinted by permission of Columbia University Press.

northern colonies, of course, were a source for lumber, naval stores, furs, whale products, and iron, and these England sorely needed to maintain her independence of European supplies. By bounties, the relaxing of trade restrictions, and the granting of favored positions in the home market, England sought to encourage these industries, partly because it required these staples and partly to divert northern capital from expanding further into shipbuilding, shipping, and manufacturing. But the policy yielded no really successful results. The advance of population into frontier zones cut down the field of operations of the fur trade. The northern merchants found more profitable outlets for their lumber in the West Indian sugar islands and in the Spanish and Portuguese wine islands off the African and European coasts. Although the production of crude iron received a stimulus due to English encouragement, most of the pigs and bars came to be absorbed in the colonies themselves so that the export of iron to England was disappointing; while the production of naval stores, despite a consistent program of bounties launched upon by England as early as 1705, never took hold in the northern colonies and therefore the plan of the Board of Trade to keep northern mercantile capitalism entirely dependent upon England completely failed.

The northern colonies, therefore, produced little for direct export to England to permit them to pay their balances; for balances there were to be paid despite the household manufacturing of textiles and the fabrication of iron goods. They were buying increasing quantities of English drygoods, hardware, notions, and house furnishings, and were thus heavy debtors on visible account (and even on invisible items, although they were using their own services of shipping, commercial exchanges, and the like) in the direct trade. Also—and this is an economic factor of the utmost significance—the northern colonies never, to any appreciable extent, presented important opportunities for English capital investment. . . . The English capital stake was largely in the South: only to a very slight degree was any of it to be found in the North. The result was the imperative necessity for the northern colonies to develop returns in order to obtain specie and bills of exchange with which to balance payments in England.

The most important of these was trade (and the subsidiary industries growing out of trade) with areas outside of England. Northern merchants and shipowners opened up regular markets in Newfoundland and Nova Scotia for their fishing tackle, salt, provisions, and rum. They established a constant and ever-growing commercial intercourse with the wine islands from which they bought their light and fortified wines direct instead of by way of England and to which they sold barrel staves, foodstuffs, and live animals. They sold fish to Spain, Portugal, and Italy. Their ports to a measurable extent during the eighteenth century (and in this way they competed directly with the English shipping fleets plying between England and the southern colonies) acted as entrepôts for the transshipment of southern staples—tobacco, hardwoods and dyewoods, indigo—to England and of rice to southern Europe.

The trade with the West Indian sugar islands—as well as the traffic in Negro slaves and the manufacture of rum, which grew out of it—became the cornerstone of the northern colonies' capitalist economy. Northern merchants, loading their small swift ships with all those necessaries the sugar planters of the West Indies were economically unable to produce—work animals for their mills; lumber for houses and outbuildings; staves, heads, and hoops for barrels; flour and salted provisions for their tables; and low-grade fish for their slaves—made regular runs from Salem, Boston, Bristol, Newport, New York, and Philadelphia originally to the British islands of Barbados, the Leeward Islands, and Jamaica, and then increasingly to the French, Spanish, Dutch, and Danish islands and settlements dotting the Caribbean. Here they acquired in return specie for the payment of their English balances, indigo, cotton, ginger, allspice, and dyewoods for transshipment to England, and, above all, sugar and molasses for conversion into rum in the distilleries of Massachusetts and Rhode Island. It was this wondrous alcoholic beverage that served as the basis of the intercourse between the northern colonies and the African coast; and in return the northern traders picked up ivory, gums, and beeswax and, most important of all, Negro slaves which were again carried to the sugar islands on that famous Middle Passage to furnish the labor supply without which the sugar-plantation economy could not survive.

The freights, commissions, and profits earned as a result of the successful conduct of trading enterprise thus furnished important sources of return through which northern merchant capitalists obtained specie and foreign bills of exchange with which to pay English balances. Shipbuilding with New England and, later, Philadelphia as the leading centers, was another source. Northern ships were sold for use in the intercolonial trade and in the local trade of the West Indies and the wine islands; also ships were frequently sold in England and southern Europe after the completion of voyages. Still another source of return was the colonial fisheries. Northern fishermen, operating in fishing craft and whalers owned by colonial merchant capitalists, fished and hunted the waters off the New England coast and increasingly penetrated northward into the Newfoundland banks.

Apparently, however, despite the complexity of all this activity still other means of obtaining remittances and finding outlets for northern mercantile capitalist accumulations had to be developed. For those already mentioned were not enough with which to pay all the English bills and to absorb all the mounting funds of the Amorys, Faneuils, and Hancocks of Boston, the Whartons, Willings, and Morrises of Philadelphia, the Livingstons and Lows of New York, the Wantons and Lopezes of Newport, and the Browns of Providence. In three illegal forms of enterprise—piracy, smuggling generally, and particularly the illicit sugar and molasses trade with the foreign West Indian islands—northern merchants found opportunities for the necessary expansion.

It is not generally appreciated to what extent piracy—at least up to the end of the seventeenth century—played a significant role in maintaining the mercantile capitalism of the northern colonies. English and colonial pirates, fitted out in the ports of Boston, Newport, New York, and Philadelphia and backed financially by reputable merchants, preyed on the Spanish fleets of the Caribbean and even boldly fared out into the Red Sea and the Indian Ocean to terrorize ships engaged in the East Indies trade; and with their ships heavily laden with plate, drygoods, and spices, they put back into colonial ports where they sold their loot and divided their profits with the merchants who had financed them. It is impossible, of course, to estimate the size of this traffic; that it was great every evidence indicates. Curtis P. Nettels, in his outstanding monograph *The Money Supply of the American Colonies Before 1720,* cites reports that single pirate ships frequently brought in cargoes valued at between £50,000 and £200,000; that New York province alone obtained £100,000 in treasure yearly from the illicit traffic; and that the greater supply of specie in the colonies before 1700 than after (after that date England began its successful war of extermination against the seafaring marauders) undoubtedly was due to the open support of piratical expeditions and the gains obtained thereby by some of the wisest mercantile heads in the northern towns.

Smuggling also contributed its share to swell the remittances the northern merchants so badly needed. Smuggling traffic could be carried on in a number of directions. In the first place, there was the illegal direct intercourse between the colonies and European countries in the expanding list of "enumerated" articles. And in the second place, ships on the homebound voyages from Europe or from the West Indies brought large supplies of drygoods, silk, cocoa, and brandies into the American colonies without having declared them at English ports and paid the duties. Most important of all, of course, was the trade with the foreign West Indian sugar islands which was rendered illegal, after 1733, as a result of the imposition by the Molasses Act of prohibitive duties on the importation into the colonies of foreign sugar, molasses, and rum. It is imperative that something be said of the productive system and the social and economic relations prevailing in the sugar islands, for just as the western lands constituted the Achilles heel of southern planter capitalism so the trade with the sugar islands—and notably that with the foreign islands—was the highly vulnerable point of northern mercantile capitalism. When England, beginning with 1763, struck at these two vital and exposed centers, it immediately threatened the very existence of free colonial enterprise.

The West Indian Trade. By the opening of the second third of the eighteenth century, the English sugar planters of the West Indies were beginning to find themselves hard pressed in the great colonial sugar market, by the steadily growing competition of the foreign sugar planters in the islands and settlements owned by the French, Spanish, Dutch, and Danes. The British sugar planters occupied a unique position in the imperial-colonial sphere. Favored from the very beginning by the tender solicitude of English imperial officialdom, supported in all their extravagant demands for protection by the great English merchant-capitalist interest allied with and dependent upon them, in time represented in Parliament itself by what today we would call a sugar bloc, the plantation lords of Barbados, the Leeward Islands, and Jamaica exerted an influence on British colonial policy that, in the words of Professor Andrews, "was probably greater than even that of politics, war, and religion." The reasons for this are not difficult to find. Sugar, even more than tobacco, was the great oversea staple of the eighteenth-century world. It was a household necessary, it had a constant and growing market everywhere in western Europe, it was the basis for the flourishing of a ramified English commercial industry made up of carriers, commission men, factors, financiers, processors, and distributors. Also, sugar was converted into molasses which in turn was distilled into rum; and it was rum that was the very heart of the unholy slave traffic and the unsavory Indian trade. Small wonder, therefore, that sugar cultivation attracted at once the concentrated attention of English mercantile capitalism: and by the time Adam Smith was writing English capitalism had succeeded in building up in the islands plantations with a capital worth of fully £60 million—a gigantic sum even in our modern imperialist age. Of this amount at least half continued to remain the stake of home English investors in long-term (land titles and mortgages) and short-term investments. When it is recalled that in the whole of the North American continental colonies the English capitalist stake at most was only one sixth as great, the reason for the favoring of the sugar colonies as against the northern commercial colonies, after 1763, is revealed in a single illuminating flash.

By the second third of the eighteenth century it was everywhere being admitted that the English sugar-planting economy was being uneconomically operated. Plantations were large and were worked by inefficient slave labor and primitive methods. Affairs of business were in the hands of paid clerks. No attention was paid to the restoration of the soil's fertility. The single crop was planted year in and year out without thought to the state of the market and mounting operating costs. The whole system was stripped of its productive capital to sustain in idleness and luxury an absentee owning class. It was the dream of every British West Indian to flee from his tropical estate and settle in England, where he could buy a country property and a seat in Parliament and play the English country gentleman. This was generally realized: by the early 1770s more than seventy plantation lords sat for country boroughs in the English Parliament and were therefore in a position to fight savagely all efforts at survival on the part of northern colonial mercantile capitalism.

This was all very well as long as nothing appeared to endanger the sugar monopoly of the English planters. But with the third decade of the eighteenth century, following the establishment of peace, such rivals appeared in the shape of foreign planters, notably the French; and the British planting interest was being threatened. The foreign planters clearly were at an advantage: their lands were newer and therefore more productive; ownership operation, on the basis of small holdings, was the rule, with therefore more efficient methods and lower operating and capital costs; they practiced diversification, and the coffee crop of some of the islands often exceeded the sugar crop. These factors, growing out of their superior economy, permitted the French and other foreign sugar planters to undersell the British. There were other reasons, implicit in the English mercantilist scheme, which strengthened further their command of the market: British sugar was compelled to pay a heavy export tax (4.5 percent) at the island ports; also, it was an "enumerated" commodity and could be sold only to England or its colonies; on the other hand, foreign sugar was free of imposts and enjoyed lower marketing costs because it reached oversea markets directly.

All this Englishmen and colonials saw. Adam Smith referred to the "superiority" of the French planters; while John Dickinson spoke of the British in the following slurring terms: "By a very singular disposition of affairs, the colonies of an absolute monarchy [France] are settled on a republican principle; while those of a kingdom in many respects resembling a commonwealth [England] are cantoned out among a few lords vested with despotic power over myriads of vassals and supported in the pomp of Baggas by their slavery."

In short, foreign sugar and molasses could be had for 25 to 40 percent cheaper: it is not hard to see, therefore, why northern colonial ship captains bought more and more of their sugar at the foreign islands. They found it possible also to develop new markets here for their flour, provisions, lumber, work animals, and fish, thus obtaining another source from which specie and bills of exchange could be derived. So great had this traffic become by the 1720s that the British planter interest took alarm and began to appeal to Parliament for succor. In 1733 Parliament yielded to pressure and passed the Molasses Act, which sought to outlaw the colonial–foreign island trade by placing prohibitive import duties on sugar, molasses, and rum. But the act did not have the desired effect because it could not be adequately enforced: the British customs machinery in the colonies was weak and venal and the naval patrols that could be allocated to this duty were inadequate because England, from 1740, engaged in foreign wars almost continuously for twenty years. Within these twenty years the illicit intercourse with the foreign West Indies took on such great proportions that it virtually became the foundation of northern colonial mercantile capitalism. By the late 1750s, when the traffic was at its height, at least 11,500 hogsheads of molasses reached Rhode Island annually from the foreign islands, as against 2500 from the British; in Massachusetts the ratio was 14,500 to 500. In Massachusetts alone there were some sixty-three distilleries by 1750 and perhaps half that number existed in Rhode Island: the manufacture of rum undoubtedly was the most important single industrial enterprise existing in New England in the second quarter of the eighteenth century. Rum was a magical as well as a heady distillation: its fluid stream reached far Guinea, distant Newfoundland, remote Indian trading posts; and it joined slaves, gold-dust, the mackerel and cod, and peltries with the fortunes of the New England trading enterprisers.

Peter Faneuil, regular church attendant, kindly, charitably disposed bachelor, was one of the greatest of these. He traded all over the world, paying English duties on his cargoes when he had to, avoiding them when he could. He was interested, of course, in rum and slaves. The distinguished historian of New England, Weeden, speaks in the following bitter terms of one of Faneuil's ships, the *Jolly Bachelor:* "Did Peter slap his fair round belly and chuckle when he named the snow *Jolly Bachelor?*—or was it the sad irony of fate that the craft deliberately destined to be packed with human pains and to echo with human groans should in its very name bear the fantastic image of the luxury-loving chief owner? If these be the sources of profit and property, where is the liberty of Faneuil Hall, where the charity of good Peter's alms?"

It is not to be wondered, therefore, that British planters kept up a constant clamor for the enforcement of the laws and the total stoppage of the foreign island trade. In this they were joined by the merchants and manufacturers whose fortunes were linked with theirs, and the bankers and *rentiers* who saw their great capital investment in the British islands threatened with destruction unless the British West Indians once more obtained a monopoly of the production of sugar and molasses. The northern colonial merchant capitalists were the foes of British prosperity. The very reasonable exposition of the situation coming from Rhode Island's governor attracted no sympathy; apparently, it was to be the British West Indies or the northern colonies, and the stake involved in the former, as far as England was concerned, was far, far greater.

Wrote Governor Stephen Hopkins to England:

> *By the best computation I have seen, the quantity of flour made in these colonies yearly is such, that after all the English inhabitants, as well of the continent as of the islands, are fully supplied, with as much as they can consume with the year, there remains a surplusage of at least one hundred thousand barrels. The quantity of beef and pork remaining after the English are in like manner supplied is very large. The fish, not fit for the European market, and the lumber produced in the northern colonies, so much exceed the market found for them in the English West Indies, that a vast surplusage remains that cannot be used. . . . From the money and goods produced by the sale of the surplusages, with many others of less consequence, sold by one means or other to the Spaniards, French, and Dutch in America, the merchants of those northern colonies are principally enabled to make their remittances to the mother country for the British manufactures consumed in them. . . .*
>
> *Supposing this intercourse of the colonies with the Spanish, French, and Dutch entirely stopped, the persons concerned in producing the surplusages will of course change the manner of their industry, and improvement and, compelled by necessity, must set about making those things they cannot live without, and now rendered unable to purchase from their mother country [i.e., manufactures].*

When, during the Seven Years' War, the colonial "Smuggling Interest" extended the bounds of its activities and openly set about supplying the French enemy of the mother country with provisions, lumber, drygoods, and the like, British sugar planters in Parliament, confronted by bankruptcy, found ready allies in outraged patriotic statesmen. Then it was that Pitt, deeply angered by knowledge of the open sale by colonial officials of commissions for flags of truce and the winking at the whole illegal practice by vice-admiralty courts, bitterly wrote to America that it was "an illegal and most pernicious trade . . . by which the enemy is, to the greatest reproach and detriment of government, supplied with provisions and other necessaries, whereby they are principally, if not alone, enabled to sustain and protract this long and expensive war." The process of repression began in 1760 with the stricter enforcement of the Acts of Trade and

Navigation; from then on, particularly after the last imperial rival, France, had been disposed of and the country at last was at peace, the screws came to be applied tighter and tighter. Soon, northern merchant capitalists, aware that every avenue of continued activity was being blocked to them, moved into the colonial revolutionary host.

The Control of the Colonial Currency. At still another point the mercantile system brought an unendurable pressure: this was in its control of the colonial currency. The colonies, it has been pointed out, found themselves constantly in a debtor status within the imperial colonial relations; and their plight was accentuated by the insistence upon the payment of colonial balances in specie and the absence of easy credit facilities. It has also been indicated how illegal activities—piracy, smuggling, trade with the foreign sugar islands—were compulsory precisely because of these unrelaxing pressures. The heavy burden of debts, therefore, the paucity of specie, and the absence of commercial banking made all the colonies steadily preoccupy themselves with the money question. Efforts to debase the currency, on the part of the colonies and, contrariwise, efforts to maintain it at a high value, on the part of England, were symptomatic of the disharmony that existed within the mercantile framework. When, in 1764, all the devices at the service of the Board of Trade having failed, Parliament passed its act (the so-called Currency Act) outlawing the use of legal-tender paper money in all the colonies, it was apparent that the crisis had been reached: whether it meant universal breakdown for the colonial economic life or not, England was going to insist that debts be paid in pounds sterling in order to protect English mercantile capitalism.

The colonies resorted to innumerable means to expand their available money supply. They employed commodity money, the assemblies fixing the value; but Parliament warned the colonists that they could not impair contracts by fixing rates for commodities contrary to those stipulated in agreements. They tried to mint their own money; but in 1684 colonial mints were forbidden. They sought to place embargoes on the exportation of coin; but beginning with 1697 the Privy Council regularly disallowed such laws. They tried, by statute, to raise the legal value of foreign coins in circulation, particularly the Spanish pieces of eight; such acts in Maryland and Virginia (and in Barbados and Jamaica) were disallowed. And when, as a result, the tobacco and sugar colonies were drained entirely of coin, in 1704 Parliament proceeded to fix a uniform value for pieces of eight in all the plantations and in 1708 prescribed prison sentences for those failing to observe the regulations.

Beginning as early as 1690, in Massachusetts, the colonies turned to the emission of paper money. This currency started out by being short-term bills of credit issued in anticipation of taxes (and therefore retirable at fixed dates after the taxes had been collected) and to be employed only for public purposes. The enactments specifically declared that the bills were not to be held as lawfully current money and could be submitted only in payment of public obligations. Within the first third of the eighteenth century, all of New England, as well as New York, New Jersey, the two Carolinas, Pennsylvania, and Maryland had emitted such bills. It was an inevitable corollary that the bills of credit next be declared legal tender not only for public but for all private transactions: the intention was a sorely needed currency expansion, to be pursued by the road of a paper inflation. The steps by which the various colonies sought to attain this end may be briefly indicated. Some tried to issue bills based not only on tax anticipations but on private land securities (utilizing the agency of public and private mortgage banks). Some pushed the dates of collection of taxes on which the bills were based so far ahead that the issues virtually became permanent paper currency. Some failed to provide adequate taxes from which bills were to be redeemed. And some colonies openly embarked on a course of repudiation, merely reissuing bills when the dates set for cancellation had arrived. Also, steps were taken to compel the acceptance of these bills as legal tender by fixing penalties to be imposed on those individuals refusing to honor them in private transactions.

The establishment of so-called public banks, which really were agencies for the issuance of notes against the security of land mortgages, was particularly common. The first such provincial institution was set up in South Carolina, and before 1750 every colony except Georgia had followed its example. Massachusetts went a step further when it permitted a group of private individuals to organize a "Land and Manufactures Bank" in 1740. This society, capitalized at £150,000, was to accept land as security for its stock and against this real estate it was to print notes to be used for lending purposes. Stockholders were to pay 3 percent interest for the privilege of putting up their land as security, to be paid either in bills of the company or in nonperishable raw materials or rough manufactures (hence the use of the term "manufactures" in the title); also, every year 5 percent of the principle of the subscription was to be amortized in the same way. Loans, too, could be paid off in bills or in the same commodities. The purpose, here, obviously, was the expansion of credit through the utilization of nonperishable commodities as a base for currency issue; and within the single year of its operation the bank succeeded in lending out and therefore issuing notes to the extent of £40,000. But Parliament insisted upon regarding the bank as a dangerous speculative enterprise and descended on it at once; it extended to it the terms of the Bubble Act of 1720 and the bank was outlawed with the ensuing ruin of many if its backers, the father of Samuel Adams among them.

A notion of the mounting size of the paper currency in circulation may be gained from the experiences of Massachusetts. When this province emitted its first bills in 1690, it was ordered that the issues should not exceed £40,000; by 1750, however, some £4,630,000 in bills had been released, of which fully half still remained outstanding. Depreciation was inevitable. In Massachusetts the value of sterling to paper money reached a maximum ratio of 11 to 1; in Connecticut it was 8 to 1; in New Hampshire it got to 24 to 1, and by 1771 sterling had vanished altogether; in Rhode Island it was 26 to 1; in North Carolina it was 10 to 1; in South Carolina it was 7 to 1. Only in New York and Pennsylvania was there some effort made to check the downward career of the bills, the depreciation here never reaching more than 25 percent.

It was the steadfast English policy to maintain a sound (that is to say, a contracted) currency in the colonies; and provincial acts were closely scrutinized from this point of view. Acts were disallowed and instructions issued, as affecting the bills of credit, therefore, on the basis of the following general principles: that the amount of bills to be issued was to be limited to the minimum requirements necessary for the legitimate needs of the colonies; that there be created adequate provisions for refunding; that the term of issues be fixed and no reissues be permitted; and that the bills could not be made legal tender for the payment of private debts. Finally, when these methods seemed to be without avail, Parliament intervened. It has already been pointed out with what swiftness Parliament acted in the case of the Massachusetts land bank. A decade later, in 1751, an act was passed forbidding the New England colonies to make any further issues of legal-tender bills of credit or bank notes; the only exceptions permitted were in the cases of issues to cover current expenses and to finance war costs. And in 1764 the Currency Act extended the prohibition to include all the colonies, even rescinding the exception in the case of military financing; further, provision was to be made for the retirement of all outstanding bills. The currency immediately began to contract until by 1774 there was not much more than £2.4 million in the colonies available for exchange and for financing the credit operations of colonial enterprise. John Dickinson was scarcely exaggerating the plight of colonial mercantile capitalism when in 1765 he wrote:

> *Trade is decaying and all credit is expiring. Money is becoming so extremely scarce that reputable freeholders find it impossible to pay debts which are trifling in comparison to their estates. If creditors sue, and take out executions, the lands and personal estates, as the sale must be for ready money, are sold for a small part of what they were worth when the debts were contracted. The debtors are ruined. The creditors get back but part of their debt and that ruins them. Thus the consumers break the shopkeepers; they break the merchants; and the shock must be felt as far as London.*

The Revolutionary Crisis

England Tightens the Screws. Such was the pattern of imperial-colonial relations which makes the events of 1763–1775 intelligible. Not human stupidity, not dreams of new splendor for the empire, not a growing dissimilarity of psychological attitudes, but economic breakdown in the mercantile system: the inability of both English mercantile capitalism and colonial mercantile and planter capitalism to operate within a contracting sphere in which clashes of interest were becoming sharper and sharper: this was the basic reason for the onset of crisis and the outbreak of revolutionary struggle. The mother country had bound the colonies to itself in an economic vassalage: opportunities for colonial enterprise were possible only in commercial agriculture (supported by land speculation) and in trade. But when the expanding commercial activities of northern merchant capitalists came into conflict with the great capitalist interest of British West Indian sugar and the related merchant and banking groups dependent upon it; when the southern tobacco and rice planters, in their role of land speculators, collided with English land speculators and the mighty fur interest; and when the colonial need to move into manufacturing and to develop adequate credit facilities for its growing enterprises threatened the very existence of English mercantile capitalism in all its ramifications: then repression, coercion, even the violence of economic extinction (as in the case of the Boston Port Bill) had to follow. There could be no accommodation possible when English statesmen were compelled to choose between supporting English mercantile capitalism and supporting colonial mercantile and planter capitalism.

As Curtis P. Nettels has so justly insisted, American scholars for more than a generation have been led astray by George Louis Beer's erroneous interpretation of the motives that prompted Pitt in 1763 to demand Canada instead of the sugar islands, Guadeloupe and Martinique, from vanquished France. The Beer argument runs as follows.

Pitt had great visions of empire; this dream and the imperial policies that stemmed from it prepared the way for conflict between colonies and mother country. For a mighty western empire, based as yet on a wilderness, demanded the formulation of a wise program with regard to the Indian problem—hence the shutting off of the lands beyond the crest of the Alleghenies to further settlement and the checks placed on the exploitation of the Indians by colonial traders. It demanded a system of defense—hence the dispatching of a British army to the colonies and provisions for its quartering and maintenance. It demanded a revenue—hence all those methods used by a hard-pressed home government to develop new sources of financing. Thus the chain of circumstances was complete; it had to snap at its weakest link—the raising of funds through tax measures among a liberty-loving and individualistic colonial people which too long had been permitted to go its own way. So Mr. Beer, and after him virtually every American colonial scholar.

The events of 1763–1775 can have no meaning unless we understand that the character of English imperial policy never really changed: that Pitt and his successors at Whitehall were following exactly the same line that Cromwell had laid down more than a century before. The purpose of their general program was to protect the English capitalist interests which now were being jeopardized as a result of the intensification of colonial capitalist competition, and

English statesmen yielded quickly when no fundamental principle was at stake but became insistent only when one was being threatened. If in the raising of a colonial revenue lay the heart of the difficulty, how are we to account for the quick repeal of the Stamp Tax and the Townshend Acts and the lowering of the molasses duty? And, on the other hand, how are we to account for the tightening of enforcement of the Acts of Trade and Navigation at a dozen and one different points, the passage of the Currency Act, the placing of iron on the "enumerated" list, English seizure of control of the wine trade, and the attempt to give the East India Company a monopoly over the colonial tea business? The struggle was not over high-sounding political and constitutional concepts: over the power of taxation or even, in the final analysis, over natural rights. It was over colonial manufacturing, wild lands and furs, sugar, wine, tea, and currency, all of which meant, simply, the survival or collapse of English mercantile capitalism within the imperial-colonial framework of the mercantilist system.

The Acts of Trade Rigorously Enforced. Even before Pitt gave up the French sugar islands in 1763 because of the insistence of the British sugar interest in Parliament, he had already moved to protect the same monopoly group through his orders to the navy to stamp out colonial smugglers operating in the illicit foreign West Indian trade. The colonial courts were directed to issue and recognize the doubtfully legal writs of assistance (general search warrants), as early as 1761. Two years later, the peacetime navy was converted into a patrol fleet with powers of search even on the high seas. In the same year, absentee officials in the customs service were ordered to their colonial posts. A vice-admiralty court was set up for all America in 1764 and the number of local admiralty courts (sitting without juries) was increased. In 1768 a new board of five customs commissioners, resident in America, was created. Statutes, orders, instructions—every conceivable weapon was employed to break up a traffic and therefore to weaken a group so dangerous to English capitalist interests. Spying was encouraged by offers to share with informers the sequestered cargoes. Customs officials were protected from damage suits for unwarranted seizures when they were declared nonliable personally and when the burden of proof was placed on the owners of vessels and goods. The stricter registration and inspection of vessels were ordered. To protect informers and make possible the easier obtaining of verdicts, it was provided that suits for the seizure of cargoes might be tried directly in the vice-admiralty court and that revenue cases might be heard in the admiralty instead of the local courts. And further to free the courts from local pressure, the payment of the judges' salaries was to be made out of customs revenues.

The revenue acts of 1764 and later were used as a screen to conceal the work of compressing the economy of colonial mercantile capitalism within even narrower limits and reducing it to an even more dependent status. The Act of 1764 and the Stamp Act of 1765 called for the payment of duties and taxes in specie, thus further draining the colonies of currency and contracting the credit base. To divert colonial capital into raw materials, the first measure increased the bounties paid for the colonial production of hemp and flax, placed high duties on the colonial importation of foreign indigo, and removed the English import duties on colonial whale fins. To cripple the trade with the foreign West Indies a high duty was fixed on refined sugar and the importation of foreign rum was forbidden altogether. Lumber was put on the "enumerated" list. To give English manufacturers a firmer grip on their raw materials, hides and skins (needed for the boot and shoe industry), pig and bar iron (needed in the wrought-iron industry), and potash and pearl ashes (used for bleaching cloth and soapmaking) were placed on the "enumerated" list. To maintain the English monopoly of the colonial finished-goods market in 1764 certain kinds of French and oriental drygoods were taxed for the first time at the point of entry; in 1765, the importation of foreign silk stockings, gloves, and mitts was altogether forbidden; also the drawbacks of duties paid on foreign goods landed in England and reexported to the colonies were rescinded. To extend the market of English merchants in Europe, in 1766 Parliament ordered that all remaining "nonenumerated" articles (largely flour, provisions, and fish) bound for European ports north of Cape Finisterre be landed first in England. And to weaken further colonial commercial activity, in 1764 high duties were placed on wines from the wine islands and wine, fruits, and oil from Spain and Portugal brought directly to America (in American ships, as a rule), while such articles brought over from England were to pay only nominal duties.

As has been said, the revenue features of these acts were quickly abandoned; the Stamp Act was repealed; and in 1770, three years after their passage, the Townshend duties on paper, paint, and glass were lifted. Only the slight tax on tea remained and even this was lightened in 1773 when the new Tea Act provided for a full drawback of English import duties on British tea shipped to the American colonies.

But it was exactly this new Tea Act which clearly revealed the intention of London: that not only was the economic vassalage of the American colonies to be continued but the interest of colonial enterprisers was to be subordinated to every British capitalist group that could gain the ear of Parliament. For, to save the East India Company from collapse, that influential organization was to be permitted to ship in its own vessels and dispose of, through its own merchandising agencies, a surplus stock of 17 million pounds of tea in America, and in this way drive out of business those Americans who carried, imported, and sold into retail channels British tea (and indeed, foreign tea, for the British tea could be sold cheaper even than the smuggled Holland article).

The merchants all over America were not slow to read the correct significance of this measure. Their spokesmen sounded the alarm. As Arthur M. Schlesinger has put it, pamphleteers set out to show "that the present project of the East India Company was the entering wedge for larger and more ambitious undertakings calculated to undermine the colonial mercantile world. Their opinion was based on the fact that, in addition to the article of tea, the East India Company imported into England vast quantities of silks, calicos and other fabrics, spices, drugs, and chinaware, all commodities of staple demand, and on their fear that the success of the present venture would result in an extension of the same principle to the sale of the other articles." The result would be, as a Philadelphia pamphleteer signing himself "A Mechanic" warned:

> *They will send their own factors and creatures, establish houses among us, ship us all other East India goods; and in order to full freight their ships, take in other kind of goods at under freight, or (more probably) ship them on their own accounts to their own factors, and undersell our merchants, till they monopolize the whole trade. Thus our merchants are ruined, ship building ceases. They will then sell goods at any exorbitant price. Our artificers will be unemployed, and every tradesman will groan under dire oppression.*

The Closing Off of the West. The southern landlords did not escape. The Proclamation Line of 1763, for the purpose of setting up temporary governments in the far western lands wrested from France after the Seven Years' War, in effect shut off the whole area beyond the crest of the Appalachians to colonial fur traders and dealers. By taking control of the region out of the hands of the colonial governors, putting it in charge of imperial agents, and ordering the abandonment of the settlements already planted, the British looked forward to the maintenance of a great Indian reservation in which the fur trade—in the interests of British concessionaires—would continue to flourish. A few years later these rigorous regulations were relaxed somewhat. But the designs of English land speculators on the area, the prohibition of free land grants, the ordering of land sales at auctions only, and the imposition of high quitrents hardly improved matters.

By 1774 the final English land policy emerged: it meant no less than the complete exclusion of colonial capital from the newly gained western domain. In the words of Professor Nettels, this program

> *closed to [colonial] speculators and settlers the territories north of the Ohio and south of Virginia, it opened only a small tract in western Virginia, it subjected all ungranted lands in the east to rigorous and hampering conditions of purchase and it deprived the landed colonies of their claims to the interior. Even the Vandalia speculators had not gained approval for their project, and despite the powerful forces making for westward expansion in Virginia that colony was denied independent access to the West. The restrictive policy applied to the thirteen colonies did not mean, however, that British investors and speculators were being Ignored. After 1763 the crown conferred numerous large tracts upon merchants, army officers, and wealthy landowners (all residents of Britain), such tracts being located in Canada, Nova Scotia, Florida, and Prince Edward Island—regions accessible to British trade and not likely to produce commodities that would compete with the products of industries in which British investors had a large stake. By opening these areas Britain created speculative opportunities for her own investors while opposing the schemes of colonial promoters to develop the trans-Allegheny West.*

The fur trade was similarly monopolized in the interest of British capital. The English conquest of Canada had resulted in the ousting of French merchants at Montreal, who controlled this lucrative traffic in the North, and their replacement by the agents of British companies. By the Quebec Act of 1774, with an eye to diverting the movement of western peltries from Philadelphia and New York to Montreal, the British provided for the regulation of traders by the governor of the province of Quebec. The intention was simple: colonial dealers in furs were to be driven out of the area north of the Ohio just as colonial land speculators (often the same persons) were to be barred from exploiting the wild lands of the West. By such restrictive and arbitrary acts the southern large planters were lost to the English cause. Their situation, already made perilous by the manipulation of the tobacco market in England and the passage of the Currency Act of 1764, was now hopeless.

Thus, colonial capitalists—whether planters, land speculators, fur dealers, or merchants—were converted from contented and loyal subjects into rebellious enemies of the crown. Tea was destroyed in Boston harbor, turned back unloaded from New York and Philadelphia, and landed but not sold in Charleston. In 1774 the First Continental Congress, to which came delegates from all the colonies, met and wrote the Continental Association, an embargo agreement, which was so successfully enforced that imports from England virtually disappeared in 1775.

The Rising of the Lower Middle Classes. The discontents of planters and merchants were not enough, in themselves, to hasten the releasing process. To be successful, assistance was required from the more numerous lower middle-class small farmers, traders, shopkeepers, artisans, and mechanics, and the working-class seamen, fishermen, and laborers. This was not difficult: for the material well-being of the lower classes was tied to the successful enterprising of the upper.

The colonies had enjoyed a period of unprecedented prosperity during the years of the war with France. The expanding market in the West Indies, the great expenditures of the British quartermasters, the illegal and contraband trade with the enemy forces—all these had furnished steady employment for workers on the fleets and in the shipyards and ports as well as lucrative outlets for the produce of small farmers. But with the end of the war and the passage of the restrictive legislation of 1763 and after, depression had set in to last until 1770. Stringency and bankruptcy everywhere confronted the merchants and big farmers. At the same time, seamen and laborers were thrown out of work; small tradesmen were compelled to close their shops; and small farmers faced ruin because of their expanded acreage, a diminished market, and heavy fixed charges made particularly onerous as a result of currency contraction. Into the bargain, escape into the frontier zones—always the last refuge of the dispossessed—was shut off as a result of the Proclamation of 1763 and the land policy of 1774. The lower middle classes and workers of the towns in almost all the colonies, beginning in 1765, organized themselves into secret societies called the "Sons of Liberty" and demonstrated and moved against the colonial agents of the crown. In these acts they were encouraged by the merchants and landlords.

It would be a mistake to assume, however, that the lower middle-class and working-class groups operated only at the behest of the colonial merchant capitalists. Under the direction of their own leaders, of whom Samuel Adams of Massachusetts was the outstanding—although some of the leaders came from the merchant class, too (Christopher Gadsden of South Carolina, John Lamb of New York, Stephen Hopkins of Rhode Island)—they perfected a powerful revolutionary weapon they sought to wield in their own interest. In 1772, at first in Massachusetts and then in all the other colonies, there began to appear the Committees of Correspondence: these conspiratorial clubs kept in constant touch with one another, intimidated royal officials and colonial placemen, and with all the devices of terror and violence on the one hand and popular appeal on the other crushed opposition and added to and solidified their ranks. They were the ones who moved against the Tea Act, who were instrumental in summoning the First Continental Congress, and who saw that the agreed-on boycott of English goods was enforced. In 1775, beginning to call themselves Committees of Safety, they mobilized the people for defense and carried on a systematic, vindicative, and successful civil war against those who remained loyal to the crown.

In effect, the committees were undermining the authority of the crown in the colonies and setting up, step by step, first in the localities and then in the provinces, revolutionary extralegal governments. The old state was disintegrating; a new revolutionary one was replacing it.

These clubs, too, were beginning to articulate those demands which later gave the lower middle classes and workers their basis for participating in the Revolution. The merchants and landlords regarded the methods of the radicals with misgivings and dread; but they dared not interfere lest, in alienating the underprivileged farmers, tradesmen, and laborers, they lose that mass support upon which their own destiny so completely was dependent.

The lower classes began to look upon the Revolution as the instrument for attaining their *own* freedom. In the *political* sphere, they wanted release from the civil disabilities of almost universal disfranchisement, unequal legislative representation for the newer areas, and an absence of local government. In colonial America, only men of sizable properties could vote and hold office; indeed, before the Revolution, the proportion of potential voters varied from one sixth to one fiftieth of the male population in the different colonies. In the *economic* sphere, the constricting hand of monopoly everywhere was to be found. On the *land,* the legal institutions of entail and primogeniture checked opportunity for younger sons. Engrossing landlords and land speculators (whether they were the crown, the proprieties, absentee owners, or the New England "common" land proprietors) prevented the settlement and improvement of small properties. In the South, the tidewater lords would not erect warehouses to encourage tobacco cultivation among the farmers of the upcountry. And in New York, inadequate boundary surveys furnished the big manor lords with an easy instrument to oppress their smaller neighbors. Everywhere, the threat of Indian risings, because a wild frontier was in the interests of the fur trade and the maintenance of land values in the settled regions, filled the days and nights of pioneers with dread.

In the *towns,* newcomers, seeking to become small tradesmen and mechanics and artisans, had been compelled to struggle against the early and established shopkeepers and craftsmen. For the old artisans and shopkeepers, not unmindful of the special positions of their fellow craftsmen in England whose privileges were protected by the livery companies and guilds, had sought to introduce guild regulations in America. In Philadelphia, Newport, and Boston, early in the eighteenth century, such enabling statutes had been passed by city councils: but they had been unsuccessful. The guild system did not take root in America. But that did not prevent the older craftsmen and shopkeepers from burdening with disabilities the later arrivals.

In all the chartered urban communities, the privilege of obtaining the "freedom of the town"—which meant the right to engage in free enterprise, whether as tradesman or artificer—was severely limited. The devices were many: sometimes being the payment of high fees, sometimes the posting of a large bond, sometimes the possession of a property qualification. There were other oppressions from which the lower middle classes suffered. Peddlers were submitted to close regulation and forced to pay sizable license fees. It was impossible to maintain city markets, for long, because small merchants here tended to compete successfully with the big ones. In New England, a small company of chandlers had got the whole whaling industry in its grip and not only choked off the competition of the lesser manufacturers but fixed the prices for the basic raw material.

Men of little property were weighed down by debts and oppressed by an inadequate currency; they were forced to support, in many of the colonies, an established church; and they were at the mercy of arbitrary executive and judicial authority. On many sides, too, they saw looming larger and larger the threat of a slave economy to the free institutions of small properties and independent craftsmen. Such were the persons who constituted the left, or radical, wing of the colonial revolutionary host.

From 1774 until the creation of new governments in the American states these radicals were in control everywhere. Joining hands across the boundaries of the provinces, they effected united action. They set up extralegal provincial congresses to supersede the assemblies; they boycotted the English military in Massachusetts when it sent out a call for mechanics; and they began secretly to form popular militias and to store up military equipment.

Upon these maneuvers the big landlords and merchants looked with alarm. Gouverneur Morris, later to become one of the patriots of the right, thus wrote to John Penn on May 20, 1774, of a New York meeting:

> *Yesterday I was present at a grand division of the city, and there . . . my fellow citizens . . . fairly contended the future forms of our government, whether it should be founded upon aristocratic or democratic principles. I stood in the balcony, and on my right were ranged all the people of property, with some few poor dependents, and on the other all the tradesmen. . . . The spirit of the English Constitution has yet a little influence left, and but a little. The remains of it, however, will give the wealthy people a superiority this time, but the mob begin to think*

and to reason. Poor reptiles! It is with them a vernal morning; they are struggling to cast off their winter's slough, they bask in the sunshine, and ere noon they will bite, depend upon it. The gentry begin to fear this. Their committee will be appointed, they will deceive the people, and again forfeit a share of their confidence. And if these instances of what with one side is policy, and with the other perfidy, shall continue to increase, and become more frequent, farewell aristocracy.

The English government met the resistance to the Tea Act and to the other oppressive British measures with what was tantamount to the imposition of an economic death sentence on the colonies. In 1774 and 1775, Parliament passed first the so-called Coercive and then the Restraining acts: they were nothing less than the opening of hostilities. One of the laws passed in 1774 closed the port of Boston; another reduced the government of Massachusetts to the status of a crown colony; another called for the furnishing of ample barracks for His Majesty's troops within twenty-four hours after they were ordered; and another, through the Quebec Act, made permanent the Proclamation Line of 1763 by putting all the far western lands north of the Ohio under the administration of Quebec Province. The Restraining Acts of 1775 cut almost all the colonies off from the northern fisheries and limited their trade entirely to Great Britain, Ireland, and the British West Indies.

The revolutionary ferment began its work. In almost all the colonies illegal congresses were called; the Second Continental Congress met; military stores were collected; and Thomas Paine wrote his stirring pamphlet *Common Sense,* to whip all those who still faltered into revolutionary enthusiasm. The Second Continental Congress struck off two declarations of freedom. The first, naturally representing the dominant interest of colonial mercantile capitalism, was embodied in a series of resolutions passed on April 6, 1776. These resolves nullified the Acts of Trade and Navigation and put an end to the colonial slave trade: and with this single blow the colonial merchants and landlords smashed the hampering chains of the imperial-colonial relations. The second, adopted by the Congress on July 4, 1776, was the Declaration of Independence: written by the radicals, this was a political manifesto which called upon the masses to defend the Revolution. The American Revolution then moved fully into the stage of armed resistance. . . .

Oliver M. Dickerson

WERE THE NAVIGATION ACTS OPPRESSIVE?

Oliver M. Dickerson, who died in 1966, was one of the leading authorities on the fiscal and commercial aspects of the American colonies. The Navigation Acts and the American Revolution, *from which the present selection is taken, is a comprehensive survey of the origins, history, and economic consequences of those acts which loomed so large in the rhetoric of colonial spokesmen. Before his retirement in 1940, Professor Dickerson taught history at Colorado State College.*

Bancroft says "American independence, like the great rivers of the country, had many sources, but the headspring which colored all the stream was the Navigation Act."[1] Other writers join in the general condemnation, but few are specific as to just who was hurt and by what provisions of the acts. Let us examine the operation of the system in detail.

Whatever may have been the opinion of some Americans in 1660 in regard to the basic law limiting the carrying trade of the British Empire to English vessels, by 1760 all opposition had disappeared, and a careful search of contemporary newspapers, pamphlets, and other publications discloses no record of anyone seriously proposing an abrogation of that law. Certainly New England, whose fishing, trading, and shipbuilding industry rested upon this law, would not be expected to ask for changes that would bring in the competition of foreign ships. The only sections of the colonial empire that could theoretically have found such a regulation even an imaginary grievance were those engaged in plantation types of industry, where markets were distant and freights heavy.

There may have been a time when freight rates were influenced by the presence or absence of the foreign-owned ships, but after 1700 the expansion of English shipping, especially from New Eng-

[1] George Bancroft, *History of the United States* (6 vols., 1st ed. New York, 1834–1874), V, 150. In the last revision "Colonial Mercantile System" is substituted for "Navigation Act" (III, 60).

land sources, had become so great that there was ample competition. American ports swarmed with shipping, some owned in England but much more of it in the colonies. In 1768 more than 2,000 vessels cleared from the American continental ports for the West Indies alone. By 1771 it required more than 1,000 vessels to serve Virginia and Maryland, and over 1,100 for the two chief ports in Massachusetts, Boston and Salem. In 1770 a total of 4,171 ships, with a combined tonnage of 488,724, cleared from the various continental ports.

The trade to the West Indies was indeed notable, employing more ships with a greater total tonnage than England was using in her trade with Holland, and far more than she used in her direct trade with Norway, Sweden, and the Eastland countries of the Baltic.

In addition, colonial shipping enabled Britain completely to dominate the Mediterranean trade. In 1768 the clearances from American ports for south Europe totaled 436 ships, with a combined tonnage of 37,093. At that time England was only using 23,113 tons in her trade to the Straits of Gibraltar, which encountered less than 1 percent of foreign competition. Clearances from America are not included in this figure, so the American tonnage is in addition to the English figure, but is included in the percentage of English ships passing the Straits.

The expansion of colonial shipping continued to the Revolution. By 1775 nearly one third of all the ships in Britain registered as English were colonial built. Instead of being oppressive the shipping clauses of the Navigation Act had become an important source of colonial prosperity which was shared by every colony. As a device for launching ships these clauses were more efficient than the fabled beauty of Helen of Troy's face.

There was another important compensation in having a shipping industry under the British flag adequate for all commercial purposes. The plantation industries, such as tobacco, rice, sugar, and indigo, had to depend upon an annual market of their staple product and an assured supply of food, clothing, tools, and other necessities that were not produced locally. This supply was dependent wholly upon the annual fleets that visited their ports. So long as England effectually controlled the seas, English shipping could serve them in time of war about as freely as in time of peace. Had they been dependent upon foreign shipping, the outbreak of a war might have meant complete suspension of their industries.

Business of any kind needs stability of conditions under which large investments of capital are made. The plantation colonies were conducted under conditions of as large individual investments of capital as were the manufacturing industries of the time. It was sounder economic practice to pay somewhat higher freight rates, if necessary, than to face the economic losses incident to a dependence upon foreign shipping; besides, there is no proof that freight rates within the British Empire were not as low after 1700 as those outside. Certainly there is no evidence in contemporary publications of any agitation to repeal this provision of the Navigation Act, nor did prominent Americans express any desire for a general relaxation of its major requirements.

Enumeration

Enumeration of commodities of colonial production has been pictured as an outstanding sin of mercantilism. The English continental colonies had three products of major importance, tobacco, rice, and indigo, included in the numerated list. All were agricultural and were grown commercially only in the southern colonies.

It should be clear that no one would engage in producing enumerated commodities unless he expected to make a profit. If he found his venture unprofitable he could shift his energies to other crops. No one was under any legal compulsion to grow the enumerated products. In spite of the extravagant language that has been used to condemn the system, the grower of enumerated commodities was not enslaved by the legal provisions of enumeration. Obviously growers continued to produce rice, indigo, and tobacco because they made larger cash profits from their cultivation than they could make by using their land, labor, and capital in any other way.

The most cursory examination of these industries reveals that each had its list of wealthy planters who had accumulated fortunes in a few years by growing the enumerated crops. These men and their families were the aristocrats of the South. No similar conditions existed elsewhere in the vast agricultural regions of the colonies. Let us examine the conditions of each industry.

Tobacco

Tobacco, the most important of all colonial exports, suffered from all the disadvantages of other agricultural crops. Late frosts could destroy the tender plants in the seed beds; and early frosts could damage the mature crop before it was harvested. Favorable seasons could produce unusually heavy yields; and heat and lack of moisture could seriously lighten a crop. There were recurring surpluses and shortages. Also there were worms, plant diseases, and soil depletion. All of these and many more were hazards that the grower had to face in colonial times and still does. All are interesting details of the burdens of the tobacco planter, but they have no possible connection with the Navigation Acts. They existed without benefit of law and always will.

Tobacco growers in many cases were debtors. That condition was not peculiar to the tobacco industry and again has no possible connection with enumeration. Farmers who engage in commercial farming always have been in debt and always will be. Farming is a business. It requires land, buildings, equipment, labor, good clothing, and shelter for those engaged in it. Costs for these have to be met for months before a crop can yield any return. Unless inherited, these things had to be supplied by the farmer himself from savings or from borrowings. Most farmers chose the latter course and hoped to make the business ultimately clear itself. In this respect tobacco raising was not different from other business enterprises.

The great assembling and processing markets were in Great Britain, as were also the bankers who supplied the essential working capital. Growing tobacco was one job, marketing it was another. Both were essential parts of the industry. . . .

The decade preceding the Revolution was one of rapid expansion for the tobacco planters. American tobacco was supplying a steadily expanding world market. The most important fact in the complicated expanding tobacco trade was the rise of Scotland as a chief primary market. Scottish imports rose from 12,213,610 pounds in 1746 to 48,269,865 pounds in 1771, a growth of more than 400 percent in twenty-five years. Finding, servicing, and holding an additional market for 36 million pounds of tobacco was a real feat of merchandising. At the same time the London merchants were increasing their importations, but at a slower rate. The merchants in the English "outports" just about held their own. From 1767 to 1771 Scotland imported nearly as much American tobacco as did London and the "outports" combined and remained the chief market to the Revolution. [Table 1] shows the course of the tobacco trade for the nine years preceding independence.

TABLE 1
Tobacco Importations into Great Britain
(in pounds)

	London	*Outports*	*Scotland*	*Total*
1767	25,723,434	13,417,175	28,937,891	68,078,500
1768	23,353,891	12,103,603	33,237,236	68,694,730
1769	24,276,259	9,480,127	....	....
1770	26,758,534	12,419,503	38,708,809	77,886,846
1771	42,952,725	15,006,771	48,269,865	106,229,361
1772	36,265,788	15,101,682	45,259,675	96,627,145
1773	37,918,111	18,010,718	44,544,230	100,473,059
1774	36,859,641	19,186,837	41,348,295	97,394,773
1775	45,250,505	10,210,997	45,863,154	101,324,656

Enumeration clearly did not hamper the expansion of the tobacco raising business in America. Any industry that enjoys an expansion of its total production of more than 50 percent in five years and holds that growth has at least the appearance of prosperity. . . .

On the eve of the Revolution America was raising tobacco for a world market, created by the merchandising skill of the English and Scottish merchants. Only a small part of the tobacco annually reaching Britain was ultimately consumed there. . . .

Western Europe was the chief market, with France, Holland, and Germany taking more than 76 million pounds in 1772, which was an average year, or more than 75 percent of the total crop exported from America. Scotland was the chief supplier for France and Ireland and a keen competitor for the German, Dutch, and Scandinavian trade. Flanders was almost entirely supplied by the English merchants.

If the tobacco planters were oppressed by enumeration they should have prospered when freed. But what happened? There was a temporary rise in exports to the pre-Revolutionary levels, but the growers quickly learned that the markets gained for them by the British, and especially by the Scotch, merchants could not be held. An attempt by Jefferson, while Minister to France, to sell tobacco directly to the French government did not succeed. The French complained that the tobacco was not up to grade and canceled the contract. Under the old plan of buying in the great central market at Glasgow they could select just the kind of tobacco that best fitted their needs. There was no such market in America and the growers had neither the experience nor the capital to set up such an organization of their own. Grading by public inspectors proved to be wholly inadequate as compared with the grading in the great merchandising and processing centers.

Instead of thriving, the decades following the Revolution show that tobacco was a sick industry, gradually losing an important part of its former export trade. The Napoleonic wars and the War of 1812 caused wide fluctuations in exportations from year to year; but when these are averaged by five-year periods the steady decline is obvious. The full story of this decline is easily read in [Table 2].

TABLE 2
Trend of American Tobacco Exports Before and After the Revolution

Years	*Average Yearly Exports in Pounds*
1767–1770	71,223,398
1771–1775	100,249,615
1790–1794	99,665,656
1795–1799	70,625,518
1800–1804	85,935,914
1805–1809	54,525,206
1810–1814	51,544,857
1815–1819	84,533,350
1820–1822	79,369,141

The same countries of Europe that bought 96,727,147 pounds of American tobacco in 1772 bought only 68,327,550 pounds fifty years later. Holland was buying only 23,692,034 pounds as contrasted with 32,631,330 in 1772. France had taken 32,414,143 pounds in 1772 but was buying only 4,665,670 fifty years later. Flanders, that had bought 5,210,565 pounds in 1772, was not even mentioned in our exports for 1822. Exports to Germany remained essentially unchanged from what they had been in 1772.

Partially to compensate for the heavy losses in our export market for tobacco in northern Europe new outlets had been found for a little more than 6 million pounds in other portions of Europe, and additional exports of 10 millions of pounds to other parts of the world. Thus there had been some development of direct new markets, but the total market for American tobacco was millions of pounds short of our exports in 1772.

Most of the loss was in drastic reductions in our exports to Scotland. Direct exports to England had shrunk from 51,367,470 pounds in 1772 to 26,740,000 in 1822, but in the same period exports to Scotland had fallen from 45,259,675 in 1772 to only 1,142,000 fifty years later.

The Revolution not only separated the American colonies from official control by the British government, it separated the tobacco planters from the great banking and marketing organizations that had developed their former world market. A very large proportion of the debts due British merchants and creditors after the Revolution were in the southern states. From what we know of the conditions of agriculture, a large percentage of these must have been advances to the tobacco planters. A total of nearly $35 million in such claims was filed before the claims commission created by the Jay Treaty and ultimately compromised in 1802 for $2,664,000. The Scottish merchants seem to have been the chief losers, since they do not again appear prominently in the world tobacco trade. It was three quarters of a century before the American tobacco industry could replace the great central marketing machinery that had been built up under enumeration.

Rice

Next to tobacco, rice was the most important commercially grown agricultural crop of the continental colonies. Like tobacco it was enumerated, but on the eve of the Revolution had a free market in Europe south of Cape Finisterre and in America south of Georgia. It was an important crop in the lowlands of South Carolina and Georgia.

It has been assumed by many writers that enumeration imposed a serious burden upon the rice planters. The ascertainable facts do not support this assumption. In the years preceding the Revolution the rice industry was prosperous and expanding. Rice exports from

Charleston, South Carolina, increased from an average of 80,631 barrels per year for the five years, 1760 to 1764, to an annual average of 120,483 barrels for the years 1770 to 1773. The exports from Georgia, the other important producer of rice, rose from an annual average of 5,152 barrels for the years 1760 to 1764 to an average of 21,910 barrels during the years 1770 to 1773. Planters made fortunes during these years.

American rice growers, like American tobacco planters, were producing for a world market. Where was that market? In 1772 rice exports from America totaled 155,741 barrels, of which 97,563 went to Great Britain, 10,066 to South Europe, and 48,112 to the West Indies. This shows that more than 60 percent of all American rice exported was finding its world market by way of Great Britain and only about 7 percent was exported to that part of Europe that was free from enumeration. . . .

What happened to America's world market for rice when the Revolution freed it from enumeration? In 1822, after the world had adjusted itself to peace, our exports of rice totaled 87,089 tierces. Of this amount 40,735 tierces went to Europe, 24,073 of which were imported by the British Isles; 15,526 went to Europe north of Cape Finisterre; and 1,136 tierces to southern Europe. Translating tierces into hundredweight we have the following results: 216,657 hundredweight exported to the British Isles in 1822, as contrasted with 468,915 in 1773; 139,734 hundredweight to continental northern Europe in 1822, as contrasted with 324,407 in 1773; and 10,224 to southern Europe in 1822, as contrasted with combined total direct exports from America and reexports from Great Britain of 69,981 in 1773. Our total European market for rice was only 366,615 hundredweight in 1822, as contrasted with 484,320 exported to the same area fifty years before.

Like the tobacco planters the rice planters faced changed conditions after the Revolution. While England remained their best market, total exports for the five years beginning in 1782 were less than half what they had been in the five-year period before the war. The war had brought to an end a long period of prosperity for the rice industry. Much of the advantage of the old central market in England was lost. Importations were burdened with new duties, although drawbacks on reexportation were permitted. Shipping regulations of other countries hampered our trade. Even our ally, France, would not admit our rice-laden ships to her ports in 1788, so that cargoes bound for that country had to be unloaded at Cowes on the Isle of Wight for transshipment to French vessels.

There is nothing in the evidence to support the theory that the rice planters were handicapped or oppressed by enumeration or that they benefited from the freedom to find markets where they could. The advantages of the one great central market still operated as the magnet to attract imports and exports. The planters not only lost a large part of their former markets, but what was even more serious, they lost the financial help they had received from the British merchants. Freedom involved the necessity of finding their own financing as well as their own markets.

Indigo

Indigo was the third most important enumerated product of the continental provinces. Unlike rice and tobacco, indigo found its ultimate market in Great Britain. It was not only enumerated but was also encouraged by a direct British bounty.

On the eve of the Revolution the indigo planters were very prosperous and production was increasing rapidly, as shown by the tables of exports reported by Sellers and by Gray. Both reports are based upon fragmentary American sources. These show that exports nearly doubled between 1765 and 1773. These estimates are too low. Actual importation by Great Britain in 1773, all certified as produced in the British plantations, was 1,403,684 pounds, or twice that reported by Gray. This is nearly three times the colonial exports reported by Macpherson for 1770, and his reports seem to be based upon official records. Any industry that was so obviously prosperous cannot be called oppressed.

The Revolutionary War quickly brought to a close this period of prosperity for the indigo planters. They soon discovered that the industry could not exist without the former bounties. British aid and encouragement were transferred to Jamaica, which was still within the empire. American production declined and just about disappeared. By 1822 the reported exports totaled only 3,283 pounds. In the meantime importations of foreign indigo had risen from zero to 1,126,928 pounds, or nearly as much as our exports were in 1773.

The Balance of Trade

The relative values of imports from Great Britain into the colonies and exports from them to the home country are frequently cited as proof of economic exploitation. In the form they are usually given they are misleading. The American colonial empire was one economic whole. The products of the West Indies were used by all of the other colonies and their products in turn supplied the essential needs of the sugar colonies. A far larger number of ships, with a greater tonnage, was used in the trade between the continental colonies and the West Indies than between the former and the mother country, and nearly as great a tonnage as was used for trade between the various continental colonial ports.

The northern colonies with their rum trade were just as much involved in the sugar industry as were the local West India planters. The colonies that supplied the millions of staves to make the sugar and molasses containers were also as directly interested in the sugar industry as were the farmers who supplied meat, grain, beans, peas, and other essential food items. The New England fishermen who marketed their fish in the West Indies may have considered themselves only seamen and fisherfolk but they were actually producing sugar as much as if they worked on the sugar plantations.

To treat imports and exports from one part of the colonial empire as a trade that should balance is as unreal as to set up a similar bookkeeping record for the external trade from New York and California. No one expects the trade of a single state of the Union with the outside world, or with any other state of the Union, to balance. It is the total trade of the United States that is important. By applying this principle to the trade between Great Britain and her American colonial empire we get the results shown in [Table 3].

From [Table 3] it is seen that total imports from the colonies exceeded total exports in two of the three years and show a small excess for the three years. It is obvious that imports from the West Indies were being paid for in part by exports to the continental colonies, who in turn supplied exports to the West Indies.

There are some items in the total trade picture that do not appear in the tables. One was the large exports of food and lumber products to southern Europe and the relatively small imports in return. This

TABLE 3
Trade Between Great Britain and the American Colonies, 1769–1771

Imported from	*1769*	*1770*	*1771*
Continental Colonies	£1,170,015	£1,129,662	£1,468,941
West Indies	2,792,178	3,131,879	2,717,194
Totals	3,962,193	4,261,541	4,186,135
Grand Total for three years			12,409,869
Exported to			
Continental Colonies	£1,604,760	£2,343,892	£4,586,882
West Indies	1,274,951	1,269,469	1,151,357
Totals	2,879,711	3,613,361	5,738,239
Grand Total for three years			12,231,311

balance in 1769 amounted to £476,052. These balances helped cover the cost of British imports each year from that area and should be credited to the total colonial exports. Adding to the value of British exports was the steady migration of capital to the continental colonies. Thousands of immigrants were moving to America with their possessions. British capital was being invested in land and various business enterprises. The vast amount of credit extended to American merchants and especially the credits advanced to the planters engaged in producing the three principal enumerated products, tobacco, rice, and indigo, had to be covered at some time by physical exports of British goods. Finally there were the costs of the British standing army and the operations of the British fleet in American waters. These included costs not covered by ordinary exports and involved the actual shipment of bullion to New York, Canada, and the West Indies in 1769 to a total of £16,651.

Limitations on Manufacturing

There were three acts that have been cited as hostile to colonial manufacturing. These are known as the woolens act, the hat act, and the iron bill. The first two applied wholly to shipments by water and the last forbade the creation of new steel furnaces, or forges equipped with tilt hammers or rolling devices for making that metal. The object of the iron bill was to encourage the colonial exportation of pig and bar iron to Britain so as to reduce the dependence upon foreign imports of these basic materials.

Did these laws materially impede the development of manufacturing in the continental colonies? Fortunately we have two thorough, objective studies on this point: one is by Victor S. Clark covering the whole field of manufactures, the other is by Arthur C. Bining dealing specifically with the iron industry. Both of these independent studies are in substantial agreement as to the basic facts. Both agree that British legislation had very little effect in retarding colonial manufacturing. We will discuss each measure separately.

Wool and Woolen Goods

The prohibitions against exporting wool and American-made woolens has generally been referred to as oppressive. The impression given is that Englishmen in America were being treated less well than those in England.

There is no foundation for this inference. England had developed the wool-growing and wool-manufacturing industry far beyond that of other countries in western Europe. It was an economic advantage of first importance—a sort of atom bomb of the seventeenth century. Under no circumstances was England willing to permit her special advantage to get away. To this end there was enacted a long series of laws regulating wool and possible wool exports, commencing with the Restoration under Charles II and extending through the reign of William III. The American woolens act was a minor item in those regulations.

The restraints imposed upon Englishmen in America who engaged in wool growing or processing were mild in comparison with those faced by Englishmen in England.

There, in addition to provisions against the export or shipment of wool similar to those in the American law, the owners of sheep had to give notice of their plans to shear sheep. They also had to report the exact number of fleeces at shearing time and give official notice of any removal from their farms, as no wool could be moved from one place to another without a permit. Buyers in certain areas had to be licensed under bond, and no raw wool could be loaded on a horse cart to be moved by land except in the daytime and at hours fixed by law. All of the above restrictions remained in force until the Revolution and are listed in the same customs manuals with the American regulations.

As has already been pointed out the prohibitions were not upon production or manufacture but upon water export of such goods. Consequently, household and neighborhood production went on unhampered, as did distribution of such products throughout the colonies and the rapidly expanding back country. Little can be added to the extensive studies of Clark. The back country clothed itself. There was very little cloth made for the market. Colonial newspapers, published in the larger port towns, printed very few advertisements of homespun cloth for sale.

There was no effort to compete commercially with imports from the home country. Textile production was still in the handicrafts stage. Weavers were not well paid and spinners very poorly paid. Working in such industries was associated with extreme poverty. It just did not pay to produce cloth under American conditions when goods of as good or better quality could be had from abroad for less money. Where family labor had no commercial value and money and money-crops were scarce there was extensive production.

American conditions remained largely unchanged long after the Revolution. In 1821 woolen goods of American production is not listed among our exports. On the other hand there appears in the list of goods imported into the United States woolen goods of various kinds to a total value of $11,971,933 out of total imports valued at $41,955,134, or nearly 30 percent of all our imports.

It is obvious that the failure of colonial America to develop a large export of woolen goods and other textiles rested upon factors entirely separate from a parliamentary act of the seventeenth century.

Hats

The hat act did prevent the shipment of hats by water and may have had a temporary effect upon a developing export trade in New England hats. But the act had no effect upon the steady development of hat manufacturing in America. It was more advantageous for hatmakers to migrate with their skills to new neighborhoods than it was to live in one place and make hats for merchants who, in turn, sold them where they could find a market. Hat manufacture, especially of wool, became widely diffused and was so far advanced that Hamilton in his "Report on Manufactures" in 1791, in discussing the wool industry, stated: "Household manufactures of this material are carried on in different parts of the United States to a very interesting extent; but there is only one branch, which as a regular business can be said to have acquired maturity. This is the making of hats." That statement could hardly have been justified concerning any other manufacturing business. The industry was better developed than any other. In 1810 Tench Coxe reported 842 hatteries operating in the United States, some of which were in the western territories of Indiana, Michigan, and Mississippi. The center of the industry was not in New England, but in Pennsylvania, where 532 operating hatteries were reported.

Iron and Steel

The law prohibiting new rolling and slitting mills, plating forges and steel furnaces, passed in 1750, is mentioned in all accounts. In some cases writers have expanded this into an instance of real oppression. Bining, who has made the most detailed study of the colonial iron industry, agrees with Clark that such legislation did not check the development of the iron industry. He even insists that on the eve of the Revolution there were more iron furnaces in operation in America than there were in England and Wales combined and that the total output was greater than that of the iron furnaces of Great Britain. Most of the pots, pans, and other hollow ware used in the colonies were made at local iron works. The growing farming, milling, and extensive wagon transportation demands for iron were absorbing most of the bar iron that could be produced. As a result the British bounties, which attracted increased colonial exports of bar iron from a bare 39 tons in 1761 to a total of 2,234 tons ten years later, proved ineffective after 1771 and exports rapidly declined. The reason was steadily growing demands for domestic use.

Most of the iron works were relatively small and were designed to supply a neighborhood market. In the main they represented personal investments. All of the large colonial iron works were erected by foreign capital and employed imported labor. All of the larger works proved financially unprofitable, largely because of the gradual exhaustion of the local supply of charcoal. That the law was not interfering with the growth of the iron industry is proved by its rapid expansion westward in Pennsylvania and by the fact that the great American Iron Company was set up in 1764 with London capital by Hasenclever, who quickly expended a total of more than a quarter

[January, 1770]
[1773(?)]

WILLIAM JACKSON,

an *IMPORTER*; at the

BRAZEN HEAD,

North Side of the TOWN-HOUSE,

and *Opposite the Town-Pump, in*

Corn-hill, BOSTON.

It is desired that the SONS and DAUGHTERS of *LIBERTY*, would not buy any one thing of him, for in so doing they will bring Disgrace upon *themselves*, and their *Posterity*, for *ever* and *ever*, AMEN.

FIGURES 1, 2, and 3. Boycott and blacklist: Three notices of colonial reactions to British policy.

The true Sons of Liberty

And Supporters of the Non-Importation Agreement,

ARE determined to reſent any the leaſt Inſult or Menace offer'd to any one or more of the ſeveral Committees appointed by the Body at Faneuil-Hall, and chaſtiſe any one or more of them as they deſerve; and will alſo ſupport the Printers in any Thing the Committees ſhall deſire them to print.

☞AS a Warning to any one that ſhall affront as aforeſaid, upon ſure Information given, one of theſe Advertiſements will be poſted up at the Door or Dwelling-Houſe of the Offender.

A LIST of the Names of *thoſe* who AUDACIOUSLY continue to counteract the UNITED SENTIMENTS of the BODY of Merchants thro'out NORTH-AMERICA; by importing Britiſh Goods contrary to the Agreement.

John Bernard,
(In King-Street, almoſt oppoſite Vernon's Head.

James McMaſters,
(On Treat's Wharf.

Patrick McMaſters,
(Oppoſite the Sign of the Lamb.

John Mein,
(Oppoſite the White-Horſe, and in King-Street.

Nathaniel Rogers,
(Oppoſite Mr. Henderſon Inches Store lower End King-Street.

William Jackſon,
At the Brazen Head, Cornhill, near the Town-Houſe.

Theophilus Lillie,
(Near Mr. Pemberton's Meeting-Houſe, North-End.

John Taylor,
(Nearly oppoſite the Heart and Crown in Cornhill.

Ame & Elizabeth Cummings,
(Oppoſite the Old Brick Meeting Houſe, all of Boſton.

Iſrael Williams, Eſq; & Son,
(Traders in the Town of Hatfield.

And, *Henry Barnes,*
(Trader in the Town of M[illegible]ro'.

million dollars on the project. It was the largest capital outlay in any colonial manufacturing venture.

Production of steel on a commercial scale came slowly. In 1810 Tench Coxe could report only four steel furnaces in the entire United States with a combined capacity of 917 tons, presumably per year.

Bining did not find a single case where any iron work was discontinued, a slitting mill or steel furnace destroyed, or even an attempted prosecution of an iron works operator. Clark also failed to find a single case in any of the other colonies. An extensive search of the Treasury papers in the Public Record Office in London by the author also failed to reveal a single such prosecution, although there is much material on other clauses of the trade and navigation laws. There is but one conclusion, and that is that the iron industry was not materially hampered by any British legislation and that its development was rapid and continuous.

Other Manufactures

British legislation did not apply to other forms of colonial manufacture except to promote them. Naval stores were encouraged by direct British bounties. The Navigation Acts directly encouraged shipbuilding and all of the allied services such as rope making, and manufacture of anchor chains, bolts, etc. American distilling of rum was on a large scale as was also sugar refining. Enormous quantities of forest products were worked up and exported to all parts of the empire and to South Europe. Millions of staves and shingles were exported annually. Much furniture shows in the list of exports coastwise and to the West Indies. Thousands of tons of bread and flour were manufactured and exported each year.

The major amount of manufactures, however, do not show in the list of exports as they were produced for domestic consumption and were sold within the colonies in the immediate vicinity where they were made.

While no case can be made for any charge that limitations on colonial manufacture were real, the measures discussed above were part of the controversy. The iron bill carried a potential threat that real interference with domestic manufactures might be attempted.

Thus it produced uneasiness in certain circles in America. The growth of colonial manufactures created a fear in England among workers, capitalists, and trading and shipping circles that unless this movement were checked in America they would lose their best markets and face a future of poverty and high taxes. This was the fear upon which Americans played with their nonimportation agreements.

Bounties

The bounty system certainly was not an item of complaint on the part of American producers. As the bounty policy was one of the most important phases of the general mercantile system, it is of course included in any general denunciation of the industrial and commercial relations of the colonies to the mother country.

The following industries were directly dependent upon such bounties: (1) naval stores, including tar, pitch, resin, turpentine, masts, spars, yards, bowsprits, and hemp; (2) lumber; (3) cooperage materials made of white oak; (4) indigo. The bounties were authorized over such periods that producers could plan production intelligently, and merchants in England could count on a continuous, artificially attracted supply of such products over a period of years. By 1765 the policy of enacting bounty laws for periods of only a few years was abandoned, and laws were passed fixing bounties for periods as great as twenty years. The total sums expended by the British government for bounties on colonial products were very large and extended over a period of nearly seventy years. They were at their highest point on the eve of the Revolution and were reported by the Comptroller General as amounting to £186,144 during the years 1761 to 1776.

Of the four groups of articles that received bounties, all were produced in colonies that revolted; and the sums expended by the British government in behalf of these industries went wholly to the continental group. It was the southern colonies, rather than the northern, that benefited most from this policy. Naval stores other than masts and spars came largely from North Carolina, South Carolina, and Georgia. Indigo grew chiefly in South Carolina and Georgia, and the most desirable lumber and cooperage materials were the products of the colonies south of Pennsylvania. New England supplied mainly masts and spars, and the bounty on these was relatively insignificant.

It should be noted that the policy of granting bounties continued until the close of the colonial period. Those on lumber and cooperage materials were adopted in the reign of George III; in fact, the first bounty on such products was expected to soften the reception of the Stamp Act in America. The framing of bounty laws in permanent form was also a characteristic feature of the legislation of his reign. No part of the commercial policy was more firmly established than that of bounties, and the sugar interests advocated them as more efficient in promoting their favorite industry than tariffs. . . .

If the bounty policy was a cause of the Revolution, it operated in a decidedly different way from what has been so confidently asserted by those who condemn the Navigation Acts. The bounty payments were a considerable burden upon the exchequer; and, when the load of taxes after 1763 became a matter of public complaint, the existence of the bounties, their continuance, and the impression made upon public opinion by the figures of total payments during the eighteenth century, became an added reason why the people in America, who apparently benefited from such bounties, should assume their fair share in the costs of empire.

To the extent that the bounties were a burden upon the British taxpayer and an excuse for taxation of the colonies by the home government, they were a cause of the Revolution. They were certainly not a cause in the sense that such payments produced discontent in America.

Several industries practically disappeared at the end of the Revolution because they could not exist without the bounties. As the beneficiaries of the bounty system were essentially all in the thirteen continental colonies that revolted, it is highly probable that the bounty phases of the navigation system produced a conservative element of loyal supporters of the imperial system—at least so far as men permitted themselves to be influenced by their direct economic interests. There may be a direct relation between the British financial encouragement of colonial industries and the loyalist movement in America. It was definitely strongest in those colonies that benefited most directly from this practice.

Preferential Tariffs

The policy of preferential tariffs and export bounties could not have been a cause of economic complaint on the part of Americans, who thus secured access to the best market in Europe on better conditions than other producers. There was no possible ground for complaint on the part of American consumers when the British government allowed drawbacks of its own import and inland duties upon goods exported from England to the colonies, or when it encouraged both production in England and colonial consumption by export bounties, as it did in many cases. These regulations gave the colonies especially favored treatment and were causes of prosperity and not of complaint.

Influence on General Prosperity

Were the navigation and trade laws so generally burdensome upon the colonies as to interfere with their development, and thus produce general poverty and distress? Again the answer must be negative; just the opposite condition existed. The colonies were prosperous and wages of labor were admittedly higher in the continental colonies than elsewhere in the world.

Population in continental America was doubling every twenty-five years, while in England it was scarcely doubling in a century. In fact the population of England seems to have doubled only once from 1066 to 1600, and again by about 1760, although a very marked increase in population was to characterize the reign of George III. In no other section of the world was there a white population expanding from natural increase so rapidly as in continental America. Marriages occurred early and families were large. The British colonies on the continent were attractive to emigrants, especially from the British Isles, and there are numerous references in the British periodicals, published in the decade 1765 to 1775, to artisans of all kinds migrating to the New World.

Another measure of their prosperity was the expansion of trade that had occurred during the eighteenth century. Other evidences of wealth were the multiplying educational institutions, churches, newspapers, magazines, and other publications. Many of the finest specimens of colonial church architecture date from the period just before the Revolution.

The wealth acquired by American merchants and planters was a real cause of jealousy on the part of residents in the mother country. There had grown up in America a new race of untitled nobility with estates and palaces that compared favorably with the possessions of the titled classes in England. Their houses were not only well, but even luxuriously, furnished. Their consumption of British and European goods was not limited to necessities, but included luxuries of all kinds. The best evidence of this is the elaborate offerings of goods, including finery of all kinds for both men and women, found in the extensive advertisements in the newspapers of the time. The population of the seaboard was no longer clothed in homespun. Many men wore silk and velvet regularly. Joseph Warren had on his usual silk waistcoat when he was killed at Bunker Hill.

One of the best tests of real prosperity is the rapidity with which a population can sink its public debts following a war. The French and Indian War had been a real world contest so far as the British Empire was concerned. Colonial exertion on the part of the northern colonists, especially, had been on a scale not unlike that of Canada and Australia in the last world war. Many of the colonies levied heavy taxes during the war, and came out with large debts. The total colonial debt according to Charles Lloyd, who prepared the statistical data for the Stamp Act, was £2.6 million. Yet this was sunk so rapidly that in 1765 it was estimated that only £767,000 remained, and the greater part of that would be sunk by 1767.

The estimate of the time within which the colonies could extinguish their remaining obligations was too optimistic; but past accomplishments made a profound impression upon people in England, who could not hope to reduce their own national debt to the level of 1754 in less than a generation.

The ability of the colonies to sink their heavy war debts at the rate of about 20 percent a year was a startling performance to thoughtful Englishmen. The economic recovery of the American continental colonies was not unlike that of the United States during the first ten years after World War I. The soreness of many British taxpayers, as they looked forward to long years of heavy taxation of their own people, while their fellow citizens across the Atlantic would soon be free from all but the lightest taxes, especially in view of their belief that the war had been fought and the burdens incurred for the benefit of the Americans, was not unlike the feeling aroused over the war debts in the years immediately following World War I. . . .

No case can be made out for the Navigation Acts as a cause of the Revolution on the grounds that such laws were economically oppressive and were steadily reducing the Americans to a condition of hopeless poverty. It is true that evidences of hard times in the colonies may be found; but such conditions were periodic and were preceded and followed by other periods of overtrading, extravagance, and luxury. There was unquestionably high taxation in some of the colonies during and after the French and Indian War. In places there were price readjustments due to deflation and the termination of large governmental activities. Such conditions were not evenly distributed. There were times when merchants and newspaper publishers complained of slow collections; but such conditions can be found in any region where credit is easy, and they can also be found at times in even the most prosperous countries. The evidence indicates far less depression in the colonies than in the home country in the same years.

It is true that after 1770 there was a serious depression in the tobacco business in a portion of Virginia, which is reflected in the newspapers. In accounting for their economic distress and suggesting possible remedies, the planters in no case charged their distress to the Navigation Acts. Their ideas of what was wrong and of proper remedies sound strangely modern. They charged their economic condition to the too easy credit supplied by the Scottish merchants, and to the organized monopoly of the buyers. One writer seriously proposed active cooperative organizations to handle their tobacco crops, with paid factors in Britain to care for their sales and arrange for their purchases.

Professor Andrews[2] and Professor Schlesinger[3] have assembled a good many items from the correspondence of merchants indicating some economic distress. Such data, however, are not convincing. The conditions complained of are local and periodic where they are not due to the chronic absence of an adequate medium of

[2] *Boston Merchants and the Non Importation Movement (Publications,* Colonial Society of Massachusetts, XIX), pp. 180–191.

[3] *The Colonial Merchants and the American Revolution* (New York, 1918), p. 106.

exchange. They should not be interpreted as indicating a general lack of prosperity for America as a whole, covering the period between 1763 and 1775. They more probably indicate that a tidal movement of prosperous and dull times was characteristic of American economic life long before the formation of the federal government.[4]

Conditions for the period as a whole must be considered. A country that was a mecca for immigrants; that was importing slaves in large numbers; that was rapidly expanding its settled area into the back country; that could order from overseas expensive marble statues of its favorite English politicians as did South Carolina and New York; that could squander large sums on the public funeral of a royal governor and bury him in a sepulcher as elaborate as was accorded to royalty in England; that could find the funds for better church buildings than it ever had before in its history; that could sink public debts more rapidly than other countries; and whose population could live on a far better scale than similar classes in any other part of the world; was not suffering from economic ills that lead to permanent poverty.

[4] This is practically conceded by Schlesinger in his account of the economic recovery after 1770. *Ibid.*, chap vi; Virginia D. Harrington, *New York Merchants on the Eve of the Revolution*, describes the periods of varying good and hard times in New York, but also advances a theory that merchants' letters are a better indication of business conditions than are the statistics of trade. She states that the bottom of the business depression in New York was in 1769, pp. 289–319.

II THE PROVOCATIONS OF BRITISH IMPERIAL POLICY AFTER 1763

Lawrence Henry Gipson

THE AMERICAN REVOLUTION AS AN AFTERMATH OF THE GREAT WAR FOR THE EMPIRE, 1754–1763

Lawrence Henry Gipson, author of The Coming of the Revolution, 1763–1775, *is best known for his multivolume* magnum opus, The British Empire before the American Revolution *(1939–1946). As one might guess from the latter title, Gipson's discussion of the events leading up to the American Revolution emphasizes the larger problems of empire that confronted the British governments of this period. Professor Gipson, who retired in 1952, taught history at Lehigh University.*

Great wars in modern times have too frequently been the breeders of revolution. The exhausting armed struggles in which France became engaged in the latter half of the eighteenth century led as directly to the French Revolution as did the First World War to the Russian Revolution; it may be said as truly that the American Revolution was an aftermath of the Anglo-French conflict in the New World carried on between 1754 and 1763. This is by no means to deny that other factors were involved in the launching of these revolutionary movements. Before proceeding with an analysis of the theme of this paper, however, it would be well to consider the wording of the title given to it.[1]

Words may be used either to disguise or to distort facts as well as to clarify them, but the chief task of the historian is to illuminate the past. He is faced, therefore, with the responsibility of using only such words as will achieve this broad objective of his calling and to reject those that obscure or defeat it. For this reason "the French and Indian War," as a term descriptive of the conflict to which we have just referred, has been avoided in this essay as well as in the writer's series on the *British Empire before the American Revolution.* This has been done in spite of the fact that it has been employed by most Americans ever since the early days of our Republic and therefore

Reprinted by permission from *Political Science Quarterly* 65, no. 1 (March 1950).

[1] This paper was read before the colonial history section of the American Historical Association in December 1948 at the Annual Meeting held in Washington.

has the sanction of long usage as well as the sanction of American national tradition assigning, as does the latter, to the Revolutionary War a position of such commanding importance as to make all other events in American history, preceding as well as following it, quite subordinate to it. In contrast to this traditional interpretation of our history one may affirm that the Anglo-French conflict settled nothing less than the incomparably vital question as to what civilization—what complex cultural patterns, what political institutions—would arise in the great Mississippi basin and the valleys of the rivers draining it, a civilization, whatever it might be, surely destined to expand to the Pacific seaboard and finally to dominate the North American continent. The determination of this crucial issue is perhaps the most momentous event in the life of the English-speaking people in the New World and quite overshadows in importance both the Revolutionary War and the later Civil War, events which, it is quite clear, were each contingent upon the outcome of the earlier crisis.

A struggle of such proportions, involving tremendous stakes, deserves a name accurately descriptive of its place in the history of the English-speaking people, and the title "the French and Indian War," as suggested, in no way fulfills this need. For the war was not, as the name would seem to imply, a conflict largely between English and French New World colonials and their Indian allies, nor was it localized in North America to the extent that the name would appear to indicate. In contrast, it was waged both before and after an open declaration of war by the British and French nations with all their resources for nine years on three oceans, and much of the land washed by the waters of them, and it ultimately brought in both Spain, allied to France, and Portugal, allied to Great Britain. While it involved, it is true, as the name would connote, wilderness fighting, yet of equal, if not greater, importance in assessing its final outcome was the pouring forth of Britain's financial resources in a vast program of shipbuilding, in the equipment and support of the British and colonial armies and the royal navy, and in the subsidization both of allies on the European continent and of the colonies in America. If it also involved the reduction of the fortress of Louisbourg, Fort Niagara, Fort Duquesne, Quebec, and Montreal in North America, each in turn to fall to British regulars aided by American provincial troops, these successes, of great significance, were, in fact, really contingent upon the resounding British naval victories in the Mediterranean, off the Strait of Gibraltar, in the Bay of Biscay, and elsewhere, that brought about the virtual extinction of the French navy and merchant marine and thereby presented to France—seeking to supply her forces in Canada and elsewhere with adequate reinforcements and matériel—a logistical problem so insoluble as to spell the doom of her North American empire and of her possessions in India and elsewhere.

If the term "the French and Indian War" meets none of the requirements of accurate historical nomenclature, neither does the term "the Seven Years' War"—a name appropriately enough employed by historians to designate the mighty conflict that raged for seven years in Germany before its conclusion in the Treaty of Hubertusburg in 1763. The principals in this war were Prussia, allied with Great Britain, Hanover, Brunswick, and Hesse facing Austria, most of the Holy Roman Empire, Russia, and Sweden, all allied with France and receiving subsidies from her. Although George II, as king of Great Britain and elector of Hanover, in the treaty of 1758 with Frederick of Prussia, promised not to conclude peace without mutual agreement with the latter, and although large subsidies were annually paid to Prussia as well as to the other continental allies out of the British treasury and troops were also sent to Germany, it must be emphasized that these aids were designed primarily for the protection of the king's German Electorate. In other words, the British alliance in no way supported the objectives of the Prussian king, when he suddenly began the German war in 1756 by invading Saxony—two years after the beginning of the Anglo-French war. In this connection it should be borne in mind that throughout the Seven Years' War in Germany Great Britain remained at peace with both Russia and Sweden and refused therefore to send a fleet into the Baltic in spite of the demands of Frederick that this be done; nor were British land troops permitted to assist him against Austria, but only to help form a protective shield for Hanover against the thrusts of the French armies. For the latter were determined not only to overrun the Electorate—something that they succeeded in doing—but to hold it as a bargaining point to be used at the conclusion of hostilities with Great Britain, a feat, however, beyond their power of accomplishment. Closely related and intertwined as were the two wars, they were, nevertheless, distinct in their beginning and distinct in their termination.

Indeed, while British historians at length were led to adopt the nomenclature applied by German and other continental historians to all hostilities that took place between 1754 and 1763 in both the Old and New Worlds, American historians, by and large in the past, have rejected, and rightly so, it seems, the name "the Seven Years' War" to designate specifically the struggle during these years in North America with the fate of that continent at stake; so likewise many of them have rejected, as equally inadmissible, the name "the French and Indian War." Instead, the late Professor Osgood employed the title "the Fourth Intercolonial War," surely not a good one; George Bancroft called the war "the American Revolution: First Phase," still more inaccurate in some respects than the names he sought to avoid; Francis Parkman, with the flare of a romanticist, was at first inclined to call it "the Old French War" but finally, under the influence of the great-man-in-history thesis, gave to his two remarkable volumes concerned with it the totally misleading name, *Montcalm and Wolfe;* finally, John Fiske, the philosopher-historian, as luminous in his views as he was apt to be careless in the details of historical scholarship, happily fastened upon the name "the Great War." In the series on the *British Empire before the American Revolution* the writer has built upon Fiske's title and has called it "the Great War for the Empire" in order to emphasize not only the fact that the war was a very great conflict both in its scope and in its lasting effects, as Fiske saw it with clearness, but also, as a war entered into specifically for the defense of the British Empire, that it was by far the most important ever waged by Great Britain to this end.

It may be pointed out that later charges, especially by American writers, that the war was begun by Great Britain with less worthy motives in mind, are not supported by the great mass of state papers and the private correspondence of British statesmen responsible for making the weighty decisions at the time—materials now available to the student which the writer has attempted to analyze in detail in the two volumes of his series that appeared under the title of *Zones of International Friction, 1748–1754.* In other words, the idea that the war was started as the result of European balance-of-power politics or by British mercantilists for the purpose of destroying a commercial rival and for conquering Canada and the French West Indies, and for expelling the French from India, rather than for the much more limited and legitimate objective of affording the colonies and particularly the new province of Nova Scotia and the Old Dominion of Virginia protection against the aggressive aims of France, must be dismissed by students brought face to face with impressive evidence to the contrary.

The development of the war into one for the military mastery of the North American continent came with the growing conviction on the part of the British ministers that nothing short of this drastic step would realize the primary aims of the government in arriving at the determination, as the result of appeals from the colonies for assistance, to challenge the right of French troops to be planted well within the borders of the Nova Scotia peninsula and at the forks of the Ohio. One may go as far as to state that the acquisition of Canada—as an objective sought by mercantilists to contribute to the wealth of Great Britain—would have seemed fantastic to any contemporary who had the slightest knowledge of the tremendous financial drain that that great possession had been on the treasury of the French king for over a century before 1754. Moreover, the motives that ultimately led, after much searching of heart, to its retention after its conquest by Great Britain were not commercial but strategic and had primarily in view the security and welfare generally of the older American colonies.

In view of these facts, not to be confused with surmises, the name "the Great War for the Empire" seems to the writer not only not inappropriate but among all the names heretofore applied to the war in question by far the most suitable that can be used by one concerned with the history of the old British Empire, who seeks earnestly to maintain that standard of exactness in terminology, as well as in other respects, which the public has a right to demand of him.

The description just given of the motives that led to the Great War for the Empire, nevertheless, runs counter, as suggested, to American national tradition and most history that has been written by American historians in harmony with it. This tradition had a curious beginning. It arose partly out of Pitt's zealous efforts to energize the colonies to prosecute the war most actively; but there also was another potent factor involved in its creation. Before the conclusion of hostilities in 1763 certain powerful commercial interests—centered particularly at Newport, Rhode Island, Boston, New

York City, and to a less extent in Philadelphia—in a desire to continue an enormously lucrative trade with the French West Indies, and therefore with the enemy, all in the face of Pitt's determination to keep supplies from the French armed forces operating in the New World, began to express themselves in terms that implied that the war was peculiarly Great Britain's war and only incidentally one that concerned her colonies and that the French, really friendly to the aspirations of British colonials, were opposed only to the mercantilistic ambitions of the mother country. By 1766—just twelve years after the beginning of the war and three years after its termination—this extraordinary tradition had become so well established that Benjamin Franklin, astonishingly enough, could actually assert in his examination before a committee of the House of Commons:

> *I know the last war is commonly spoke of here as entered into for the defence, or for the sake of the people of America; I think it is quite misunderstood. It began about the limits between Canada and Nova Scotia, about territories to which the crown indeed laid claim, but were not claimed by any British colony. . . . We had therefore no particular concern or interest in that dispute. As to the Ohio, the contest there began about your right of trading in the Indian country, a right you had by the Treaty of Utrecht, which the French infringed . . . they took a fort which a company of your merchants, and their factors and correspondents, had erected there to secure that trade. Braddock was sent with an army to retake that fort . . . and to protect your trade. It was not until after his defeat that the colonies were attacked. They were before in perfect peace with both French and Indians. . . .*

By the beginning of 1768 the tradition had been so extended that John Dickinson—voicing the popular American view in his highly important *Letters from a Farmer in Pennsylvania,* no. 8—felt that he not only could affirm, as did Franklin, that the war was strictly Britain's war and fought for selfish purposes, but could even insist that the acquisition of territory in North America as the result of it "is greatly injurious to these colonies" and that they therefore were not under the slightest obligation to the mother country.

But to return to the last phases of the Great War for the Empire. The British customs officials—spurred into unusual activity in the face of Pitt's demand for the strict enforcement of the Trade and Navigation Acts in order to break up the pernicious practice of bringing aid and comfort to the enemy—were led to employ writs of assistance for the purpose of laying their hands upon goods landed in American ports and secured in exchange for American provisions sent for the most part either directly or indirectly to the French West Indies. Although in the midst of hostilities, most of the merchants in Boston showed bitter opposition to the writs and equally ardent support of James Otis's declaration made in open court in 1761 that Parliament, acting within the limits of the constitution, was powerless to extend the use of these writs to America, whatever its authority might be in Great Britain. The importance of this declaration lies not so much in its immediate effect but rather in the fact that it was indicative of the line of attack that not only Otis would subsequently follow but also the Adamses, Hawley, Hancock, and other popular leaders in the Bay Colony during the developing crisis, in the laying down of constitutional restrictions upon the power of Parliament to legislate for America. Further, it is clear that, even before the Great War for the Empire had been terminated, there were those in the province who had begun to view Great Britain as the real enemy rather than France.

Just as definitely as was the issue over writs of assistance related to the war under consideration was that growing out of the twopenny acts of the Virginia Assembly. In search of funds for maintaining the frontier defensive forces under the command of Colonel George Washington, the Assembly was led to pass in 1755 and 1758 those highly questionable laws as favorable to the tobacco planters as they were indefensibly unjust to the clergy. Even assuming the fact that these laws were war measures, and therefore in a sense emergency measures, it was inconceivable that the Privy Council would permit so palpable a violation of contractual relations as they involved. The royal disallowance of the laws in question opened the way for Patrick Henry, the year that hostilities were terminated by the Peace of Paris, not only to challenge in the Louisa County courthouse the right of the King in Council to refuse to approve any law that a colony might pass that in its judgment was a good law, but to affirm that such refusal was nothing less than an act of tyranny on the part of the king. It was thus resentment at the overturning of Virginia war legislation that led to this attack upon the judicial authority of review by the Crown—an authority exercised previously without serious protest for over a century. It should also be noted that the Henry thesis helped to lay the foundation for the theory of the equality of colonial laws with those passed by Parliament, a theory of the constitution of the empire that most American leaders in 1774 had come to accept in arguing that if the king could no longer exercise a veto over the acts of the legislature of Great Britain, it was unjust that he should do so over those of the colonial assemblies.

But the most fateful aftermath of the Great War for the Empire, with respect to the maintenance of the historic connection between the mother country and the colonies, grew out of the problem of the control and support not only of the vast trans-Appalachian interior, the right to which was now confirmed by treaty to Great Britain, but of the new acquisitions in North America secured from France and Spain. Under the terms of the royal Proclamation of 1763, French Canada to the east of the Great Lakes was organized as the Province of Quebec; most of old Spanish Florida became the Province of East Florida; and those areas, previously held by Spain as well as by France to the west of the Apalachicola and to the east of New Orleans and its immediate environs, became the Province of West Florida. The Proclamation indicated that proper inducements would be offered British and other Protestants to establish themselves in these new provinces. With respect to the trans-Appalachian region, however, it created there a temporary but vast Indian reserve by laying down as a barrier the crest of the mountains beyond which there should be no white settlement except by specific permission of the Crown.

The Proclamation has been represented not only as a blunder, the result largely of carelessness and ignorance on the part of those responsible for it, but also as a cynical attempt by the British ministry to embody mercantilistic principles in an American land policy that in itself ran counter to the charter limits of many of the colonies and the interests in general of the colonials. Nevertheless, this view of the Proclamation fails to take into account the fact that it was the offspring of the war and that the trans-Appalachian aspects of it were an almost inevitable result of promises made during the progress of hostilities. For both in the Treaty of Easton in 1758 with the Ohio Valley Indians, the treaty ratified by the Crown, and in the asseverations of such military leaders as Colonel Bouquet, these Indians were assured that they would be secure in their trans-Appalachian lands as a reward for deserting their allies, the French. As a sign of good faith, the lands lying within the bounds of Pennsylvania to the west of the mountains, purchased by the Proprietors from the Six Nations in 1754, were solemnly released. Thus committed in honor in the course of the war, what could the Cabinet Council at its termination do other than it finally did in the Proclamation of 1763? But this step not only was in opposition to the interests of such groups of land speculators as, for example, the Patrick Henry group in Virginia and the Richard Henderson group in North Carolina, both of whom boldly ignored the Proclamation in negotiating with the Cherokee Indians for land grants, but also led to open defiance of this imperial regulation by frontiersmen who, moving beyond the mountains by the thousands, proceeded to settle within the Indian reserve—some on lands previously occupied before the beginning of the late war or before the great Indian revolt in 1763, and others on new lands.

The Proclamation Line of 1763 might have become an issue, indeed a most formidable one, between the government of Great Britain and the colonials, had not the former acquiesced in the inevitable and confirmed certain Indian treaties that provided for the transfer of much of the land which had been the particular object of quest on the part of speculators and of those moving westward from the settled areas to establish new homes. Such were the treaties of Hard Labor, Fort Stanwix, Lochaber, and the modification of the last-named by the Donelson agreement with the Cherokees in 1771. Nor did the regulation of the trans-Appalachian Indian trade create serious colonial irritation, especially in view of the failure of the government to implement the elaborate Board of Trade plan drawn up in 1764. The same, however, cannot be said of the program put forward by the ministry and accepted by Parliament for securing the means to maintain order and provide protection for this vast area and the new acquisitions to the north and south of it.

Theoretically, it would have been possible for the government of Great Britain to have dropped onto the lap of the old continental colonies the entire responsibility for maintaining garrisons at various strategic points in North America—in Canada, about the Great Lakes, in the Ohio and Mississippi valleys, and in East and West Florida. In spite, however, of assertions made by some prominent colonials, such as Franklin, in 1765 and 1766, that the colonies would be able and were willing to take up the burden of providing for the defense of America, this, under the circumstances, was utterly chimerical, involving, as it would have, not only a vast expenditure of funds but highly complicated intercolonial arrangements, even in the face of the most serious intercolonial rivalry such as that between Pennsylvania and Virginia respecting the control of the upper Ohio Valley. The very proportions of the task were an insuperable obstacle to leaving it to the colonies; and the colonies, moreover, would have been faced by another impediment almost as difficult to surmount—the utter aversion of Americans of the eighteenth century, by and large, to the dull routine of garrison duty. This was emphasized by the Massachusetts Bay Assembly in 1755 in its appeal to the government of Great Britain after Braddock's defeat to send regulars to man the frontier forts of that province; the dispatches of Colonel George Washington in 1756 and in 1757 respecting the shameful desertion of militiamen, ordered to hold the chain of posts on the western frontier of Virginia in order to check the frightful French and Indian raids, support this position, as does the testimony in 1757 of Governor Lyttelton of South Carolina, who made clear that the inhabitants of that colony were not at all adapted to this type of work. The postwar task of garrison duty was clearly one to be assumed by regulars held to their duty under firm discipline and capable of being shifted from one strategic point to another as circumstances might require. Further, to be effective, any plan for the defense of the new possessions and the trans-Appalachian region demanded unity of command, something the colonials could not provide. Manifestly this could be done only through the instrumentalities of the mother country.

The British ministry, thus confronted with the problem of guaranteeing the necessary security for the extended empire in North America, which it was estimated would involve the annual expenditure of from three to four hundred thousand pounds for the maintenance of ten thousand troops—according to various estimates made by General Amherst and others in 1764 and to be found among the Shelburne Papers—was impelled to raise the question: Should not the colonials be expected to assume some definite part of the cost of this? In view of the fact that it was felt not only that they were in a position to do so but that the stability of these outlying possessions was a matter of greater concern and importance generally to them, by reason of their proximity, than to the people of the mother country 3,000 miles away, the answer was in the affirmative.

The reason for this is not hard to fathom. The nine years of war had involved Britons in tremendous expenditures. In spite of very heavy taxation during these years, the people were left saddled at the termination of hostilities with a national debt of unprecedented proportions for that day and age of over £140 million. It was necessary not only to service and to retire this debt, in so far as was possible, but also to meet the ordinary demands of the civil government and to maintain the navy at a point of strength that would offer some assurance that France and Spain would have no desire in the future to plan a war to recover their territorial losses. In addition to all this, there was now the problem of meeting the charges necessary for keeping the new possessions in North America under firm military control for their internal good order and for protection from outside interference.

It may be noted that before the war the British budget had called for average annual expenditures of £6.5 million; between the years 1756 and 1766 these expenditures mounted to £14.5 million a year on the average and from the latter date to 1775 ranged close to £10 million. As a result, the annual per capita tax in Great Britain, from 1763 to 1775, without considering local rates, was many times the average annual per capita tax in even those American colonies that made the greatest contribution to the Great War for the Empire, such as Massachusetts Bay and Connecticut—without reference to those colonies that had done little or nothing in this conflict, and therefore had accumulated little in the way of a war debt, such as Maryland and Georgia. The student of the history of the old British Empire, in fact, should accept with great reserve statements to the contrary—some of them quite irresponsible in nature—made by Americans during the heat of the controversy, with respect to the nature of the public burdens they were obliged to carry in the years preceding the outbreak of the Revolutionary War. In this connection a study of parliamentary reimbursement of colonial war expenses from 1756 to 1763 in its relation to public debts in America between the years 1763 and 1775 is most revealing. As to American public finance, all that space will here permit is to state that there is abundant evidence to indicate that, during the five-year period preceding the outbreak of the Revolutionary War, had the inhabitants of any of the thirteen colonies, which therefore included those of Massachusetts Bay and Virginia, been taxed in one of these years at the average high per capita rate that the British people were taxed from 1760 to 1775, the proceeds of that one year's tax not only would have taken care of the ordinary expenditures of the colony in question for that year but also would have quite liquidated its war debt, so little of which remained in any of the colonies by 1770. Well may John Adams have admitted in 1780 what was equally true in 1770: "America is not used to great taxes, and the people there are not yet disciplined to such enormous taxation as in England."

Assuming, as did the Grenville ministry in 1764, the justice of expecting the Americans to share in the cost of policing the new possessions in North America, the simplest and most obvious way, it might appear, to secure this contribution to a common end so important to both Americans and Britons was to request the colonial governments to make definite grants of funds. This was the requisition or quota system that had been employed in the course of the recent war. But the most obvious objections to it were voiced that same year by Benjamin Franklin, who, incidentally, was to reverse himself the following year in conferring with Grenville as the Pennsylvania London agent. In expressing confidentially his personal, rather than any official, views to his friend Richard Jackson on June 25, 1764 he declared: "Quota's would be difficult to settle at first with Equality, and would, if they could be made equal at first, soon become unequal, and never would be satisfactory." Indeed, experience with this system in practice, as a settled method of guaranteeing even the minimum essential resources for the end in view, had shown its weakness and utter unfairness. If it could not work equitably even in war time, could it be expected to work in peace? It is, therefore, not surprising that this method of securing even a portion of the funds required for North American security should have been rejected in favor of some plan that presented better prospects of a definite American revenue.

The plan of last resort to the ministry was therefore to ask Parliament to act. That Grenville, however, was aware that serious objections might be raised against any direct taxation of the colonials by the government of Great Britain is indicated by the caution with which he approached the solution of the problem of securing from America about a third of the total cost of its defense. The so-called Sugar Act first of all was passed at his request. This provided for import duties on certain West Indian and other products. Colonial import duties imposed by Parliament, at least since 1733, were no innovation. But the anticipated yield of these duties fell far short of the desired £100,000. He therefore, in introducing the bill for the above act, raised the question of a stamp duty but requested postponement of parliamentary action until the colonial governments had been consulted. The latter were thereupon requested to make any suggestions for ways of raising an American fund that might seem more proper to the people than such a tax. Further, it would appear —at least, according to various London advices published in Franklin and Hall's *Pennsylvania Gazette*—that proposals were seriously considered by the Cabinet Council during the fall of 1764 for extending to the colonies representation in Parliament through the election of members to the House of Commons by various colonial assemblies. However, it is quite clear that by the beginning of 1765 any such proposals, as seem to have been under deliberation by the ministry, had been put aside when Grenville at length had become convinced that representation in Parliament was neither actively sought nor even desired by Americans. For the South Carolina Commons House of Assembly went strongly on record against this idea in September 1764 and was followed by the Virginia House of Burgesses in December. In fact, when in the presence of the London colonial agents the minister had outlined the objections raised by Americans to the idea of such representation, no one of them, including Franklin, was prepared to deny the validity of these objections. That he was not mistaken in the opposition of Americans at large to sending members to Parliament, in spite of the advocacy of this by James Otis, is clear in the resolutions passed both by other colonial assemblies than the ones to which reference has been made and by the Stamp Act Congress in 1765. Indeed, in 1768 the House of Representatives of Massachusetts Bay went so far in its famous Circular Letter framed in opposition to the Townshend duties as to make clear that the people of that colony actually preferred taxation by Parliament without representation to such taxation with representation.

When—in view of the failure of the colonial governments to suggest any practicable, alternate plan for making some contribution to the postwar defensive program in North America—Grenville finally urged in Parliament the passage of an American stamp bill, he acted on an unwarranted assumption. This assumption was—in paraphrasing the minister's remarks to the colonial agents in 1765—that opposition to stamp taxes, for the specific purpose in mind, would disappear in America both in light of the benefits such provision would bring to colonials in general and by reason of the plain justice of the measure itself; and that, in place of opposition, an atmosphere of mutual goodwill would be generated by a growing recognition on the part of Americans that they could trust the benevolence of the mother country to act with fairness to all within the empire. Instead, with the news of the passage of the act, cries of British tyranny and impending slavery soon resounded throughout the entire eastern Atlantic American seaboard. What would have been the fate of the empire had Grenville remained in office to attempt to enforce the act, no one can say. But as members of the opposition to the Rockingham ministry, he and his brother, Earl Temple, raised their voices —one as a commoner, the other as a peer—in warning that the American colonies would inevitably be lost to the empire should Parliament be led to repeal the act in the face of colonial resistance and the pressure of British merchants. Had Parliament determined, in spite of violence and threats of violence, to enforce the act, it might have meant open rebellion and civil war, ten years before it actually occurred. Instead, this body decided to yield and, in spite of the passing of the so-called Declaratory Act setting forth its fundamental powers to legislate on all matters relating to the empire, suffered a loss of prestige in the New World that was never to be regained.

But the Stamp Act was not the sole object of attack by colonials. To many of them not only the Sugar Act of 1764 but the whole English prewar trade and navigation system was equally, if not actually more, obnoxious. Indeed, the unusual energy displayed by the navy and the customs officials, spurred into action by Pitt during the latter years of the war—bringing with it the condemnation in courts of vice-admiralty of many American vessels whose owners were guilty of serious trade violations, if not greater crimes—generated a degree of antagonism against the whole body of late seventeenth- and early eighteenth-century restrictions on commercial intercourse such as never had previously existed. It is not without significance that the greatest acts of terrorism and destruction during the great riot of August 1765 in Boston were directed not against the Massachusetts Bay stamp distributor but against those officials responsible for encouraging and supporting the enforcement, during the late war, of the various trade acts passed long before its beginning in 1754. The hatred also of the Rhode Island merchants, as a group, against the restrictions of the navigation system as well as against the Sugar Act of 1764, remained constant. Moreover, in December 1766 most of the New York merchants, over two hundred in number, showed their repugnance to the way that this system was functioning by a strongly worded petition to the House of Commons in which they enumerated an impressive list of grievances that they asked to be redressed. Even Chatham, the great friend of America, regarded their petition "highly improper: in point of time most absurd, in the extent of their pretensions, most excessive; and in the reasoning, most grossly fallacious and offensive." In fact, all the leading men in Great Britain supported the system of trade restrictions.

Nevertheless, the determination of the government—in view especially of the great financial burdens that the late war had placed upon the mother country—to enforce it now much more effectively than had been done before 1754, and to that end in 1767 to pass appropriate legislation in order to secure funds from the colonies by way of import duties so that public officials in America might be held to greater accountability when paid their salaries by the Crown, could have only one result: the combined resistance of those, on the one hand, opposed to any type of taxation that Parliament might apply to America and of those, on the other, desiring to free the colonies of hampering trade restrictions.

The suggestion on the part of the Continental Congress in 1774 that Americans would uphold the British navigation system, if exempted from parliamentary taxation, while a shrewd gesture to win support in England, had really, it would seem, no other significance. For it is utterly inconceivable that the Congress itself, or the individual colonial governments, could have set up machinery capable of preventing violations of the system at will on the part of those whose financial interests were adversely affected by its operation. Moreover, it is obvious that, by the time the news had reached America that Lord North's ministry had secured the passage of the Coercive Acts—for the most part directed against Massachusetts Bay for the defiant destruction of the East India Company's tea—leading colonials, among them Franklin, had arrived at the conclusion that Parliament possessed powers so very limited with respect to the empire that without the consent of the local assemblies it could pass neither constitutional nor fiscal legislation that affected Americans and the framework of their governments. It is equally obvious that this represented a most revolutionary position when contrasted with that held by Franklin and the other delegates to the Albany Congress twenty years earlier. For it was in 1754 that the famous Plan of Union was drawn up there and approved by the Congress—a plan based upon the view that Parliament, and not the Crown, had supreme authority within the empire, an authority that alone was adequate in view of framers of the Plan to bring about fundamental changes in the constitutions of the colonies in order legally to clothe the proposed union government with adequate fiscal as well as other powers.

In accounting for the radical change in attitude of many leading colonials between the years 1754 and 1774 respecting the nature of the constitution of the empire, surely among the factors that must be weighed was the truly overwhelming victory achieved in the Great War for the Empire. This victory not only freed colonials for the first time in the history of the English-speaking people in the New World from dread of the French, their Indian allies, and the Spaniards, but, what is of equal significance, opened up to them the prospect, if given freedom of action, of a vast growth of power and wealth with an amazing westward expansion. Indeed, it is abundantly clear that a continued subordination of the colonies to the government of Great Britain was no longer considered an asset in the eyes of many Americans by 1774, as it had been so judged by them to be in 1754, but rather an onerous liability. What, pray tell, had the debt-ridden mother country to offer in 1774 to the now geographically secure, politically mature, prosperous, dynamic, and self-reliant offspring along the Atlantic seaboard, except the dubious opportunity of accepting new, as well as retaining old, burdens? And these burdens would have to be borne in order to lighten somewhat the great financial load that the taxpayers of Great Britain were forced to carry by reason of obligations the nation had assumed both in the course of the late war and at its termination. If many Americans thought they had a perfect right to profit personally by trading with the enemy in time of war, how much more deeply must they have resented in time of peace the serious efforts made by the home government to enforce the elaborate restrictions on commercial intercourse? Again, if, even after the defeat of Colonel Washington at Great Meadows in 1754, colonials such as Franklin were opposed to paying any tax levied by Parliament for establishing a fund for the defense of North America, how much more must they have been inclined to oppose such taxation to that end with the passing in 1763 of the great international crisis?

At this point the question must be frankly faced: If France had won the war decisively and thereby consolidated her position and perfected her claims in Nova Scotia, as well as to the southward of the St. Lawrence, in the Great Lakes region, and in the Ohio and Mississippi valleys, is it at all likely that colonials would have made so fundamental a constitutional issue of the extension to them of the principle of the British stamp tax? Would they have resisted such a tax had Parliament imposed it in order to provide on an equitable basis the maximum resources for guaranteeing their safety, at a time when they were faced on their highly restricted borders by a militant, victorious enemy having at its command thousands of ferocious redskins? Again, accepting the fact of Britain's victory, is it not reasonable to believe that, had Great Britain at the close of the triumphant war left Canada to France and carefully limited her territorial demands in North America to those comparatively modest objectives that she had in mind at its beginning, there would have been no very powerful movement within the foreseeable future toward complete colonial autonomy—not to mention American independence? Would not Americans have continued to feel the need as in the past to rely for their safety and welfare upon British sea power and British land power, as well as upon British resources generally? In other words, was Governor Thomas Hutchinson of Massachusetts Bay far mistaken when, in analyzing the American situation late in 1773, he affirmed in writing to the Earl of Dartmouth:

> *Before the peace [of 1763] I thought nothing so much to be desired as the cession of Canada. I am now convinced that if it had remained to the French none of the spirit of opposition to the Mother Country would have yet appeared & I think the effects of it [that is, the cession of Canada] worse than all we had to fear from the French or Indians.*

In conclusion, it may be said that it would be idle to deny that most colonials in the eighteenth century at one time or another felt strongly the desire for freedom of action in a wider variety of ways than was legally permitted before 1754. Indeed, one can readily uncover these strong impulses even in the early part of the seventeenth century. Yet Americans were, by and large, realists, as were the British, and under the functioning of the imperial system from, let us say, 1650 to 1750 great mutual advantages were enjoyed, with a fair division, taking everything into consideration, of the financial burdens necessary to support the system. However, the mounting Anglo-French rivalry in North America from 1750 onward, the outbreak of hostilities in 1754, and the subsequent nine years of fighting destroyed the old equilibrium, leaving the colonials after 1760 in a highly favored position in comparison with the taxpayers of Great Britain. Attempts on the part of the Crown and Parliament to restore by statute the old balance led directly to the American constitutional crisis, out of which came the Revolutionary War and the establishment of American independence. Such, ironically, was the aftermath of the Great War for the Empire, a war that Britons believed, as the Earl of Shelburne affirmed in 1762 in Parliament, was begun for the "security of the British colonies in N. America. . . ."

Bernhard Knollenberg

BRITISH PROVOCATIONS IN THE MOVEMENT FOR INDEPENDENCE

Educated at Earlham College and at Harvard University, Bernhard Knollenberg has, even while making major contributions to the writing of American history, pursued several nonacademic careers. (He has been an attorney with a New York law firm, a librarian at Yale University, an administrator in the Lend-Lease Administration, an intelligence worker in the O.S.S.) In the work from which this selection is taken, he argues that a major cause of colonial discontent was the series of judgments and decisions made by British policy makers of the period.

While the British Stamp Act of 1765 greatly contributed to and touched off the colonial uprising of 1765–1766, the colonists had been brought to the brink of rebellion by a number of other provocative British measures from 1759 to 1764, most of which persisted after the Stamp Act was repealed in 1766 and contributed to the mounting colonial discontent culminating in the American Revolution of 1775–1783.

From 1759 to 1763 the chief causes of colonial discontent were:

The Privy Council's disallowance in 1759 of an important Virginia act accompanied by an order to the governor of the colony forbidding him to sign any bill passed by the legislature of the colony repealing or amending an existing act, unless the bill contained a clause suspending its operation until approved by the Privy Council in England. Since many acts would be wholly or nearly useless if suspended until thus approved, this order struck at the very roots of self-government in Virginia. Soon afterward Massachusetts and South Carolina were likewise alarmed by steps taken to extend the order to these colonies;

Issuance in 1761 of general writs of assistance empowering officers of the English customs service in Massachusetts to break into and search homes and stores for supposed smuggled goods;

Issuance of an order by the Privy Council in 1761 forbidding governors of the royal colonies to issue judicial or other commissions not revocable at the pleasure of the king, an order particularly disturbing in New York and New Jersey because the judges of the Supreme Court in these colonies had heretofore been granted tenure during good behavior;

The activities from 1759 onward of Thomas Secker, archbishop of Canterbury, assisted by the Society for the Propagation of the Gospel in Foreign Parts of which he was president, in planting a Church of England mission church in Cambridge near Harvard College, fountainhead of the Congregational clergy in eastern New England; in procuring the disallowance by the Privy Council of a Massachusetts act to establish a Congregational missionary society for work among the American Indians; and in attempting to secure the establishment of Church of England bishops in the colonies.

The Treaty of Paris between Great Britain and France and Spain, signed at Paris in February 1763, laid the basis for reestablishing cordial relations between Great Britain and the colonies. For the colonists were highly pleased and grateful to the British Government, as they had every reason to be, for the removal of the French threat to the security of the British colonies in North America by insisting on France's cession of the whole of Canada. But the favorable effect of the treaty on colonial opinion was almost immediately impaired by fresh and even more provocative British measures affecting the colonies.

The first was a movement in 1763 for rigid enforcement of the whole range of acts of Parliament restricting colonial trade, including the hitherto unenforced Sugar Act of 1733 imposing a prohibitive duty on imports of foreign colonial molasses. The enforcement of this would seriously cripple if not destroy the extremely important trade of the northern British colonies with the foreign colonial possessions in the West Indies and South America. This trade not only furnished the molasses which was the backbone of the flourishing northern colonial rum industry and was widely used for sweetening, but gave northern colonial farmers, fishermen and lumbermen a favorable market for their surplus farm produce, fish, and lumber.

Irritating under any circumstances, the new measure was particularly so because it was implemented by sending a squadron of British warships to American waters as an arm of the English customs service. Even when British warships were in American waters to defend the colonies in time of war, impressment of colonial seamen to fill gaps in the crews from death and desertion had caused serious trouble. Now, with the ships in constant attendance on an obnoxious mission, impressment and other incidents connected with their presence were a source of acute friction.

Rigorous enforcement of the Sugar Act was accompanied by rigorous enforcement of long unenforced acts of Parliament prohibiting (with certain exceptions) the cutting of white pine trees in the colonies.

Even more serious and far-reaching was the passage by Parliament, in April 1764, of an act, the American Act of 1764, imposing new restrictions on colonial trade and levying taxes in the colonies to support an enlarged British standing army in America without consulting the colonial governments as to the number or composition and distribution of the troops and without offering commissions to any former colonial officers, many of whom had served creditably in the recent French and Indian War. So long as Great Britain paid the entire cost of the British forces stationed in America, the colonists had little cause for complaint if not consulted on these points; but when called upon to support or help support the British troops in America, it was unreasonable not to give them a share in determining the number, distribution, and kind of troops needed for their protection and in the apportionment of commissions.

The failure to consult the colonial governments was particularly galling because at the very time the new policy of taxing the colonists for the support of the British army in America was put into effect, the army was miserably failing to protect the colonial frontiers from the ravages of the western Indians in an uprising (Pontiac's Rebellion) attributable largely to blunders of the British commander in chief in North America, General Sir Jeffrey Amherst.

Furthermore, though in the Act of Union of England and Scotland, the Scots were protected not only by representation in Parliament but by a provision permanently limiting the proportion of the total land tax to be imposed on Scotland, neither the American Act itself nor any statement in Parliament concerning it offered assurance that, having established the precedent of taxing the colonies, Parliament would not shift an ever-increasing proportion of the imperial tax burden from British to colonial taxpayers. Moreover, since the colonies were now to be taxed for imperial purposes, they had reason to expect an offset by amelioration of the restrictions imposed by

Parliament on colonial trade, whereas, far from easing existing restrictions, Parliament made them more onerous than ever.

Had the provocative measures from 1759 to 1764 been distributed over a long period, the effect of each might have rippled away before the next was felt; but, concentrated in the span of a few years, all contributed to the colonial fear that the British government would go further and further in depriving the colonists of the large measure of self-government in internal affairs they had so long enjoyed and justly valued.

This fear became conviction on Parliament's passing the colonial Stamp Act of 1765. Warned by a resolution of the House of Commons in 1764 and by their agents in London that a bill for such an act would probably be introduced in the next session of Parliament, the legislatures of the leading North American colonies petitioned against the proposed new act, only to have their petitions rejected and the act adopted by an overwhelming majority in both Houses. This was the last straw. There now seemed no other way to halt further British encroachment on colonial self-government than to resist the execution of this latest measure, even at the risk of war.

As indicated by the foregoing discussion, I differ from the view presented by Professor Charles Andrews in his well-known Presidential address to the American Historical Association in 1925, "The American Revolution: An Interpretation." The manifestations of colonial discontent in the half century preceding the Revolution were, said Andrews, "the outward and visible signs of an inward factual divergence. . . . On one side was the immutable stereotyped system of the mother country, based on precedent and tradition and designed to keep things comfortably as they were; on the other, a vital, dynamic organism, containing the seed of a great nation, its forces untried, still to be proved. It is inconceivable that a connection should have continued long between two such yokefellows, one static, the other dynamic, separated by an ocean and bound only by the ties of a legal relationship."

To me, on the contrary, it seems reasonably clear that until the adoption of the provocative British measures from 1759 to 1765, . . . the stereotyped system of British government, based on precedent and tradition and designed to keep things comfortably as they were, was, on the whole, satisfactory to the colonial "yokefellows." Far

FIGURE 4. The Boston Massacre. March 5, 1770. Colored line engraving, 1770. (*The Granger Collection*)

from being bound only by the ties of a legal relationship, they were, in most cases, bound also by a powerful bond of sentiment woven from many strands: a feeling for England as the ancestral homeland ("home" as many still called it); a strong sense of family kinship with its people; a common language, literature, and system of law; loyalty to a common sovereign. Had the relationship not been disturbed by the many new and vexing British measures introduced from 1759 to 1765 and afterward continued or renewed, it might, I think, have endured (subject to occasional political readjustments notably such as were made a half century later in the British Empire and in Great Britain itself) for many generations, perhaps even to this day. . . .

As to the failure of the island colonies and the newly acquired mainland colonies to resist the Stamp Act, the reasons for this are, I think, pretty clear. Enforcement of the prohibitive duty on foreign colonial molasses imposed by the Sugar Act of 1733 and perpetuated at a lower but still heavy rate by the American Act of 1764, far from injuring the West Indians as it did the mainland colonists, was for their benefit. Furthermore, Great Britain granted a large tariff preference in favor of British colonial over foreign sugar, and, since the British demand for sugar had long outstripped the British colonial sugar supply, the tariff differential in favor of British colonial sugar was effective in raising the price of sugar in the British market far above the world price. Because of its costliness to British consumers, the high protective tariff in favor of British colonial sugar had long been under fire, and, if Parliament was seriously antagonized, would almost certainly be reduced or repealed. Finally, apart from economic considerations there was a compelling reason for the British West Indian colonists to remain quiet, since, outnumbered seven to one by their slaves and in constant fear and danger of slave insurrection, they were utterly dependent on the continued protection of the British army and navy.

Bermuda, the Bahamas, and Nova Scotia, though not benefited by the British tariff differential on sugar, were, like the West Indian colonies, exceptionally dependent on the British navy and army for protection. Moreover, they were politically and economically backward; Nova Scotia received direct financial aid from Parliament; and Bermuda and the Bahamas were isolated from the currents of opinion and protest through which the leaders in the mainland colonies aroused and encouraged each other. Grenada, East Florida, and West Florida, formed out of the territory ceded by France and Spain in 1763, were too sparsely peopled and politically undeveloped (they did not even have representative assemblies yet) to resist. And Quebec, the colony formed from eastern Canada, though more populous than the other new colonies, was equally backward in political development.

As to the . . . question why so many British measures obnoxious to the North American colonists were taken at this particular time, no summary answer is possible. . . . Many factors were involved. The most important, I believe, was the distracted state of British politics and government following the death in 1760 of George II, a state attributable chiefly to the shift in power from the experienced duke of Newcastle and William Pitt to George III's inexperienced favorite, Lord Bute, and the audacity and art of the archdemagogue John Wilkes. . . .

III THE SOCIAL BASIS OF REVOLUTIONARY POLITICS

Carl Becker

THE SPIRIT OF '76

Carl Lotus Becker, professor of history at Cornell from 1917 until his death in 1945, is as widely known as any American historian. He was the author of classic works in the history of ideas (The Heavenly City of the Eighteenth Century Philosophers) *and in the writing of history* (Every Man His Own Historian) *as well as in American history itself. The essay reprinted here presents his imaginative recreation of the thoughts of the American colonists on the eve of the Revolution.*

Last October Mr. Lyon asked me to come down to the Brookings School and tell you about the Spirit of '76. I suspected that he hadn't any clear notion of what was meant by the phrase "Spirit of '76," and I was positive I hadn't. I was therefore about to decline the invitation when, rummaging among my papers, I came upon an old and imperfect manuscript which seemed providentially designed to throw some light on this obscure subject. The manuscript bore the date of 1792, but who may have written it I was unable to determine. There are obviously some pages missing, and the tale ends suddenly as if never quite finished. But such as it is I have transcribed it, and I give it to you for what it may be worth. The title of the manuscript is "Jeremiah Wynkoop."

Jeremiah Wynkoop

During the war of independence I not infrequently heard zealous patriots say that Mr. Wynkoop was not as warm in the cause as he should be. The charge has lately been revived by those who had no great liking for Mr. Wynkoop's Federalist principles. Mr. Wynkoop was of course not alone in being thus distinguished. It is now said of many men who were never suspected of being Tory that they look back with regret to the old days before the breach with Britain. It is said of them, to employ a phrase now becoming current, that they were never really inspired by the true spirit of '76. For my part, I suspect that, in recalling the desperate days of the war, we are likely to invest the so-called spirit of '76 with a glamor which it did not have at the time. Be that as it may, I knew Jeremiah Wynkoop as an honest man and a genuine patriot. I was his closest friend, intimate enough to know better than most the difficulties that confronted him and the sentiments that determined his conduct. And so I think it worth while, now that the man is dead, to set down a plain tale of his activities and opinions from the beginning of the quarrel in 1763 to the final breach in 1776. This I do, not only for old friendship's sake and as a justification of Mr. Wynkoop, but as a contribution to the history of those troubled times; for Jeremiah Wynkoop was fairly representative, both in his station in life and in his opinions, of that considerable class of substantial men who did as much as any other class, and I think more than any other class, to enable these states to maintain their liberties against British tyranny.

Born of rich middle class parents of genuine Dutch-American stock, Jeremiah was educated at Kings College, then recently established. In fact we both entered the College the year it was founded, and graduated with the first class in 1758. Jeremiah then spent two years in the office of William Moore reading law, a profession which he nevertheless abandoned for the trade. Taking over a profitable business upon the sudden death of his father, he rapidly achieved a notable success in commerce, chiefly in West Indian ventures, and was already known, in 1765, as a leading merchant in New York, where he had offices near the wharves, and a town house, inherited from his father, on the Bowling Green. But Jeremiah, being much given to study and the reading of books, preferred to live away from the distractions of the city, and had in fact for some years resided in the country, out Greenwich Village way, where he possessed a fine estate which had come to him as part of the generous dowry of his wife, the daughter of old Nicholas Van Schoickendinck, a great landowner in the province.

Mr. Wynkoop was much given to the reading of books, as I have said; and it is necessary to dwell on this matter a little since it helps to explain his opinions and conduct. Of all books, histories of the ancient and the modern times were his favorite study. It was an interest which he acquired in college, and never afterward lost. In college of course we all read the standard Greek and Roman writers, and acquired the usual knowledge of classical history. To admire the classical poets and essayists was nothing out of the way for young men in college, but the ancient civilization fascinated Jeremiah more than most of us, and I recall that he devoured every book on that subject which the college afforded, and many others which he bought or borrowed. The Parallel Lives of Plutarch he knew almost by heart, and was never weary of discanting on the austere morality and virtuous republicanism of those heroic times. For Jeremiah a kind of golden age was pictured there, a lost world which forever disappeared when Caesar crossed the Rubicon. The later Roman times never interested him much—"five hundred years," he used to say, "in which the civilized world groaned under the heavy hands of tyrants, relieved only by the reigns of five good emperors." Still less was he interested in the Dark Ages, when the light of learning and the spirit of liberty were submerged by feudal anarchy and ecclesiastical superstition. But the story of modern times fascinated Jeremiah as much as the story of the ancient world because all its significance seemed to lie in the slow and painful emergence from that long mediaeval night, through the recovery of the wisdom of the ancients, the progress of natural philosophy, and the struggle for political liberty.

All these matters I recall we used to discuss at great length, so that I was perfectly familiar with Jeremiah's reflections on history. At that time his ideas seemed to me wonderfully novel and interesting, but I have since thought them, in a vague general way at least, those of most cultivated Americans. Be that as it may, all the significance of history appeared to Mr. Wynkoop to lie in the age-long conflict between Truth and Error, between Freedom and Oppression. And for this reason he opined that the central event of modern times was the struggle of the last century between the English people and the Stuart kings. With the history of that heroic time he was entirely familiar, and in a less degree I was too. Our heroes were Pym and Eliot, and John Hampden, imprisoned for refusing to pay a twenty shilling tax. Cromwell we admired as the man of iron who had forever laid the ghost of the Divine Right doctrine, and whose mistakes were later corrected by the liberal Whigs who called in Dutch William to replace the last of the Stuarts. We knew the great charters of liberty—the Magna Charta, the Petition of Right and the Bill of Rights. We knew our Milton, the man who defended the authority of elected magistrates, and erected an impregnable bulwark against the denial of free speech. We knew our Grotius, who had discovered in right reason the foundation of civil and international society. Above all we knew our Locke, and especially his second discourse on Civil

Government, in which he so eloquently defended the Revolution of '88 as an act of reasonable men defending their natural rights against the usurping king who had broken the original compact.

Much as Jeremiah admired England as the home of political liberty, he was thoroughly American, and it was always his idea that America had played a most notable part in the great modern struggle against the oppression of Church and State. He used to find great satisfaction in recalling that our ancestors, at the hazard of their lives and fortunes, had braved the terrors of the new world in pursuit of religious and political liberty; that they had persisted, often at the point of failure, in the desperate determination to transform the inhospitable wilderness into a land fit for human habitation; and he would point out that they had succeeded beyond any reasonable expectation, so much so that these thirteen colonies were now the most fortunate and the freest countries in the world—thirteen communities living in peace and content, happily without kings, neither burdened with an idle aristocracy nor menaced by a depraved populace, with a press uncensored, and many religious faiths deprived of the power of persecution and long habituated to the spirit of toleration. For my part I used to complain sometimes that after all we were only "provincials," remote from the center of things. I used to express the wish that fate had set us down in London, nearer Piccadilly and the Beefsteak Club. But Jeremiah would have none of such repining. Provincials we might be in a geographical sense, he would say, but spiritually we were at "the center of the world, in the direct line of those heroes and martyrs who since the beginning of time have done battle for the dignity and happiness of mankind against the leagued assailants of both."

Here some pages are missing in the manuscript. It goes on as follows.

". . . are become so populous and wealthy that we are as indispensable to Britain as Britain is to us. The time is surely approaching when this vast country will be the center of power and wealth of the Empire. We are now freed from the French menace. The peace will be an enduring one, and the two branches of the English race will continue in the future as in the past to exemplify to the world those incomparable blessings that are the prerogatives of free peoples."

Such was Jeremiah Wynkoop's conception of history in general and of the part which Britain and America had played in the story of human progress. With him it was a kind of philosophy, a religion indeed, the only religion really that he had. I don't mean that he was of the atheistical school of thought. He believed indeed in the existence of the Deity as the First Cause and Original Contriver of the universe; and this was in fact the very reason why he found so much delight in the study of history. History was God's revelation of the meaning of life and of human destiny on earth, making plain the gradual progress and the ultimate triumph of Truth and Freedom. And this I think was the secret of his profound loyalty to both Britain and America; these were in his view the promised lands, the homes of the chosen peoples whose mission it was to lead mankind toward the final goal.

Nothing at all events was farther from his thought in 1763 than that there could be any serious differences between the two peoples who were so bound together by ties of blood and affection, by mutual respect, and by the common tradition of . . .

Another break in the manuscript here.

In the year 1765 Mr. Wynkoop shared the general feeling of apprehension which for two years had been steadily increasing on account of the measures, as unprecedented as they were unfortunate, of the king's minister, Mr. George Grenville. The chief of these measures were undoubtedly the Sugar Act of the last, and the Stamp Act of the then present year. On the nature and effects of these measures Mr. Wynkoop had read and reflected as much as a busy man well could do. The Sugar Act, obviously designed to placate the British West Indian sugar planters, was certain, as indeed it was intended, to put obstacles in the way of the island trade with New York and New England. In that trade Mr. Wynkoop was personally interested. It is true, as indeed he was careful to tell me, that his profits for the last year were much as usual; but it had been abundantly demonstrated in pamphlets that the Sugar duties were bound to have a disastrous effect on American trade in general; would, for example, undermine the New England rum industry and thereby depress the fisheries and the African trade; would diminish the exports of lumber and grain from New York and Pennsylvania; would above all, since the new duties were to paid in silver, drain the colonies of their small store of hard money and thereby make it difficult for American merchants to settle their balances due in London on account of imported British manufactures.

No one doubted, at least no one in America, that the Sugar Act was unwise in point of policy, calculated to defeat the very end intended. Yet there it was, an act of Parliament imposing duties for the regulation of trade, and we could not deny that Parliament had long exercised without opposition the right to regulate trade. But I recall Mr. Wynkoop's pointing out to me one novel feature of the act, which was the declared purpose, expressed in the preamble, of raising a revenue in "his Majesty's dominions in America, for defraying the expenses of defending, protecting, and securing the same." For some reason Mr. Wynkoop disliked the term "dominions," always preferring the term "colonies." But he disliked still more the term "securing." For two years ministers had been prone to talk of laying restrictions on his Majesty's dominions for their better security. This idea Mr. Wynkoop disliked extremely. I remember his saying that the term "free-born Englishmen" had always given him great satisfaction, that he had always supposed that Americans were possessed of all the rights of Englishmen born within the realm; and indeed I knew him well enough to know that he harbored the firm conviction that Americans were not only as free as Englishmen but even a little freer, a degree less subservient to aristocrats and kings, a degree more emancipated from custom and the dead hand of the past. I often heard him compare the Assembly of New York, chosen by the free suffrages of the people, with the British Parliament in which so often the members were chosen by irresponsible Peers and Borough-mongers—compare them of course to the disadvantage of the latter. To suppose that Parliament was now bent upon restricting the dearly bought and well deserved liberties of America was to Jeremiah, as indeed it was to all of us, an alien and distressing thought.

We could scarcely therefore avoid asking the question: "What constitutional right has the British Parliament to legislate in restraint of American liberties?" We never doubted that we were possessed of liberties, and no American, certainly no American as well informed as Mr. Wynkoop, needed to be told that there was a British Constitution which guaranteed the rights of Englishmen. Yet, as I recall those early years, I must confess that we were somewhat perplexed, had a little the air of groping about in the dark for the precise provisions of the British Constitution. The spirit of the British Constitution we knew was to be found in the Magna Charta and the Bill of Rights. Rights were indeed of its very essence; and to Mr. Wynkoop at least it was incredible that there was not to be found in it an adequate guarantee of the rights which Americans ought to enjoy. I remember his reading to me certain passages from the pamphlets of Stephen Hopkins and Governor Hutchinson—pamphlets which he thought expressed the American view very adequately. "What motive," Mr. Hopkins asked, "can remain to induce the Parliament to hedge the principles and lessen the rights of the most dutiful and loyal subjects—subjects justly entitled to ample freedom, who have long enjoyed and not abused, their liberties?" This passage I think expressed Mr. Wynkoop's state of mind very well in the year of the Sugar Act. His state of mind was one of amazement, the state of mind of a man who is still at the point of asking questions—Why? For what reason?

Meantime the Stamp Act, presenting the question more clearly, did much to clarify our ideas on the matter of American taxation; and certainly Mr. Wynkoop was never in doubt as to the unconstitutionality of that famous measure. In those days I was much at Mr. Wynkoop's house, and I remember one day in November, 1765, sitting with him and his father-in-law, old Nicholas Van Schoickendinck, discussing the state of the nation. Even old Nicholas had been startled out of his customary complacency by the furious excitement occasioned by the Stamp Act.

"The Act is unconstitutional, sir," Mr. Wynkoop had just declared, somewhat dogmatically it must be confessed, and for perhaps the third time. "There can be no question about that I think. It is not only contrary to precedent, but is destructive of British liberty, the fundamental principle of which is that Englishmen may not be taxed without their own consent. We certainly never gave our assent to the Stamp Act."

"I won't say no to that," old Nicholas remarked. "And if we had done no more than to protest the measure I should be well content."

"Little good protests would have done, sir. We protested before the bill was passed, and without effect. Mr. Grenville would not hear our protests, and now he finds the act virtually nullified. I can't say I regret it."

"Nullified!" Old Nicholas exclaimed with some asperity. "A soft word for a nasty business. Mr. Grenville finds his law 'nullified,' you say. But in getting the law nullified we get half the windows of the Broad Way smashed too, and Governor Colden gets his chariot burned. For my part I don't know what Mr. Colden's chariot had to do with the devilish stamps—it wasn't designed to carry them."

"Very true, sir, I admit. And regrettable enough, all this parading and disturbance. But if Ministers will play with oppression the people will play with violence. Similar incidents occurred in England itself in the last century. Let Mr. Grenville beware of playing the role of Strafford. God knows I am no friend of rioting. I have windows too. But a little rioting may be necessary on occasion to warn ministers that legislative lawlessness is likely to be met by popular violence."

Mr. Wynkoop had perhaps a little the air of talking to convince himself rather than old Nicholas. Old Nicholas at least was not convinced.

"Tush!" he exclaimed irritably. "That's a new word, 'popular.' You young fellows have picked up a lot of precious democratical phrases, I must say. Who are 'the people' you talk so loosely about? Another word for 'populace' or I miss my guess. Don't delude yourself by supposing that it was hatred of the Stamps that made them break Mr. Livingston's windows and burn Mr. Colden's chariot. They hate Mr. Livingston and Mr. Colden because they are men of substance and standing. It is not windows they aim at but class privileges, the privileges of my class and yours, the class that always has, and I trust always will, govern this province. The bald fact is that a mob of mechanics and ne'er-do-wells, led by obscure fellows like John Lamb and Isaac Sears who have hitherto doffed their caps and known their places, are now aiming to control the city through their self constituted committees. Sons of Liberty, they call themselves; sons of anarchy, in fact. I wish as much as you to preserve our liberties. But I warn you that liberty is a sword that cuts two ways, and if you can't defend your rights against ministerial oppression without stirring the 'people,' you will soon be confronted with the necessity of defending your privileges against the encroachments of the mob on the Bowling Green."

Old Nicholas stopped to light his pipe, and after a few puffs added:

"You don't associate with *Mr.* John Lamb, do you? You ain't one of the Liberty Boys who erect poles and break windows, I hope."

Mr. Wynkoop laughed off the sarcasm.

"Certainly not, sir. I don't know the fellow Lamb, never saw him in fact, although I am told, and believe, that he is an honest, worthy man. The danger you mention has of course occurred to me, but I think you probably exaggerate it. Let Britain repeal the Stamp Act, as she must do, and the populace will be quiet enough."

We sat until a late hour. I took but little part in the discussion, enjoying nothing better than to listen to the good natured wrangling of these two friends. During the course of the evening each repeated, many times over, his former argument, all without rancor, but all equally without effect. Except in opinion, they were not divided; and at last, pledging one another courteously in a glass of stiff toddy, we separated for the night.

During the following months Mr. Wynkoop continued firm in the defence of American rights. He agreed, as all the substantial merchants did, not to use the stamps, which was indeed not possible since none were to be had. Yet he would do no business without them. Let the courts close, he said. Let his ships stand idle in harbor, a year, two years, let them rot there rather than submit to an unconstitutional measure. So I often heard him declare roundly, sitting at dinner sipping his madeira. . . .

Again something missing from the manuscript.

. . . secret misgivings, during the long cold winter, by the continued disturbances in the streets, and by the clamor of those, mostly of the common sort, who demanded that the courts should open and denounced the merchants for timidly refusing to do business without stamps. The Sons of Liberty were saying that the stopping of business was all very well for gentlemen of fortune, but that it was ruining the people who must starve unless business went on as usual. The Sons of Liberty were grown more hostile to the merchants than they were to ministers, and they even hinted that the better sort were by their timidity betraying the cause. Meantime Old Nicholas appeared to enjoy the situation, and never lost an opportunity of asking him, Jeremiah Wynkoop, whether he hadn't yet joined the Liberty Boys, and why after all he didn't send his ships out, clearance papers or no clearance papers.

Mr. Wynkoop was therefore immensely relieved when the British Parliament finally repealed the hateful measure, thus at once justifying his conduct and restoring his confidence in the essential justice of Britain. He had now, I recall, rather the better of the argument with Old Nicholas (the two were forever disputing) and pointed out to him ever so often that a little firmness on America's part was all that was needful to the preservation of her liberties. For two years he went about his business and pleasure with immense content. I dare say he easily forgot, as men will do, the distasteful incidents of the Stamp Act struggle, and allowed his mind to dwell chiefly on its satisfactions. He often spoke of the principle, "No taxation without representation," as being now fully established; often expressed his gratification that, by taking a firm and sensible stand, he and his substantial friends had brought Britain to recognize this principle; so that by the mere passing of time as it were these ideas acquired for Jeremiah a certain axiomatic character. I was never so sure of all this, and sometimes called his attention to the Declaratory Act as evidence that Britain still claimed the right of binding the colonies in all matters whatsoever. Needless to say, old Nicholas called his attention to the Declaratory Act oftener than I did. But Mr. Wynkoop would not take the Declaratory Act seriously. It was, he said, no more than a bravely flying banner designed to cover a dignified retreat from an untenable position; and he had no fear that Britain, having confessed its error by repealing the Stamp Act, would ever again repeat it.

It presently appeared that the British government could commit errors without repeating itself. In 1767, following the mysterious retirement and delphic silences of Mr. Pitt, Mr. Charles Townshend had come forward, no one knew on whose authority, and promised the House to obtain a revenue from America without doing violence to her alleged rights. The Americans, he said, had drawn a distinction between "internal" and "external" taxes, denying the former but admitting the latter. This distinction Mr. Townshend thought "perfect nonsense," but was willing to humor Americans in it; which he would do by laying an external tax on the importation of glass, lead, paper, and tea. These duties, which would bring into the Exchequer about £40,000, the Americans must on their own principles, Mr. Townshend thought, admit to be constitutional.

It may strike my readers as odd that any one could have been surprised by anything Mr. Townshend took a notion to; but we were indeed not then as well aware of the man's essential frivolity as we have since become. I recall at all events that Mr. Wynkoop followed the proceedings in the House with amazement; and when we learned, one day in 1768, that Mr. Townshend had actually blarneyed the House into passing the Tea Act, the whole business struck Jeremiah as preposterous—"doubtless one of those deplorable jokes," I remember his saying, "which Mr. Townshend is fond of perpetrating when half drunk." I had some recollection that in the time of the Stamp Act troubles certain writers had hinted at a distinction between "internal" and "external" taxes; and Mr. Wynkoop admitted that some such distinction may have been made. But he said that for his part he thought little of such subtle distinctions, agreeing rather with Mr. Pitt that the real question was whether Parliament could "take money out of our pockets without our consent" by any tax whatsoever. There was, however, a difficulty in taking so advanced a position at that time, and as usual it was old Nicholas, always quick to perceive difficulties, who pointed it out.

"I fancy," Old Nicholas had said, "that every act in regulation of trade takes money out of our pockets, but I don't imagine you have yet become so ardent a Son of Liberty as to deny Parliament the right of regulating our trade."

At that time we were all reading Mr. Dickinson's Letters of A Pennsylvania Farmer, and Mr. Wynkoop, who read everything, was able to meet that objection.

"The essential question," he said, "is whether an act of Parliament is laid primarily for the regulation of trade or for the raising of a revenue. If for the latter, it is a tax. The intention of the framers must decide, and there can be no question that the Tea Act is a tax since the framers expressly declare its purpose to be the raising of a revenue."

"A fine distinction, that! But it would be easy for the framers of an act to levy duties on imports with the real intention of raising a revenue, all the while professing loudly their intention of regulating trade. What then?"

"Americans would not be so easily deceived, sir. The nature of the Act would reveal the real intention clearly enough."

"Ha! You would determine the nature of an act by the intention of the framers, and the intention of the framers by the nature of the act. Excellent! That is the logic of your Pennsylvania Farmer. The New Englanders are still more advanced, I see. They are now saying that our rights are founded on a law of Nature, and God only knows what that is. God and Mr. Adams—it's the same thing, I dare say."

"The New Englanders are likely to be a little rash, sir, I think," Mr. Wynkoop admitted. "The argument of their Mr. Adams is complicated, and I fear too subtle to be easily followed. I'm not sure I understand it."

"Well, never mind. You will all understand it soon enough. First you say that Britain has no right to lay internal taxes. Then that she has no right to levy taxes of any sort. Next you will be saying that Parliament has no right of legislation for the colonies on any matter whatsoever. And as you can't derive that from precedent you will derive it from the law of nature."

Mr. Wynkoop smiled at this outburst.

"I have no fear of its coming to that," he said. "The Tea Act is not really an act of Britain; it is Mr. Townshend's foolish hobby. A firm and sensible resistance on our part will effect its repeal. But if one could conceive Britain to be so blind as to push matters to extremes—well, I don't know. If it were really a choice between admitting that Parliament has a right of making all laws for us or denying that she has a right of making any laws for us, it would be a hard choice, but should we not be forced to choose the latter alternative? What other answer could we make?"

"You may well ask! What answer will you make when your precious Adams comes out with a declaration of independency from Great Britain?"

"Independence!" Mr. Wynkoop exclaimed. "Good God, sir, what an idea!"

And indeed, at that time, the idea of separation from Great Britain struck us all as fantastic.

A firm and sensible resistance, Jeremiah had maintained, would bring a repeal of the Townshend duties, as it had formerly brought a repeal of the Stamp Act. When it was learned that Lord North, on March 5, 1770, had moved the repeal of all the Townshend duties save that on tea, Mr. Wynkoop could with some reason say, and did say, that events had proved the justice of his view. And Mr. Wynkoop felt, rightly enough, although he modestly refrained from boasting of it, that he had contributed to this happy result. With no more than the grudging consent of old Nicholas, he had taken a leading part in organizing the Merchant's Association—an agreement not to import any goods from Great Britain so long as the Townshend duties should be in force. That Association had been faithfully kept by the New York merchants of substance and standing. Mr. Wynkoop had himself kept it to the letter, and had sacrificed much in doing so. He told me that his enlarged stock of goods, ordered in anticipation of the agreement, had soon been sold out—at high prices indeed, but not sufficiently high to recoup him for his subsequent losses. For four months last past business had been dull beyond all precedent—scarcely a ship moving; debts not to be collected; money hardly to be had at any price; and the poorer sort of people in dire need for want of employment.

There were indeed plenty of unscrupulous men who had done well enough, who had even profited while pretending to defend their country's rights. The Boston and Philadelphia merchants, as was definitely known in New York, had observed the Association none too well; and even in New York men of no standing had done a thriving business in the smuggling way, especially in Holland tea. Obviously the longer the Association was maintained by honest merchants, the more unscrupulous smugglers would profit by it. We were therefore somewhat surprised to learn that the Boston merchants were in favor of maintaining the Association in full vigor, in spite of Lord North's concessions, so long as the 3d duty on tea was retained. This policy was also advocated by the dishonest beneficiaries of the system in New York, who made use of agitators like Mr. MacDougall to stir up the Mechanics Association and the populace generally against the Merchants, their argument being that our liberties were as much endangered by the 3d duty on tea as they had been by all the Townshend duties.

I am not so sure now that they were wrong, but at that time all of the substantial merchants of New York were strong for a modification of the Association. Mr. Wynkoop, I recall, took a leading part in the affair. He was much irritated with the Boston merchants whom he described as being more active in "resolving what to do than in doing what they had resolved." His opinion was that the Association no longer served any "purpose other than to tie the hands of honest men to let rogues, smugglers, and men of no character plunder their country." Besides, he was much gratified, as all the merchants were, by the recent act of the British government permitting the issue in New York of a paper currency, which was so essential to business prosperity. And therefore, in view of the fact that Britain had taken the first step by repealing the major part of the Townshend duties, it seemed to him the part of wisdom for the colonies to make some concession on their part. The New York merchants of standing were I think generally of Mr. Wynkoop's opinion; and at all events, after taking a canvass of the city, they resolved to abandon the old Association, agreeing for the future to import all commodities, "except teas and other articles that are or may be subject to an importation duty." Some were apprehensive lest New York might find itself alone in this action, and thereby suffer the stigma of having deserted the cause. But in the event it proved otherwise, as Mr. Wynkoop had anticipated. In spite of protests from Boston and Philadelphia, the merchants of those cities followed the lead of New York. Demonstrations in the streets soon subsided, importation became general, business revived, and the controversy with Britain seemed definitely closed.

The years of '71 and '72 were quiet years—ominously so as it proved. But in those days we all nourished the conviction that the controversy with Britain was definitely closed. Nothing occurred to remind us of it even, unless it would be the annual celebrations of the repeal of the Stamp Act, or the faint reverberations, always to be heard in any case, of political squabbles in the Massachusetts Bay. Then, out of a clear sky as it seemed, the storm burst—the landing of the tea ships, the destruction of the tea in Boston harbor, and the subsequent meeting of the Philadelphia Congress. These events, all occurring in rapid succession, seemed to fall like so many blows on Mr. Wynkoop's head, and I recall his saying to me . . .

Here the manuscript breaks off again, and there are evidently some pages missing.

. . . return from Philadelphia, I met him at his father's house where we were to take dinner, as often happened. Arriving early, we had a long talk while waiting for old Nicholas to come down. I found Mr. Wynkoop in low spirits, an unusual thing for him. It may have been no more than a natural weakness after the excitement of attending the Congress, but to my accustomed eyes his low spirits seemed rather due to the uncomfortable feeling that he had been elbowed by circumstances into a position which he never intended to occupy. I was eager for the details of the Congress, but he seemed unwilling to talk of that, preferring rather to dwell upon the events leading up to it—matters which we had threshed out many times before. It was as if Mr. Wynkoop wished to revive the events of the last year and his own part in them, as if, feeling that he might and perhaps should have followed a different line of conduct, his mind was eagerly engaged in finding some good reasons for the line of conduct which he had followed in fact. What first gave me this notion was his saying, *apropos* of nothing.

"I will confess to you, what I would not to another, that if I could twelve months ago have foreseen the present situation I should probably not have attended the Congress."

The remark alarmed me. Mr. Wynkoop's admiration for Britain and his faith in her essential justice were always stronger than mine. For my part I doubted not, from the moment of the passing of the Coercive Acts, that we were in for it, that Britain would not back down again, and that we must either break with her or submit to her demands. My decision was made. I would go with America when the time came for the final breach, I knew that; and above all things I wished Mr. Wynkoop, who was my closest friend, to throw the weight of his powerful interest on the side of my country. But I knew him well enough to be sure that if he now convinced himself that it would come to a breach with Britain he would probably wash his hands of the whole business. What I counted on was a certain capacity in the man, I won't say for deceiving himself, but for convincing himself that what he strongly desired would somehow come to pass. I therefore did what I could to convince him, or rather to help him convince himself, that his past and present conduct was that of a wise and prudent man.

"No man can foresee the future," I remarked, somewhat sententiously.

"That is true," he said. "And even could I have foreseen the future, I fail to see how I could have acted differently, at least not honorably and with any satisfaction to myself. It is past a doubt that Britain, in authorizing the India Company to sell its teas in America, deliberately sought to raise the issue with America once more. It was a challenge, and so insidiously contrived that America had no choice but submission or a resort to a certain amount of violence. Once landed the teas were bound to be sold, since even with the 3d duty they were offered at a less price than the Holland teas. The issue could not be met by commercial agreements, still less by argument. Well, we sent the teas back to London. The Massachusetts people threw theirs into the harbor. Violence, undoubtedly. I had no part in it, but what could be done? Who after all was responsible for the violence? Let ministers who revived an issue happily settled answer that."

"There is no doubt in my mind," I said, "that Britain welcomed the violence in Boston harbor as a pretext for strong measures."

"It seems incredible," Mr. Wynkoop resumed, "but what else can we think? Hitherto it might be said of ministers that they blundered, that they did not know the consequences of their acts. But not on this occasion. They knew perfectly the temper of America; and in any case the destruction of a little tea was surely a mild offense compared with the abrogation of the Massachusetts Charter and the closing of Boston harbor. To subject a loyal province to military despotism, and then deliberately to set about starving the people into submission reveais a vindictiveness foreign to the British character. I can't think the Coercive Acts represent the will of the English people, and I am confident, always have been, that the sober second thought of the nation will repudiate these acts of ministerial despotism."

It was not the first time I had heard Mr. Wynkoop express that sentiment.

"I trust it may prove so," I said. "At least we have done our part. No one can say that the Congress has countenanced rash measures. It has merely adopted a commercial agreement, a measure which we have frequently resorted to before. I don't see how it could have done less."

Mr. Wynkoop seemed a little uncertain of that.

"Yes," he said. "I suppose we could not have done less; Heaven knows we have shown a proper restraint. And I may say that what little influence I have had has always been exerted to that end."

I knew well enough what he was thinking of. After the tea episode there were rash spirits who talked of resort to arms, and even hinted at independence. There were such men even in New York. They had formed the Committee of 25, but fortunately the more moderate minded had got the committee enlarged to 51; and Mr. Wynkoop, together with Mr. Jay and Mr. Alsop and other men of substance, had consented to serve on the Committee of 51 in order to prevent the firebrands from carrying the province into violent measures. Old Nicholas had advised against it.

"Beware of meddling with treason," I recall hearing him say to Mr. Wynkoop at that time.

"Precisely my idea," Mr. Wynkoop had replied, with the smile he always had for old Nicholas' penchant for using stronger terms than the occasion warranted. "I wish to steer clear of treason, or anything remotely approaching it. But it is plain to be seen that New York will support Boston in some fashion, plain to be seen that she will send delegates to Philadelphia. Suppose I and all moderate men follow your advice and wash our hands of the affair? What then? Then the Mechanics will take the lead and send MacDougall and Sears and men of their kidney to Philadelphia, with instructions for vigorous measures. Vigorous measures! God only knows what measures they may be for!"

It was to keep New York from violent measures of all sorts that Mr. Wynkoop had consented to serve on the Committee of 51; it was for that reason he had gone to Philadelphia. I knew that better than most, and I knew that that was what he was now thinking of.

"I am very glad you went to Philadelphia," I said.

"What else could I have done?" he exclaimed. "I have asked myself that a dozen times without finding any answer. But about the Association I don't know. You say it is a moderate measure, but after all it was the measure of the New Englanders, and among the moderates of Philadelphia it was commonly thought to be perhaps too vigorous. I was opposed to it. I voted against it. And having done so perhaps I was ill advised to sign it. I don't know."

I was about to make some reply, when old Nicholas came into the room, and I fancied I could see Mr. Wynkoop stiffen to defend his conduct against inevitable sarcasms.

"Fine doings!" Old Nicholas growled. "The New Englanders had their way, as I expected. I warned you against meddling with treason."

"Treason's a strong word, sir."

"The Association smells of it."

"I cannot think so, sir. The Association is a voluntary agreement not to do certain things; not to import or to export certain goods after a certain date. No law that I know of compels me to import or to export."

"No law requires you to import or to export, very true. But does any law require *me not* to import or export? Certainly no law of the British Parliament or of New York Province obliges me. But suppose I exercise my lawful privilege of importing after the date fixed? What then? Will not your Association compel me not to import, or try to do so? Are not your committees pledged to inspect the customs, to seize my goods, and to sell them at public auction for the benefit of the starving mechanics of Boston? I tell you your Association erects a government unknown to the law; a government which aims to exert compulsion on all citizens. When I am given a coat of tar for violating the Association, will you still say it is a *voluntary* Association?"

"I think little compulsion will be necessary," Mr. Wynkoop replied. "The continent is united as never before; and when the British people realize that, and when British merchants find markets wanting, ministers will be made to see reason."

"You signed the Association, I hear."

"I did, sir. I was opposed to it as Mr. Jay was, but when it was finally carried we both signed it. Once adopted as expressing the policy of Congress, it seemed useless to advertise our divisions, and so weaken the effect of the measures taken. Congress has decided. The important thing now is not what policy Congress should have adopted; the important thing now is for all to unite in support of the policy which it has in fact adopted. If the Colonies present a united front to Britain, as they will do, Britain must yield."

"My advice," old Nicholas said as we went into dinner, "is to drop it. And don't say I didn't warn you."

Over our after dinner wine the matter was gone into at greater length. I said but little, no more than to throw in a remark now and then to keep the argument alive; for I felt that the opposition of old Nicholas would do more to keep Mr. Wynkoop in the right frame of mind than anything I could say. Be that as it may, I left the house well satisfied; for whether it was the dinner, or the wine, or the truculent arguments of old Nicholas, or all of these combined, I felt sure that the total effect of the evening had been to confirm

Mr. Wynkoop in the conviction that the Association was a wise measure, well calculated to bring Britain to terms.

As Mr. Wynkoop had anticipated, little compulsion was necessary to secure the observance of the Association; the threat of confiscation, on the authority of the Committee of 60, of which Mr. Wynkoop was a member, was quite sufficient, save in the case of certain obstinate but negligible traders. And at first it seemed to many that the measures taken would produce the desired effect, for in February Lord North introduced his famous Resolution on Conciliation. I thought the Resolution signified little or nothing, and when in April the news came from Lexington I was not much surprised. It meant war to a certainty, and my first thought was to learn what Mr. Wynkoop would make of it. Curiously enough, with that faculty he had for moulding the world close to the heart's desire, Mr. Wynkoop found some satisfaction in this untoward event. War with Great Britain—no, he would not pronounce the word prematurely. He spoke of the Lexington affair as a repetition of the Boston Massacre, seemingly more serious only because America was now prepared to defend its liberties with arms in its hands. I was delighted that he could take it so; for it convinced me that we might still carry him along with us. The Assembly of New York was too lukewarm to be depended on, half the members or more being frankly Tory, so that we found it convenient to organize a Provincial Congress, composed of delegates elected under the supervision of the Committees, in order to take charge of affairs and keep New York in line with the continent. The most advanced party was already suspicious of Mr. Wynkoop's loyalty; but the moderate men saw the wisdom of winning his support if possible. Mr. Jay and Mr. Alsop were especially keen to have Mr. Wynkoop serve in the Provincial Congress, and they asked me to do what I could to obtain his consent to stand as a candidate.

I did what I could, and I flatter myself that my representations had some influence with him. Knowing his admiration for Mr. Jay, I put it to him as a thing strongly urged by that gentleman.

"Mr. Jay thinks it the more necessary," I said to Mr. Wynkoop, "for men of your sound and moderate views to serve, since the Mechanics are every day gaining headway, and at the same time many men of standing are withdrawing altogether. There is a twofold danger to meet; we must keep the province loyal to the cause, and we must prevent the levelling ideas of the New Englanders from gaining the ascendancy here. If men of your standing refuse to direct the affairs of the colony in these crucial times we shall surely succumb to one or the other of these evils."

"I understand that very well," Mr. Wynkoop replied, "but the decision is not, as you know, an easy one for me."

"Your difficulties are appreciated, and by no one more than by Mr. Jay and all his friends. But it is precisely for that reason, as they point out, that we need your support. Old Nicholas is known to be Tory, and it is much commented on that the Van Schoickendinck Interest is largely lukewarm if not actually hostile. The family Interest is a powerful one, and if you are cordially with us it will do much to bring over many who are hesitating. Your responsibility is the greater, as Mr. Jay rightly says, because of the fact that you will carry with you, one way or another, a great number."

"It is very flattering of Mr. Jay to say so."

Mr. Wynkoop had a great respect for Mr. Jay's judgment—had always had. He consented to stand, and was elected. Throughout the summer of 1775 he attended the sessions of the Provincial Congress faithfully, giving his support to those who were endeavoring to hold the province to a sane middle course—enforcing the Association; raising a militia for defense; keeping the door carefully open for conciliation. Old Nicholas charged him with being too much led about by Mr. Jay. Mr. Wynkoop naturally replied that the notion was ridiculous. What kept him to the mark I feel sure was the feeling that his views and his conduct had been hitherto justified by events, and were now justified by Lord North's Resolution on Conciliation. On this he placed all his hopes. Unacceptable Lord North's Resolution was, he told me on one occasion; but he regretted that the Congress at Philadelphia had seen fit to pronounce it "unseasonable and insidious." When bargains are to be struck, Mr. Wynkoop said, politicians do not offer everything at the first approach. The Resolution proved, he thought, that Lord North was preparing to retreat, as gracefully as possible no doubt. Meantime the policy adopted by the Philadelphia Congress Mr. Wynkoop thought eminently satisfactory; the Resolution on Taking up Arms was admirably phrased to convince Britain that America would defend her rights; the Petition to the King admirably phrased to prove her loyalty.

Throughout the summer and autumn Mr. Wynkoop therefore held the same language to men of extreme views—to the over timid and to the over zealous: the Petition's the thing, he said; it will surely effect the end desired.

Hope delayed makes the heart sick, it has been said. But I think this was not the effect on Mr. Wynkoop. On the contrary, I am sure that for four months he found peace of mind by looking forward to the happy day when the king would graciously make concessions. I had little expectation of any concessions, and it was no great shock to me when the news arrived in November that the king had not even deigned to receive the Petition, much less to answer it. But I knew it would be a heavy blow to Mr. Wynkoop; and when the British government, placing an embargo on American trade, proclaimed America to be in a state of rebellion, it is not too much to say that Mr. Wynkoop's little world of opinion and conduct, held together by recollection of the past and hope for the future, was completely shattered. For a month I saw him scarcely at all. He rarely went abroad, even to attend the Provincial Congress. He must have sat at home in seclusion, endeavoring to adjust his thought to the grim reality, gathering together as best he could the scattered fragments of a broken faith.

During the winter of '76 I saw him more frequently. We often discussed the situation at length. The time for discussion, for discussion of the past that is, seemed to me to be over. But Mr. Wynkoop was seemingly more interested in discussing what had happened than in discussing what ought now to be done. At first this puzzled me; but I soon found the explanation, which was that he knew very well what had to be done; or at least what he had to do, and was only engaged in convincing himself that it had been from the first inevitable, that the situation that now confronted him was not of his making. His one aim from the first, he said, and he said it many times, was to prevent the calamity now impending. I know not how many times he reviewed his past conduct. Short of tamely submitting to the domination of Parliament, he was forever asking, what other course could America have followed but the one she had followed? What other course could he have followed? If America had appealed, not to force but to reason, was this not due to the efforts of men of substance and standing, men of Mr. Wynkoop's class? If Mr. Wynkoop and all his kind had washed their hands of the affair, would not the populace and their hot headed leaders long since have rushed America into violence, and so have given Britain's measures the very justification which they now lacked?

In all this I quite agreed with Mr. Wynkoop. I assured him that his conduct had always been that of a wise and prudent man, and that if events had disappointed the expectations of prudent men, the fault was clearly not his. Responsibility lay with the British government, with those mad or unscrupulous ministers who, wittingly or unwittingly, were betraying the nation by doing the will of a stubborn king. Mr. Wynkoop found consolation in the thought that since ministers had appealed to the sword, the decision must be by the sword. Fight or submit, they had said. The alternative was not of America's choosing, nor of Mr. Wynkoop's choosing. Could America submit now? Could Mr. Wynkoop submit now? Whatever he might have done a year ago, two years ago, could he now tamely submit, bowing the head like a scared school boy, renouncing the convictions of a lifetime, advising the friends with whom he had been associated on committees and congresses to eat their words, to cry out for mercy, saying that they did not mean what they said, saying that it was only a game they were playing. "I have made commitments," Mr. Wynkoop often said to me. "I have given hostages." This was true, and this I think was the consideration of greatest weight with him; he could not deny his words and renounce his friends without losing his self respect.

War with Great Britain! Mr. Wynkoop was forced to pronounce the word at last. But independence! That was the hardest word of all. Yet the word was in the air, passing from mouth to mouth behind closed doors and in the open streets. I had long since accustomed myself to the idea, but Mr. Wynkoop hated the thought of it, said he had never desired it, did not now desire it—"unless," he admitted as a kind of after thought, "the Britain I have always been loyal to proves an illusion." It was this notion, I think, that enabled Mr. Wynkoop to reconcile himself to the policy of separation. The Britain of his dreams was an illusion. The Britain he had known did not exist. In those days we were all reading the fiery papers of Mr. Paine entitled *Common Sense.* I know that Mr. Wynkoop read them, and I fancy that they helped him to see Britain in her true colors.

"I like neither the impudence of the man's manner nor the uncompromising harshness of his matter," Mr. Wynkoop once said to me. "Yet it seems that events give only too much foundation for his assertion that we have deluded ourselves in proclaiming the advantages of the connection with Britain. I can't agree with him that the loyal and respectful tone of our pamphlets and petitions is no more than mawkish sentiment; but I do wonder if the alleged benefits of the union with Britain are but figments of the imagination. It is hard to think so. And yet what now are those benefits? We must surely ask that."

Thus in the long winter of '76 Mr. Wynkoop repaired the illusions by which he lived, reconciling himself to the inevitable step. At this time he saw little of Mr. Van Schoickendinck—it was too painful for both of them, I dare say. At least their last conversation I know (it was by Jeremiah's express invitation that I was present) was a trying one. It was on the 30th of May that we found old Nicholas in the hall of his house, standing, leaning on his cane, evidently much moved.

"I asked you to come," old Nicholas said after greeting us a little stiffly, "because I must know what you purpose to do. General Howe is about to take New York. The Philadelphia Congress is about to declare a separation from Great Britain. The so-called Provincial Congress of New York will hesitate, but it will probably support the measure. Am I to understand that you will burn your bridges and side with the rebels?"

With great seriousness and gravity, Mr. Wynkoop replied:

"I wish you to believe, sir, that I have given the matter every consideration in my power; and it seems to me that I can't do other than go with America. America is my country, and yours too, sir."

"America *is* my country." The voice of old Nicholas was shrill. "I have no great love for Britishers, as you know. Damn them all, I say! But I am too old to meddle with treason. Especially when it can't come to any good. Either we shall be crushed, in which case our last state will be worse than our first; or we shall succeed, in which case we shall be ruled by the mob. Which is better, God knows. What I can't see is why you have allowed the fanatics to run away with the cart. Fight if you must, but why close the door to reconciliation by declaring an independency?"

"We can't fight without it, sir. That's the whole truth of the matter. I was much against it, and so were most. But the necessity is clear. First we refused to trade, hoping that Britain would make terms as she had formerly done. Instead of making terms Britain closed our ports and prepared to make war. To fight we must have supplies and munitions. We must have money. We can get none of these things without reviving trade; and to revive trade we must have allies, we must have the support of France. But will France aid us so long as we profess our loyalty to Britain? France will give money and troops to disrupt the British empire, but none to consolidate it. The act of separation will be the price of a French alliance."

"Am I to understand that the act of separation is not to be seriously made, except to buy French assistance? That you will let France go by the board as soon as Britain is willing to negotiate?"

Mr. Wynkoop did not at once reply. After a moment he said,

"No, I would not say that, sir. The act of separation is intended for Britain's benefit too. It will make it plain that we mean what we say—that we mean to defend our liberties to the last ditch if necessary. Yet I hope, and believe, in spite of all, that it will not come to that."

For a long moment old Nicholas stood stiff and silent. Suddenly extending his hand, but turning his face away, he said,

"Well, good bye. Our ways part then."

"Don't say that, sir."

"I must say it. I must remain as I began—a loyal British subject. You have ceased to be one. I am sorry to have seen this day. But I must submit to necessity, and you must too."

Slowly old Nicholas ascended the stairs, tapping each tread with his cane. Half way up, he cried out, as if in anger,

"Good bye, I say!"

"God keep you, sir," was all Mr. Wynkoop could find to reply.

Mr. Wynkoop afterwards told me that he spent a sleepless night in his half-abandoned house. In anticipation of General Howe's arrival he had already begun to move his effects out of the city, into Westchester County, near White Plains, where the Provincial Congress was adjourned to meet on July 2. With the business of settling his personal affairs to the best advantage he was so fully occupied that he did not attend the Congress on the opening days. But on the afternoon of the 9th of July he took his place, a little late. Slipping quietly into a vacant chair just in front of me, he was handed a copy of "A Declaration by the Representatives of the

United States of America, in Congress Assembled." The chairman of a committee, appointed to report on the validity of the reasons given for separation from Great Britain, was reading the document. We listened to the felicitous and now familiar phrases—"hold these truths to be self-evident"—"just powers from the consent of the governed"—"right of the people to alter or abolish it"—

"Who are the people?" I heard Mr. Wynkoop murmur to his neighbor.

His neighbor, not hearing or not understanding him, whispered behind his hand,

"This is not an easy time for you, I dare say. Mr. Van Schoickendinck can't be induced to join us." The last a statement rather than a question.

"No," Mr. Wynkoop said. "He will go Tory. He will not oppose us. His sympathies are with us really, I think. He is thoroughly American, with no great love for Britain. But he is old—he will go Tory."

"The Declaration will carry, I think."

"Yes."

"It seems well phrased. Jefferson's pen, I understand."

Presently the chairman, having finished the reading of the Declaration, read the report of the committee. "While we lament the cruel necessity which has made that measure unavoidable, we approve the same, and will, at the risk of our lives and fortunes, join with the other colonies in supporting it."

The report of the committee was carried, unanimously, a bare majority being present.

Whereupon a member begged leave, before proceeding to other routine business, to make a few remarks. Permission being granted, the member spoke of the decisive step which had just been taken; of the solemn crisis which confronted all America; of the duty of meeting that crisis with high courage, with the indomitable perseverance of freemen fighting for their liberties. "The time for discussion is over," he said. "The time for action has come. Once thoroughly united, we cannot fail, and if we triumph, as we shall, a grateful posterity will recall these days, and do honor to the patriotic men whose conduct was inspired by the spirit of freedom. God grant we may so act that the spirit of freedom will ever be synonymous with the spirit of '76!"

In the perfunctory applause which greeted these remarks, Mr. Wynkoop joined, as heartily I think, as . . .

Here, most unfortunately, the manuscript ends. What the conclusion of the story may have been, if indeed it ever was concluded, will probably never be known.

James Truslow Adams

THE ROLE OF MERCHANTS AND RADICALS

James Truslow Adams, although widely known as an American historian, was a stockbroker by profession from 1900 until shortly before World War I, during which he served in Military Intelligence. Between the end of the war and his death in 1949 he wrote many notable works, including Revolutionary New England, 1691–1776 *(1923),* New England in the Republic, 1776–1850 *(1926),* Provincial Society, 1690–1763 *(1927), and, of course, the well-known work from which this selection is taken.*

Except for sections on the frontier which suffered from Indian raids, the colonies had not been the seat of any of the military operations of the Seven Years' War, which ended, as far as America was concerned, in 1760. As always happens in a war, a good many new fortunes had been built up. Privateering frequently proved exceedingly profitable, and the great prizes brought in encouraged speculation. Army contracts—such, for example, as one for 2 million pounds of beef and 2 million pounds of bread, among other supplies—lined the pockets of the contractors, who always emerge rich from such troubled periods. Business of all sorts had come to be conducted on a much larger scale, and we can clearly trace the growing connection between business leaders and subservient or participating legislatures, even one so close to the people as that of Connecticut. Lawyers were rising into prominence as business affairs became larger and more complex, and they also began to appear in legislatures.

For a while the farming and laboring classes had shared in the wartime prosperity; the farmer had got wartime prices and the laborer's wages had risen rapidly as the scarcity of labor had increased and floods of paper money had worked their usual inflation. But when the bubble broke, all of these classes suffered severely. Taxes had risen rapidly with the debts contracted by the several colonies. The currency became heavily depreciated. General business fell off sharply. The price of farm produce crashed. Many of the laborers and farmers had to abandon their homes. There was a severe decline in the price of farm land in the older settlements, many foreclosures of mortgages, lawsuits for debts which wiped out all equities. Once more the frontier seemed to offer the only hope to many of the poor who could not weather the storm.

But in 1763 came a stunning blow. England by proclamation forbade any colonials to cross the watershed of the mountains to settle. This was the British government's solution of the Indian problem, one of the first which required to be settled with respect to the new Canadian and western territory. The Ministers feared—not without good cause, as Pontiac's conspiracy was to show—that, with the savages already hostile to the English regime and perhaps stirred up by the French, there would be constant trouble on the frontier if the settlers pressed into the Indian hunting grounds. The valuable fur trade had to be preserved, and England had no wish to garrison a frontier of perhaps twelve hundred miles. As a temporary expedient, the government lit upon the idea of holding back immigration to the western country, and, in order to keep the Indians quiet, to erect for the present a large Indian territory. Unfortunately, with the procrastination in government affairs characteristic of the times, what was intended to be only a temporary expedient was never seriously considered again. The Americans felt that they had given considerable help in conquering America from the French, and were furious at being told that they must not enter the promised land. The population was doubling every twenty to twenty-five years. The postwar suffering was keenly felt. Canute might as well have commanded the waves not to advance as for the British government to forbid the Americans, in their distress, to seek new fortune across the mountains—except that the waves would not have resented it, whereas the colonists did.

. . . [T]here was plenty of resentment on the frontier in any case—

resentment against New England land speculators, against the all-engrossing land-grabbers in New York, against the new slavocracy in the South; resentment on the part of the new immigrants against those who had cheated and ill-used them; resentment against the landlords of England by the Scotch-Irish. Typical of the feeling of the latter was the inscription that was carved on the tombstone of one of them in the Shenandoah Valley. "Here lies," so it read, "the remains of John Lewis, who slew the Irish Lord, settled Augusta County, located the town of Staunton, and furnished five sons to fight the battles of the American Revolution." There is ample evidence that the frontier was full of combustible material—lawless, resentful, radical, and independent. Moreover, in the older settlements the poorer people were full of trouble and grievances at this time and quite ready to father them upon anyone. Even the rich were beginning to feel hard times. If more grievances came, it would not be very difficult to stir sedition into a flame. There was a flare-up in 1761 when the Courts in Boston were asked by the revenue officers to issue new "writs of assistance," all the old ones having expired with the death of George II. These were of the nature of general search warrants, not naming the particular place to be searched or the object to be searched for, and had been used for some years, at the suggestion of Pitt, chiefly to try to prevent the illicit trade between Boston merchants and the French enemy, which had been prolonging the war. James Otis, who argued against them in a fiery speech, although he lost his case, took the proper ground that they were destructive of liberty, and John Adams once said that the American Revolution began then and there.

The first move made by the English government to reorganize the administration of the empire was along the lines of old legislation accepted by the colonists in principle though not complied with in practice. In 1764, in an effort to secure some customs revenue, which heretofore had sufficed only to pay a quarter of the cost of collection, the Sugar Act was passed by Parliament, followed by two others in the next two years.

These three acts might have seriously demoralized commerce, but as their incidence happened to be almost wholly on the trade carried on by New England, the issue was not felt by all the colonies. The Stamp Act in 1765, however, as being internal taxation, affected every colony alike, though not to equal extent financially, as did also the Townshend Acts of 1767, which included duties on imports of manufactured articles from Great Britain. Moreover, both these last were especially designed to transfer a revenue from the colonies in sterling or bills of exchange, when it was difficult enough to find sufficient of either to make good the annual adverse balance of trade. They also marked a new sort of legislation, different from the mere trade regulation of old.

The excitement during these years was intense. The economic structure of the colonies, already seriously affected, was threatened with ruin. Business grew rapidly worse, and the passage of the Stamp Act had given a focus for every possible form of discontent. The reaction expressed in varying tones from Patrick Henry's well-known speech up to the dignified papers drawn up by representatives of the various colonies in the Stamp Act Congress, as well as the mobbing and burning of houses in various towns, made the British government realize it had gone too far as a matter of expediency. Both the Sugar Act and the Stamp Act were soon repealed, and in 1770, after a non-importation agreement, enforced in the colonies, had reduced imports from Great Britain by nearly half, the Townshend Acts also were largely modified, leaving only a trifling tax on tea as a symbol of the power of Parliament. The much disliked act quartering British soldiers on the colonists where garrisons were maintained was also allowed to lapse without being reenacted. The British government pledged itself to attempt to raise no further revenue in America; the non-importation agreements were rescinded; and American imports from England rose from £1,634,000 in 1769 to £4.2 million in 1771. Here and there in various colonies there were local grievances against England, but prosperity had returned to America, and the wealthy, as well as many of the classes dependent on them, were inclined to forget the quarrel with the mother country.

Meanwhile, however, much that was ominous for the future had happened. The merchant and other wealthy and conservative classes had been chiefly anxious to avoid trouble and merely to get the obnoxious acts rescinded. The English mind which America inherited has nearly always preferred adjustment and working compromises to declarations of abstract principles. The wealthy men had been willing to fight their cause on the grounds that the new laws were inexpedient and that they would damage the business interests of England as well as their own, a line of argument in which they received the cordial support of the mercantile interests in London who did business with them, and who agreed with their point of view. In fact, the repeal of the various acts was due more to the English mercantile influence brought to bear on Parliament than to either the mobbing or the constitutional arguments in America. What the English merchants and the richer men in the colonies wanted above all was good business and as little political friction as possible.

On the other hand, as we have seen, there was a vast mass of smouldering discontent among the poorer people everywhere in America. The line of economic class cleavage was beginning to be more clearly defined, and the lower in the scale were beginning to look to men from among their own ranks to lead them politically. When, for example, Patrick Henry tried to secure the passage of his Stamp Act resolutions in the Virginia House of Burgesses, he was unanimously backed by the poor electors, whereas he had to overcome the almost solid resistance of the rich. However, the greatest master in manipulating the masses whom America has ever seen, except possibly Bryan, arose in Boston. Opinions will always differ regarding Samuel Adams, but there can be no difference of opinion as to his consummate ability as a plotter of revolution. In all else he was a failure throughout his life. Before the years in which his manipulation of the inflammable material among the public was to give him a lasting place in American history, he had failed in law and business and public office. In after years, when constructive work had to be done in Congress in constitution making or as governor of his new state, he played a wholly insignificant part. He could tear down, but not build up. He was a fanatic, as most men are who change history, and with a fanatical hatred of England he strove to break all ties with her. Had he lived a century earlier he would have been one of the stern Puritan leaders of the type of Endicott, unyielding, persecuting, convinced to the very marrow of his bones of the infallibility of his own beliefs. But although he was a Puritan of the Puritans, the times had changed. They had become political, and in Adams's mind England and her rule had become the principle of evil in the lives of the people of God, to be fought day and night and with every weapon in his arsenal. Even when others had no wish to secede from the empire, but merely to be left in peace or to have certain inimical laws repealed, Adams early conceived the belief that the one end to work for was immediate and complete independence.

As he surveyed the field of public opinion in which he would have to operate, he saw clearly the two classes of rich and poor and realized that their interests were different. The rich were conservative, the poor radical; the rich were desirous of as little change as possible, the poor clamored for any change that would better their condition; the rich would be influenced mainly by arguments of compromise and expediency, the poor by appeals to their rights for a greater share in the political and economic life of their communities. If these two classes could be brought to work together, public opinion would be a unit, but if they could not, then the greater reliance must be placed on the poorer classes, who constituted the overwhelming mass of the population and who could more readily be stirred to anger and radical action. From about 1761 until independence was declared by the colonies in 1776, Adams worked ceaselessly for the cause to which he had devoted his life, manipulating newspapers and town meetings, organizing committees for correspondence throughout the colonies, even bringing about happenings which would inflame public opinion. At one period it looked as though his efforts would be in vain, but in the end the stupidity of the British government won the day for him.

It is a great mistake to think of public opinion as united in the colonies and as gradually rising against British tyranny. Public opinion is never wholly united, and seldom rises to a pitch of passion without being influenced—in other words, without the use of propaganda. The Great War taught that to those who did not know it already.

The years preceding the final secession of the colonies may be divided into three periods. During the first, from the passage of the Sugar Act to the practical repeal of all obnoxious legislation in 1770, the different groups were by force of circumstances united in opposition to the policy of England. The merchants needed no propaganda to realize that their business was being seriously interfered with, though they cared little about the popular catchwords that were being used by the new leaders of the people to inflame them. The Stamp Act, however, with its threat of internal taxation, did, during its one brief year of life, bring the whole problem for a while from the realm of mere business to that of constitutional questioning. But by 1770 the merchants' grievances were settled, and from then until 1773 all desire for agitation and "rocking the boat" disappeared among the richer classes. Up to that point, the popular anger had served their own cause. For the next three years their cause was peace, and popular agitation and attacks on England became a menace and not a help to them.

From the first, Adams and those working with him had realized the necessity of democratic slogans in the creation of a state of mind. While the merchants were busy pointing out to their London correspondents that the new laws would hurt the business of all alike, Adams at once struck boldly out to inflame the passions of the crowd by threatening that it was to be reduced to the "miserable state of tributary slaves," contrasting its freedom and moral virtue with the tyranny and moral degradation of England. He proclaimed that the mother country was bent on bringing her colonies to a condition of "slavery, poverty and misery," and on causing their utter ruin, and dinned into the ears of the people the words "slavery and tyranny" until they assumed a reality from mere reiteration. His political philosophy was eagerly lapped up by a populace smarting under hard times and resentful of colonial even more than imperial conditions of the moment. The establishment of government by free consent of all had become imbedded in the mind of the average man, as an essential part of the American dream. Adams himself had seen the vision, but had glimpsed it with the narrowness and bitterness with which the more bigoted Puritans had seen the vision of an unloving and revengeful Hebrew Jehovah. Like them he felt that he alone, and those who believed as he did, were in possession of the truth, and that those who differed from him were enemies of truth and God. Because, however, the American dream had so deeply affected the hopes and aspirations of the common men, the more radical among them, in town and on frontier, echoed with wild enthusiasm such pronouncements of Adams as that "the natural liberty of man is to be free from any superior power on earth, and not to be under the will or legislative authority of man, but only to have the law of nature for his rule."

Such talk as this could only make England fearful of how far the people might try to put such precepts into practice. The upper classes in the colonies also began to be uneasy. Up to 1770, when their own grievances were redressed, they might allow such ideas to be disseminated, considering themselves in control of the situation, but after that it became clear that they were losing control. Whereas such men as John Hancock and John Adams wanted quiet, and retired from public affairs to the management of their own, Sam Adams and the lesser radicals worked harder than ever to keep public opinion inflamed.

With the upper classes become lukewarm or hostile to his continued propaganda, with the obnoxious legislation repealed or modified, he had to trust to generalizations and emotional appeals. A good example of his use of the latter was the affair called the "Boston Massacre." As part of the general imperial policy following the war, the British government had stationed some regiments in Boston. They were under good officers and good discipline, and there was no more reason why they should have made trouble there than in any provincial garrison town of England. Adams, however, was continually stirring up the public mind against them; John Adams reported finding him one Sunday night "preparing for the next day's newspaper—a curious employment, cooking up paragraphs, articles, occurrences, etc., working the political engine." Finally, one March evening, as a result of more than usual provocation given by taunting boys to soldiers on duty, an unfortunate clash occurred. There was confusion, a rioter's shout to "fire" was mistaken for an officer's command, and several citizens were killed. The officer surrendered to the civil authorities, was tried, defended by John Adams and Josiah Quincy, Jr., and acquitted. But Samuel Adams at once saw the value of the incident. Every emotion of the mob was played upon. The affair was termed a "massacre," and in the annual speeches given for a number of years to commemorate its anniversary the boys and men who had taken part in the mobbing were described as martyrs to liberty and the soldiers as "bloody butchers." Although there is no recorded instance of a soldier having offered the slightest affront to any Boston girl, orators ranted about "our beauteous virgins exposed to all the insolence of unbridled passion—our virtuous wives, endeared to us by every tender tie, falling a sacrifice to worse than brutal violence, and perhaps, like the famed Lucretia, distracted with anguish and despair, ending their wretched lives by their own fair hands." At the request of the citizens the troops were removed from the city, but such talk, which served its intended purpose, was kept up for years after. The incident was unimportant in itself, and its chief interest is in how the radicals, after having provoked it, made use of it.

America was, indeed, more or less in ferment, quite aside from the question of Anglo-American relations. Pennsylvania was almost on the verge of civil war, feeling having become extremely embittered between the older and newer sections of the colony. The rich seaboard counties had not only been unwilling to help protect the frontier in the late war, but were controlling all the political machinery for their own benefit, the 16,000 voters in the three eastern counties having twice as many members of the Assembly as the 15,000 in the five western counties. To some extent the mechanics in Philadelphia were making common cause with the frontiersmen against the moneyed class. In Virginia, there was similar feeling between classes and sections, the tidewater counties controlling the much more populous frontier ones. In North Carolina, civil war did actually break out after several years of agitation, and the frontiersmen set up their own organization of "Regulators" to prevent, among other things, the collection of taxes by the men of the eastern counties who controlled the legislature and graft of the colony, and who succeeded in putting down the insurrection only after three years' effort ending in a bloody campaign in 1772.

The Seven Years' War had left society disorganized and unstable. The rich, from 1764 to 1770, had their grievances against England, grievances that were real and deep, but they were also beginning to watch with alarm the rise of radical sentiment among their own people. Everywhere thoughtful, farseeing men were thinking—thinking of the constitutional relations with the mother country which had permitted so serious a crisis to arise as that from which they believed they had just happily emerged; thinking also of the problems of government in the colonies and of what might be in store for conservatism and wealth if the people, by continuing to press their demands for greater share in ruling themselves, should oust their old leaders who had been used to being in control. The more they pondered the Anglo-American constitutional relation, however, the more it became apparent that if the question should ever have to be forced to an issue, the only ground to take would be the broad one of the rights of man as man. Sam Adams was right in that. They had tried to argue from charter rights, and soon found that ground too narrow. Their rights as Englishmen afforded a wider scope, but argument thence tended toward a bog of legalistic confusion. If Parliament should try inimical legislation again, and if a situation should arise calling for a denial of its power to legislate, the broadest rights of man would be none too broad to provide standing room for argument. But this would play right into the hands of the discontented populace, who were already getting too obstreperous, demanding new rights, asking more representation, refusing to pay taxes, getting a bit too much into the habit of backing up their demands by mobbing, even plunging a colony like North Carolina into civil war. It was all bad for business, thought the rich, and holding back the development of the country. However, the quarrel with England was made up for the present. English merchants had seen the light. Perhaps, with better times in America, these agitations on the frontiers and by the lower classes in the big towns would die down, if only men like Sam Adams would know when to stop and would quit throwing oil on the flames. The rich determined to sit on the lid, and carry out a policy of business and politics as usual. Sam Adams and his group also continued their agitation as usual.

For three years, from 1770, in spite of constant discussion in pamphlets and newspapers and declaimings by radicals, things seemed to be getting better. The frontiersmen and town radicals were doing a lot of talking, but getting nowhere. The Regulators' insurrection had been put down. Then suddenly the British government made a colossal blunder which could never be retrieved. Sam Adams saw to that.

The East India Company had accumulated a huge and partly unsalable store of tea, and was on the brink of bankruptcy. In order to prevent the catastrophe, which would have been a financial one of the first magnitude, the British government, with perfectly good intentions from an English point of view, but with an ignorance and a carelessness which are beyond condonation, gave the [East] India Company what was practically a monopoly of selling tea in America. By the elimination of the American merchants as middlemen, the price of tea to the American consumer was expected to be cut in half; but considering the delicacy of Anglo-American relations, and the fact that the American merchant and business class was the chief reliance of England in America, to have struck a blow at it in favor of an English business concern revealed in a flash both the stupidity of the men in power with whom Americans had to deal and the unthinking selfishness of English policy with regard to the colonies. The fat was in the fire now with a vengeance. For three years the conservatives had been trying to maintain good relations with England and at the same time to combat what they considered the dangerous rising tide of radicalism in their own colonies. Now they were forced once more into opposition to England and so into unwilling alignment with the radicals.

The rest of the story is well known by every schoolboy—how the tea was shipped over and refused admittance at every port; how Adams's followers in Boston raided the tea ship and threw fifty thousand dollars' worth of tea into the waters of the harbor; how Parliament, when it heard of the deed, passed acts closing the port to commerce except in food, until the tea should be paid for, voiding the Massachusetts charter, and placing the colony under the immediate control of the Crown, ordering that British officers or soldiers should be tried only in England (or in a colony other than Massachusetts) for anything done in the line of duty, and providing that troops should be quartered again in the colonies. "The die is cast," wrote George III to Lord North; "the colonies must either triumph or submit."

It is possible that a peaceful solution might have been found when the dull wits of the British Cabinet had become aware of the extent of feeling aroused in America, and of the fact that they had forced the whole population into a united front. But this would have been possible only had the tea not been destroyed, an act that many loyal Americans condemned. Adams had seized his chance. Fifty thousand dollars' worth of British private property destroyed and indemnity refused; Parliament would have to retaliate. If the retaliation should be heavy enough, the door might be closed to peaceful settlement. The retaliation came, swift and crushing, and the colonies were aflame with sympathy for Massachusetts. In the next three years the progress of events was inevitable in its sequence, given all the factors involved. The petitions and their rejections, the calling of Congress, the bloodshed at Lexington and Concord, the final Declaration of Independence in 1776, and the military events of the struggle are too familiar to need retelling.

What concern us more particularly are the abiding influences upon American character and thought.

We have already seen how the wilderness and the colonists' need of erecting governments for themselves had given a considerable spur to the spread of democracy and the belief in government only by the consent of the governed. The colonies, however, had been far from democratic, and with the accumulation of wealth had been growing less so. Belief was still general among the upper classes that political power should rest in the hands of the wellborn or the rich, who had knowledge, experience, and a property stake in the community. Many of the poorer classes, especially as we look further to the south from New England and out on any part of the frontiers, were shiftless, illiterate, rather lawless. To increase the political power of such people seemed to the conservatives like inviting anarchy and the spoliation of property. On the other hand, during the gradual shift in the grounds for arguing the constitutional relations toward Parliament, it had been found necessary to base the argument at last squarely on the rights of man. "When, in the course of human events," in the words of the great Virginian, it became necessary to inform the world why they were taking up arms against England, the signers of the Declaration had to announce the theory of these rights to all mankind—mankind including their own "lower classes" at home in America. "We hold these truths to be self-evident," wrote Jefferson in words which rang through the continent, "that all men are created equal; that they are endowed by their Creator with certain inalienable rights; that among these are life, liberty, and the pursuit of happiness. That, to secure these rights, governments are instituted among men, deriving their just powers from the consent of the governed; that, whenever any form of government becomes destructive of these ends, it is the right of the people to alter or to abolish it."

Nothing here about the rich or the wellborn; and, as Sam Adams said, the people recognized "the resolution as though it were a decree promulgated from heaven." The upper classes were thinking of their independence as against the exercise of legislative power by Parliament. The lower classes were thinking not only of that, but of their relations to their colonial legislature and governing class. "No taxation without representation." If that were true as between England and America, why not also as between poor Western frontier counties and rich Eastern seaboard ones, as between the town mechanic and the town merchant, as between the laborer and the planter?

If, as the king had said, the die was cast in imperial relations, so had it also been in American political philosophy. For a dozen years, men like Adams had been dinning this idea of the rights of man as man into the ears of the people. The conservatives had first been of the party, then fallen off, then again had to join it, and now at last the voice of united America in Congress had announced to the world the political equality of all men as the creed of the continent. The dam had been dynamited. After the announcement that all men are created equal, that all men have rights, that all men may revolt against conditions, there could be no turning back. The quarter of a century from the beginning of active agitation against England until the adoption of the Federal Constitution afforded an incomparable schooling in political discussion and training for an entire people, and for the burning into their minds and hearts of the democratic dogma.

Jesse Lemisch

JACK TAR IN THE STREETS: MERCHANT SEAMEN IN THE POLITICS OF REVOLUTIONARY AMERICA

Professor Lemisch, who studied with Edmund S. Morgan, is widely known as one of the ablest exponents of what is sometimes called a radical, revisionist interpretation of colonial history. The article reprinted here is a trenchant statement of his thesis that the lower classes played an independent and autonomous role in the revolutionary movement, and were neither mere pawns manipulated by merchants and other upper-class elements nor rabble indulging in mindless or senseless violence. This viewpoint conflicts not only with the orthdox loyalist conception, of course, but, more importantly, with the views of historians such as James Truslow Adams.

The merchant marine was a place full of forces beyond the seaman's control: death and disease, storms, and fluctuations in employment. Indeed, the lack of "old salts" in Morison's merchant marine might reflect a somber irony: Was the average seaman young because mobility rapidly brought him to another trade or because seamen died young? A man in jail, said Dr. Johnson, was at least safe from drowning, and he had more room, better food, and better company. The Quaker John Woolman was one of the few sensitive enough to see that if the "poor bewildered sailors" drank and cursed, the fault lay not so much in themselves as in the harsh environment and the greed of employers. Nor was the road up through the hawsehole so easy as Morison asserts. That the few succeeded tells us nothing of the many; only the successful left autobiographies. Perhaps the sons of merchants and shipmasters made it, along with the captain's brother-in-law and those who attended schools of navigation, but what of the "poor lads bound apprentice" who troubled Woolman, those whose wages went to their masters? What of the seamen in Morison's own Boston who died too poor to pay taxes and who were

From *William and Mary Quarterly,* 3d ser. 25 (July 1968): 371–407. (Abridged. Footnotes omitted, except where referring to issues in this volume.)

a part of what James Henretta has called "the bottom" of Boston society? What of those who went bankrupt with such frequency in Rhode Island? Why, at the other end of the colonies, did Washington's uncle warn that it would be "very difficult" to become master of a Virginia vessel and not worth trying?

The presence of such men, fugitives and floaters, powerless in a tough environment, makes *wanderlust* appear an ironic parody of the motives which made at least some men go to sea. Catch the seaman when he is not pandering to your romanticism, said former seaman Frederick Law Olmsted a century later, and he will tell you that he hates the sight of blue water, he hates his ship, his officers, and his messmates—and he despises himself. Melville's Ishmael went to sea when he felt grim, hostile, and suicidal: "It is a way I have of driving off the spleen." No matter what we make of Ishmael, we cannot possibly make him into one of Morison's "adventure-seeking boys." Others, perhaps, but not Ishmael. The feelings of eighteenth-century Americans toward seafaring and seamen, and what evidence we have of the reasons men had for going to sea indicate that there were many like Ishmael in the colonial period, too, who left the land in flight and fear, outcasts, men with little hope of success ashore. These were the dissenters from the American mood. Their goals differed from their fellows ashore; these were the rebels, the men who stayed on to become old salts.

Admiralty law treated seamen in a special way, as "wards." Carl Ubbelohde says that seamen favored the colonial Vice Admiralty Courts as "particular tribunals in case of trouble," and Charles M. Andrews and Richard B. Morris agreed that these courts were "guardians of the rights of the seamen." The benefits of being classified as a "ward" are dubious, but, regardless of the quality of treatment which admiralty law accorded to seamen, it certainly does not follow that, all in all, the colonial seaman was well treated by the law. Indeed, if we broaden our scope to include colonial law generally, we find an extraordinarily harsh collection of laws, all justifying Olmsted's later claim that American seamen "are more wretched, and are governed more by threats of force than any other civilized laborers of the world." There are laws providing for the whipping of disobedient seamen and in one case for their punishment as "seditious"; laws prohibiting seamen in port from leaving their vessels after sundown and from traveling on land without certificates of discharge from their last job; laws empowering "every free white person" to catch runaway seamen. We find other laws, less harsh, some seeming to protect the seaman: laws against extending credit to seamen and against arresting them for debt, and against entertaining them in taverns for more than one hour per day; laws against selling them liquor and prohibiting them from playing with cards or dice; laws waiving imprisonment for seamen convicted of cursing; laws requiring masters to give discharge certificates to their seamen and laws prohibiting hiring without such certificates. Finally, there are laws which clearly do help the seaman: laws requiring masters to provide "good and sufficient diet and accommodation" and providing for redress if the master refused; laws providing punishment for masters who "immoderately beat, wound, or maim" their seamen; laws providing that seamen's contracts be written.

These harsh or at best paternalistic laws add up to a structure whose purpose is to assure a ready supply of cheap, docile labor. Obedience, both at sea and ashore, is the keystone. Charles Beard at his most rigidly mechanistic would doubtless have found the Constitution merely mild stuff alongside this blatantly one-sided class legislation. Today's historians of the classless society would do well to examine the preambles of these laws, written in a more candid age, by legislatures for which, even by Robert Brown's evidence, most seamen could not vote.[1] Again and again these laws aim to inhibit acts of seamen which may do "prejudice to masters and owners of vessells" or constitute a "manifest detriment of . . . trade." The seamen's interests are sacrificed to the merchants', and even the laws

[1] Robert E. Brown, *Middle-Class Democracy and the Revolution in Massachusetts, 1691–1780* (Ithaca, 1955), 27–30, acknowledges that the "city proletariat" constituted "the largest disfranchised group" and strongly implies that itinerant seamen could not vote. Even so, Brown has stated the case too optimistically. By including propertied captains under the ambiguous label "mariner," he has disguised the fact, legible in his own evidence, that the "mariners" who could vote were captains and the common seamen could not. See John Cary, "Statistical Method and the Brown Thesis on Colonial Democracy, With a Rebuttal by Robert E. Brown," *Wm. and Mary Qtly.*, 3d Ser., XX (1963), 257. For Brown's acknowledgment of the error see *ibid.*, 272. Arthur M. Schlesinger, *The Colonial Merchants and the American Revolution, 1763–1776* (New York, 1918), 28, includes seamen in a list of those who were "for the most part, unenfranchised." For an assertion that "sailors" could vote based on evidence that *masters* could compare Jacob R. Marcus, *Early American Jewry* (Philadelphia, 1953), II, 231; and B. R. Carroll, ed., *Historical Collections of South Carolina* (New York, 1836), II, 441.

which seem friendly to the seaman benefit the master. Laws against giving credit, arresting, and suing aim to keep the seaman available rather than involved in a lawsuit or imprisoned; the certificates and written contracts seek to prevent desertion and to protect the master against what would today be called a "strike"; the laws protecting seamen against immoderate punishment and requiring adequate food and accommodation are implicitly weak in that they require that dependents make open complaint against their superiors. Sometimes this limitation is made explicit, as in a South Carolina law of 1751 whose stated purpose is "TO DISCOURAGE FRIVOLOUS AND VEXATIOUS ACTIONS AT LAW BEING BROUGHT BY SEAMEN AGAINST MASTERS AND COMMANDERS."

Thus if we think of Jack Tar as jolly, childlike, irresponsible, and in many ways surprisingly like the Negro stereotype, it is because he was treated so much like a child, a servant, and a slave. What the employer saw as the necessities of an authoritarian profession were written into law and culture: the society that wanted Jack dependent made him that way and then concluded that that was the way he really was.

Constantly plagued by short complements, the Royal Navy attempted to solve its manning problems in America, as in England, by impressment. Neil Stout has recently attributed these shortages to "death, illness, crime, and desertion" which were in turn caused largely by rum and by the deliberate enticements of American merchants. Rum and inveiglement certainly took a high toll, but to focus on these two causes of shortages is unfairly to shift the blame for impressment onto its victims. The navy itself caused shortages. Impressment, said Thomas Hutchinson, caused desertion, rather than the other way around. Jack Tar had good reasons for avoiding the navy. It would, a young Virginian was warned, "cut him and staple him and use him like a Negro, or rather, like a dog"; James Otis grieved at the loss of the "flower" of Massachusetts's youth "by ten thousands" to a service which treated them little better than "hewers of wood and drawers of water." Discipline was harsh and sometimes irrational, and punishments were cruel. Water poured into sailors' beds, they went mad, and died of fevers and scurvy. Sickness, Benjamin Franklin noted, was more common in the navy than in the merchant service and more frequently fatal. In a fruitless attempt to prevent desertion, wages were withheld and men shunted about from ship to ship without being paid. But the accumulation of even three or four years' back wages could not keep a man from running. And why should it have? Privateering paid better in wartime, and wages were higher in the merchant service; even laborers ashore were better paid. Thus Stout's claim that the navy was "forced" to press is only as accurate as the claim that the South was forced to enslave Negroes. Those whose sympathies lie with the thousands of victims of this barbaric practice—rather than with naval administrators—will see that the navy pressed because to be in the navy was in some sense to be a slave, and for this we must blame the slave owners rather than the slaves.

Impressment angered and frightened the seamen, but it pervaded and disrupted all society, giving other classes and groups cause to share a common grievance with the press-gang's more direct victims: just about everyone had a relative at sea. Whole cities were crippled. A nighttime operation in New York in 1757 took in 800 men, the equivalent of more than one quarter of the city's adult male population. Impressment and the attendant shortage of men may have been a critical factor in the stagnancy of "the once cherished now depressed, once flourishing now sinking Town of Boston." H.M.S. *Shirley*'s log lists at least 92 men pressed off Boston in five months of 1745–1746; *Gramont* received 73 pressed men in New York in three days in 1758; *Arethusa* took 31 in two days off Virginia in 1771. Binges such as these left the communities where they occurred seriously harmed. Preachers' congregations took flight, and merchants complained loudly about the "many Thousands of Pounds of Damage." "Kiss my arse, you dog," shouted the captain as he made off with their men, leaving vessels with their fires still burning, unmanned, finally to be wrecked. They took legislators and slaves, fishermen and servants. Seamen took to the woods or fled town altogether, dreading the appearance of a man-of-war's boat—in the words of one—as a flock of sheep dreaded a wolf's appearance. If they offered to work at all, they demanded inflated wages and refused to sail to ports where there was danger of impressment. "New York and Boston," Benjamin Franklin commented during the French and Indian War, "have so often found the Inconvenience of . . . Station Ships that they are very indifferent about having them: The Pressing of their Men and thereby disappointing Voyages, often hurting their Trade more than the Enemy hurts it." Even a ferryboat operator complained as people shunned the city during a press; food and fuel grew short and their prices rose.

From the very beginning the history of impressment in America is a tale of venality, deceit, and vindictiveness. Captains kept deserters and dead men on ships' books, pocketing their provision allowances. In 1706 a captain pressed men and literally sold them to short-handed vessels; his midshipman learned the business so well that after his dismissal he became a veritable entrepreneur of impressment, setting up shop in a private sloop. Another commander waited until New York's governor was away to break a no-press agreement and when the governor returned he seriously considered firing on the Queen's ship. In Boston in 1702 the lieutenant-governor *did* fire, responding to merchants' complaints. "Fire and be damn'd," shouted the impressing captain as the shots whistled through his sails. The merchants had complained that the press was illegal under 1697 instructions which required captains and commanders to apply to colonial governors for permission to press. These instructions, a response to complaints of "irregular proceedings of the captains of some of our ships of war in the impressing of seamen," had clearly not put an end to irregularities. In 1708 a Parliament fearful of the disruptive effect of impressment on trade forbade the practice in America. In the sixty-seven years until the repeal in 1775 of this "Act for the Encouragement of the Trade to America" there was great disagreement as to its meaning and indeed as to its very existence. Did the Sixth of Anne, as the act was called, merely prohibit the navy from impressing and leave governors free to do so? At least one governor, feeling "pinioned" under the law, continued impressing while calling it "borrowing." Was the act simply a wartime measure, which expired with the return of peace in 1713? Regardless of the dispute, impressment continued, routine in its regularity, but often spectacular in its effects.

Boston was especially hard-hit by impressment in the 1740s, with frequent incidents throughout the decade and major explosions in 1745 and 1747. Again and again the town meeting and the House of Representatives protested, drumming away at the same themes: impressment was harmful to maritime commerce and to the economic life of the city in general and illegal if not properly authorized.

In all this the seaman himself becomes all but invisible. The attitude towards him in the protests is at best neutral and often sharply antagonistic. In 1747 the House of Representatives condemned the violent response of hundreds of seamen to a large-scale press as "a tumultuous riotous assembling of armed Seamen, Servants, Negroes, and others . . . tending to the Destruction of all Government and Order." While acknowledging that the people had reason to protest, the House chose to level *its* protest against "the most audacious insult" to the governor, Council, and House. And the town meeting, that stronghold of democracy, offered its support to those who took "orderly" steps while expressing its "Abhorence of such Illegal Criminal Proceedings" as those undertaken by the seamen "and other persons of mean and Vile Condition."

Protests such as these reflect at the same time both unity and division in colonial society. All kinds of Americans—both merchants and seamen—opposed impressment, but the town meeting and the House spoke for the merchant, not the seaman. They opposed impressment not for its effect on the seaman but for its effect on commerce. Thus their protests express antagonism to British policy at the same time that they express class division. These two themes continue and develop in American opposition to impressment in the three decades between the Knowles Riots of 1747 and the Declaration of Independence.

During the French and Indian War the navy competed with privateers for seamen. Boston again protested against impressment, and then considered authorizing the governor to press, "provided said Men be impressed from inward-bound Vessels from Foreign Parts only, and that none of them be Inhabitants of this Province." In 1760 New York's mayor had a naval captain arrested on the complaint of two shipmasters who claimed that he had welched on a deal to exchange two men he had pressed for two others they were willing to furnish. With the return of peace in 1763 admirals and Americans alike had reason to suppose that there would be no more impressment. But the Admiralty's plans for a large new American fleet required otherwise, and impressment began again in the spring of 1764 in New York, where a seven-week hot press was brought to a partial stop by the arrest of one of the two offending captains. In the spring and summer a hunt for men between Maine and Virginia by four naval vessels brought violent responses, including the killing of a marine at New York; another fort, at Newport, fired on another naval vessel.

Along with the divisions there was a certain amount of unity. Seamen who fled after violently resisting impressment could not be found—probably because others sheltered them—and juries would not indict them. Captains were prevented from impressing by the threat of prosecution. And in 1769 lawyer John Adams used the threat of displaying the statute book containing the Sixth of Anne to frighten a special court of Admiralty into declaring the killing of an impressing lieutenant justifiable homicide in necessary self-defense.

There were two kinds of impressment incidents: those in which there was immediate self-defense against impressment, usually at sea, and those in which crowds ashore, consisting in large part of seamen, demonstrated generalized opposition to impressment. This is what the first kind of incident sounded like: a volley of musketry and the air full of langrage, grapeshot, round shot, hammered shot, double-headed shot, even rocks. "Come into the boat and be damned, you Sorry Son of a Whore or else Ile breake your head, and hold your tongue." Small arms, swords and cutlasses, blunderbusses, clubs and pistols, axes, harpoons, fishgigs, twelve-pounders, six-pounders, half-pounders. "You are a parsill of Raskills." Fired five shots to bring to a snow from North Carolina, pressed four. "You have no right to impress me. . . . If you step over that line . . . by the eternal God of Heaven, you are a dead man." "Aye, my lad, I have seen many a brave fellow before now."

Here is hostility and bloodshed, a tradition of antagonism. From the beginning, impressment's most direct victims—the seamen—were its most active opponents. Bernard Bailyn's contention that "not a single murder resulted from the activities of the Revolutionary mobs in America" does not hold up if extended to cover resistance to impressment; there were murders on both sides. Perhaps the great bulk of incidents of this sort must remain forever invisible to the historian, for they often took place out of sight of friendly observers, and the only witness, the navy, kept records which are demonstrably biased and faulty, omitting the taking of thousands of men. But even the visible records provide a great deal of information. This much we know without doubt: seamen did not go peacefully. Their violence was purposeful, and sometimes they were articulate. "I know who you are," said one, as reported by John Adams and supported by Thomas Hutchinson. "You are the lieutenant of a man-of-war, come with a press-gang to deprive me of my liberty. You have no right to impress me. I have retreated from you as far as I can. I can go no farther. I and my companions are determined to stand upon our defence. Stand off." (It was difficult for Englishmen to fail to see impressment in such terms—even a sailor *doing* the pressing could feel shame over "fighting with honest sailors, to deprive them of their liberty.")

Ashore, seamen and others demonstrated their opposition to impressment with the only weapon which the unrepresentative politics of the day offered them—riot. In Boston several thousand people responded to a nighttime impressment sweep of the harbor and docks with three days of rioting beginning in the early hours of November 17, 1747. Thomas Hutchinson reported that "the lower class were beyond measure enraged." Negroes, servants, and hundreds of seamen seized a naval lieutenant, assaulted a sheriff and put his deputy in the stocks, surrounded the governor's house, and stormed the Town House where the General Court was sitting. The rioters demanded the seizure of the impressing officers, the release of the men they had pressed, and execution of a death sentence which had been levied against a member of an earlier press-gang who had been convicted of murder. When the governor fled to Castle William—some called it "abdication"—Commodore Knowles threatened to put down what he called "arrant rebellion" by bombarding the town. The governor, who, for his part, thought the rioting a secret plot of the upper class, was happily surprised when the town meeting expressed its "Abhorence" of the seamen's riot.

After the French and Indian War press riots increased in frequency. Armed mobs of whites and Negroes repeatedly manhandled captains, officers, and crews, threatened their lives, and held them hostage for the men they pressed. Mobs fired at pressing vessels and tried to board them; they threatened to burn one, and they regularly dragged ships' boats to the center of town for ceremonial bonfires. In Newport in June 1765, 500 seamen, boys, and Negroes rioted after five weeks of impressment. "Sensible" Newporters opposed impressment but nonetheless condemned this "Rabble." In Norfolk in 1767 Captain Jeremiah Morgan retreated, sword in hand, before a mob of armed whites and Negroes. "Good God," he wrote to the governor, "was your Honour and I to prosecute all the Rioters that attacked us belonging to Norfolk there would not be twenty left unhang'd belonging to the Toun." According to Thomas Hutchinson, the *Liberty* Riot in Boston in 1768 may have been as much against impressment as against the seizure of Hancock's sloop: *Romney* had pressed before June 10, and on that day three officers were forced by an angry crowd "arm'd with Stones" to release a man newly pressed from the Boston packet. *Romney* pressed another man, and on June 14, after warding off "many wild and violent proposals," the town meeting petitioned the governor against both the seizure and impressment; the instructions to their representatives (written by John Adams) quoted the Sixth of Anne at length. On June 18 two councillors pleaded with the governor to procure the release of a man pressed by *Romney* "as the peace of the Town seems in a great measure to depend upon it."

There were other impressment riots at New York in July of 1764 and July of 1765; at Newport in July of 1764; at Casco Bay, Maine, in December 1764. Incidents continued during the decade following, and impressment flowered on the very eve of the Revolution. Early in 1775 the practice began to be used in a frankly vindictive and political way—because a town had inconvenienced an admiral, or because a town supported the Continental Congress. Impresses were ordered and took place from Maine to Virginia. In September a bundle of press warrants arrived from the Admiralty, along with word of the repeal of the Sixth of Anne. What had been dubious was now legal. Up and down the coast, officers rejoiced and went to work.

Long before 1765 Americans had developed beliefs about impressment, and they had expressed those beliefs in words and deeds. Impressment was bad for trade and it was illegal. As such, it was, in the words of the Massachusetts House in 1720, "a great Breach on the Rights of His Majesties Subjects." In 1747 it was a violation of "the common Liberty of the Subject," and in 1754 "inconsistent with Civil Liberty, and the Natural Rights of Mankind." Some felt in 1757 that it was even "abhorrent to the English Constitution." In fact, the claim that impressment was unconstitutional was wrong. (Even Magna Charta was no protection. *Nullus liber homo capiatur* did not apply to seamen.) Instead impressment indicated to Benjamin Franklin "that the constitution is yet imperfect, since in so general a case it doth not secure liberty, but destroys it." "If impressing seamen is of right by common law in Britain," he also remarked, "slavery is then of right by common law there; there being no slavery worse than that sailors are subjected to."

For Franklin, impressment was a symptom of injustice built into the British Constitution. In *Common Sense* Tom Paine saw in impressment a reason for rejecting monarchy. In the Declaration of Independence Thomas Jefferson included impressment among the "Oppressions" of George III; later he likened the practice to the capture of Africans for slavery. Both "reduced [the victim] to . . . bondage by force, in flagrant violation of his own consent, and of his natural right in his own person."

Despite all this, and all that went before, we have thought little of impressment as an element in explaining the conduct of the common man in the American Revolution.[2] Contemporaries knew better. John Adams felt that a tactical mistake by Thomas Hutchinson on the question of impressment in 1769 would have "accelerated the revolution. . . . It would have spread a wider flame than Otis's ever did, or could have done."[3] Ten years later American seamen were being impressed by *American* officers. The United States Navy had no better solution for "public Necessities" than had the Royal Navy. Joseph Reed, president of Pennsylvania, complained to Congress of "Oppressions" and in so doing offered testimony to the role of *British* impressment in bringing on revolution. "We cannot help observing how similar this Conduct is to that of the British Officers during our Subjection to Great Brittain and are persuaded it will have the same

[2] James Fulton Zimmerman, *Impressment of American Seamen* (New York, 1925), esp. 11–17, treats the practice as almost nonexistent before the Revolution, giving the pre-Revolutionary phenomenon only the briefest consideration, and concluding, on the basis of speculative evidence, that impressment was rare in the colonies. The author does not understand the Sixth of Anne and thinks it was repealed in 1769. Clark, "Impressment of Seamen," in *Essays to Andrews,* 202; Paine, *Ships and Sailors of Salem,* 65; George Athan Billias, *General John Glover and his Marblehead Mariners* (New York, 1960), 31; Bridenbaugh, *Cities in Revolt,* 114–117, 308–310; Bernhard Knollenberg, *Origin of the American Revolution: 1759–1766* (New York, 1961), 12, 179–181, all see impressment as contributing in some way to the revolutionary spirit.

[3] Adams, ed., *Works of Adams,* II, 226*n.* Neil Stout, "Manning the Royal Navy," 182–184, suggests that impressment did not become a "great issue" of the American Revolution because American "radicals" did not *make* an issue of it and especially because of the failure of John Adams's attempt to make a *"cause celebre"* in 1769. Stout's approach sides with the navy and minimizes the *reality* of impressment as a grievance. Its implication is that the seaman had in fact no genuine grievance and that he acted in response to manipulation.

unhappy effects viz., an estrangement of the Affections of the People from the Authority under which they act which by an easy Progression will proceed to open Opposition to the immediate Actors and Bloodshed." Impressment had played a role in the estrangement of the American people from the British government. It had produced "Odium" against the navy, and even six-year-olds had not been too young to have learned to detest it. The anger of thousands of victims did not vanish. Almost four decades after the Declaration of Independence an orator could still arouse his audience by tapping a folk-memory of impressment by the same "haughty, cruel, and gasconading nation" which was once again trying to enslave free Americans.[4]

The seamen's conduct in the 1760s and 1770s makes more sense in the light of previous and continued impressment. What may have seemed irrational violence can now be seen as purposeful and radical. The pattern of rioting as political expression, established as a response to impressment, was now adapted and broadened as a response to the Stamp Act. In New York General Gage described the "insurrection of October 31, 1765, and following as "composed of great numbers of Sailors." The seamen, he said, were "the only People who may be properly Stiled Mob," and estimates indicate that between a fifth and a fourth of New York's rioters were seamen. The disturbances began among the seamen—especially former privateersmen—on October 31. On November 1 they had marched, led primarily by their former captains; later they rioted, led by no one but themselves. Why? Because they had been duped by merchants, or, if not by merchants, then certainly by lawyers. So British officials

[4] William M. Willett, *A Narrative of the Military Actions of Colonel Marinus Willett, Taken Chiefly from his own Manuscript* (New York, 1831), 149–151. On the level of leadership impressment was not a major cause of the American Revolution. But the extent to which the articulate voice a grievance is rarely an adequate measure of the suffering of the inarticulate. Since it is unrealistic to suppose that the victims of impressment forgot their anger, the question becomes not, why was impressment irrelevant to the American Revolution—for it had to be relevant, in this sense—but, rather, why were the articulate not *more* articulate about the seamen's anger? In part, perhaps, because much impressment took place offshore and was invisible to all but the seamen directly involved. But the leaders had always perceived even visible impressment more as an interference with commerce than as a form of slavery. As the Revolution approached, impressment as human slavery interested them even less than Negro slavery did; the gap between Jack Tar and the men who made laws for him continued. The failure of the elite to see impressment more clearly as a political issue means only that they failed, as we have, to listen to the seamen.

believed—aroused by these men who meant to use them, the seamen themselves had nothing more than plunder on their minds. In fact, at that point in New York's rioting when the leaders lost control, the seamen, who were then in the center of town, in an area rich for plunder, chose instead to march in an orderly and disciplined way across town to do violence to the home and possessions of an English major whose provocative conduct had made him the obvious political enemy. Thus the "rioting" was actually very discriminating.

Seamen and non-seamen alike joined to oppose the Stamp Act for many reasons, but the seamen had two special grievances: impressment and the effect of England's new attitude toward colonial trade. To those discharged by the navy at the end of the war and others thrown out of work by the death of privateering were added perhaps 20,000 more seamen and fishermen who were thought to be the direct victims of the post-1763 trade regulations. This problem came to the fore in the weeks following November 1, 1765, when the Stamp Act went into effect. The strategy of opposition chosen by the colonial leadership was to cease all activities which required the use of stamps. Thus maritime trade came to a halt in the cities. Some said that this was a cowardly strategy. If the Americans opposed the Stamp Act, let them go on with business as usual, refusing outright to use the stamps. The leaders' strategy was especially harmful to the seamen, and the latter took the more radical position—otherwise the ships would not sail. And this time the seamen's radicalism triumphed over both colonial leadership and British officials. Within little more than a month the act had been largely nullified. Customs officers were allowing ships to sail without stamps, offering as the reason the fear that the seamen, "who are the people that are most dangerous on these occasions, as their whole dependance for a subsistence is upon Trade," would certainly "commit some terrible Mischief." Philadelphia's customs officers feared that the seamen would soon "compel" them to let ships pass without stamps. Customs officers at New York yielded when they heard that the seamen were about to have a meeting.

Customs officers had worse luck on other days. Seamen battled them throughout the 1760s and 1770s. In October 1769 a Philadelphia customs officer was attacked by a mob of seamen who also tarred, feathered, and nearly drowned a man who had furnished him with information about illegally imported goods. A year later a New Jersey customs officer who approached an incoming vessel in Delaware Bay had *his* boat boarded by armed seamen who threatened to murder him and came close to doing so. When the officer's son came to Philadelphia, he was similarly treated by a mob of seamen; there were 1,000 seamen in Philadelphia at the time, and according to the customs collector there, they were "always ready" to do such "mischief." This old antagonism had been further politicized in 1768 when, under the American Board of Customs Commissioners, searchers began to break into sea chests and confiscate those items not covered by cockets, thus breaking an old custom of the sea which allowed seamen to import small items for their own profit. Oliver M. Dickerson has described this new "Invasion of Seamen's Rights" as a part of "customs racketeering" and a cause of animosity between seamen and customs officers.

Many of these animosities flared in the Boston Massacre. What John Adams described as "a motley rabble of saucy boys, negroes and molattoes, Irish teagues and out landish jack tarrs," including twenty or thirty of the latter, armed with clubs and sticks, did battle with the soldiers. Their leader was Crispus Attucks, a mulatto seaman; he was shot to death in front of the Custom House. One of the seamen's reasons for being there has been too little explored. The Massacre grew out of a fight between workers and off-duty soldiers at a ropewalk two days before. That fight, in turn, grew out of the long-standing practice in the British army of allowing off-duty soldiers to take civilian employment. They did so, in Boston and elsewhere, often at wages which undercut those offered to Americans—including unemployed seamen who sought work ashore—by as much as 50 percent. In hard times this led to intense competition for work, and the Boston Massacre was in part a product of this competition. Less well known is the Battle of Golden Hill, which arose from similar causes and took place in New York six weeks before. In January 1770 a gang of seamen went from house to house and from dock to dock, using clubs to drive away the soldiers employed there and threatening anyone who might rehire them. In the days of rioting which followed and which came to be called the Battle of Golden Hill, the only fatality was a seaman, although many other seamen were wounded in the attempt to take vengeance for the killing. The antipathy between soldiers and seamen was so great, said John

Adams, "that they fight as naturally when they meet, as the elephant and Rhinoceros."

To wealthy Loyalist Judge Peter Oliver of Massachusetts, the common people were only "Rabble"—like the "Mobility of all Countries, perfect Machines, wound up by any Hand who might first take the Winch." The people were "duped," "deceived," and "deluded" by cynical leaders who could "turn the Minds of the great Vulgar." Had they been less ignorant, Americans would have spurned their leaders, and there would have been no Revolution. I have tested this generalization and found it unacceptable, at least in its application to colonial seamen. Obviously the seamen did not cause the American Revolution. But neither were they simply irrational fellows who moved only when others manipulated them. I have attempted to show that the seaman had a mind of his own and genuine reasons to act, and that he did act—purposefully. The final test of this purposefulness must be the Revolution itself. Here we find situations in which the seamen are separated from those who might manipulate them and thrown into great physical danger; if they were manipulated or duped into rebellion, on their own we might expect them to show little understanding of or enthusiasm for the war.

To a surprising extent American seamen remained Americans during the Revolution. Beaumarchais heard from an American in 1775 that seamen, fishermen, and harbor workers had become an "army of furious men, whose actions are all animated by a spirit of vengeance and hatred" against the English, who had destroyed their livelihood "and the liberty of their country." The recent study of Loyalist claimants by Wallace Brown confirms Oliver Dickerson's earlier contention that "the volumes dealing with loyalists and their claims discloses an amazing absence of names" of seamen. From a total of 2,786 Loyalist claimants whose occupations are known Brown found only 39, 1.4 percent, who were seamen (or pilots). (It is possible to exclude fishermen and masters but not pilots from his figures.) In contrast, farmers numbered 49.1 percent, artisans 9.8 percent, merchants and shopkeepers 18.6 percent, professionals 9.1 percent, and officeholders 10.1 percent. Although as Brown states, the poor may be underrepresented among the claimants, "the large number of claims by poor people, and even Negroes, suggests that this is not necessarily true."

An especially revealing way of examining the seamen's loyalties under pressure is to follow them into British prisons. Thousands of them were imprisoned in such places as the ship *Jersey,* anchored in New York harbor, and Mill and Forton prisons in England. Conditions were abominable. Administration was corrupt, and in America disease was rife and thousands died. If physical discomfort was less in the English prisons than in *Jersey,* the totality of misery may have been as great, with prisoners more distant from the war and worse informed about the progress of the American cause. Lost in a no-man's-land between British refusal to consider them prisoners of war and Washington's unwillingness in America to trade trained soldiers for captured seamen, these men had limited opportunities for exchange. Trapped in this very desperate situation, the men were offered a choice: they could defect and join the Royal Navy. To a striking extent the prisoners remained patriots, and very self-consciously so. "Like brave men, they resisted, and swore that they would never lift a hand to do any thing on board of King George's ships." The many who stayed understood the political signficance of their choice as well as the few who went. "What business had he to sell his Country, and go to the worst of Enemies?" Instead of defecting they engaged in an active resistance movement. Although inexperienced in self-government and segregated from their captains, on their own these men experienced no great difficulties in organizing themselves into disciplined groups. "Notwithstanding they were located within the absolute dominions of his Britanic majesty," commented one, the men "adventured to form themselves into a republic, framed a constitution and enacted wholesome laws, with suitable penalties." Organized, they resisted, celebrating the Fourth of July under British bayonets, burning their prisons, and escaping. Under these intolerable conditions, seamen from all over the colonies discovered that they shared a common conception of the cause for which they fought.

At the Constitutional Convention Benjamin Franklin spoke for the seamen:

> *It is of great consequence that we shd. not depress the virtue and public spirit of our common people; of which they displayed a great deal during the war, and which contributed principally to the favorable issue of it. He related the honorable refusal of the American seamen who were*

> *carried in great numbers into the British prisons during the war, to redeem themselves from misery or to seek their fortunes, by entering on board of the Ships of the Enemies to their Country; contrasting their patriotism with a contemporary instance in which the British seamen made prisoners by the Americans, readily entered on the ships of the latter on being promised a share of the prizes that might be made out of their own Country.*

Franklin spoke *against limiting* the franchise, not *for broadening* it: he praised the seamen, but with a hint of condescension, suggesting that it would be prudent to grant them a few privileges. A decade later a French traveler noticed that "except the laborer in ports, and the common sailor, everyone calls himself, and is called by others, a *gentleman.*" Government was still gentleman's government: more people were defined as gentlemen, but Jack Tar was not yet among them.

Bernard Bailyn has recently added needed illumination to our understanding of pre-Revolutionary crowd action. Bailyn has disagreed with Peter Oliver and with modern historians who have concurred in describing pre-Revolutionary rioters as mindless, passive, and manipulated: "far from being empty vessels," rioters in the decade before the outbreak of fighting were "politically effective" and "shared actively the attitudes and fears" of their leaders; theirs was a " 'fully-fledged political movement.' "[5] Thus it would seem that Bailyn has freed himself from the influential grasp of Gustave Le Bon.[6] But Bailyn stopped short of total rejection. Only in 1765, he says, was the colonial crowd "transformed" into a political phenomenon. Before then it was "conservative"—like crowds in seven-

[5] Bailyn, ed., *Pamphlets,* 581–583, 740 n. 10; Bailyn quotes the last phrase from George Rudé, "The London 'Mob' of the Eighteenth Century," *Historical Journal,* II (1959), 17. Bailyn is here contending that the post-1765 crowd was more highly developed than its English counterpart which was, according to Rudé, not yet "a fully-fledged political movement." See also Gordon S. Wood, "A Note on Mobs in the American Revolution," *Wm. and Mary Qtly.,* 3d Ser., XXIII (1966), 635–642.

[6] See Gustave Le Bon, *The Crowd* (New York, 1960). For a critique of interpretations of the American Revolution which seem to echo Le Bon, see Lemisch, "American Revolution," in Bernstein, ed., *Towards a New Past, passim.* Two useful discussions which place Le Bon and those he has influenced in the context of the history of social psychology (and of history) are George Rudé, *The Crowd in History* (New York, 1964), 3–15, and Roger W. Brown, "Mass Phenomena," in Gardner Lindzey, ed., *Handbook of Social Psychology* (Cambridge, Mass., 1954), II, 833–873. Both Rudé and Brown describe Le Bon's bias as "aristocratic." Also relevant are some of the studies in Duane P. Schultz, ed., *Panic Behavior* (New York, 1964), especially Alexander Mintz, "Non-Adaptive Group Behavior," 84–107.

teenth- and eighteenth-century England, aiming neither at social revolution nor at social reform, but only at immediate revenge. Impressment riots and other "demonstrations by transient sailors and dock workers," Bailyn says, expressed no "deep-lying social distress" but only a "diffuse and indeliberate antiauthoritarianism"; they were "ideologically inert."[7]

Other historians have seen the colonial seamen—and the rest of the lower class—as mindless and manipulated, both before and after 1765.[8] The seeming implication behind this is that the seamen who demonstrated in colonial streets did so as much out of simple vindictiveness or undisciplined violence as out of love of liberty. Certainly such motivation would blend well with the traditional picture of the seaman as rough and ready. For along with the stereotype of Jolly Jack—and in part belying that stereotype—is bold and reckless Jack, the exotic and violent. Jack *was* violent; the conditions of his existence were violent. Was his violence nonpolitical? Sometimes. The mob of seventy to eighty yelling, club-swinging, out-of-town seamen who tried to break up a Philadelphia election in 1742 had no interest in the election; they had been bought off with money and liquor.

Other violence is not so clear-cut. Edward Thompson has seen the fighting out of significant social conflict in eighteenth-century England "in terms of Tyburn, the hulks and the Bridewells on the one hand; and crime, riot, and mob action on the other." Crime and violence among eighteenth-century American seamen needs reexamination from such a perspective. Does "mutiny" adequately describe the act of the crew which seized *Black Prince,* renamed it

[7] Bailyn ed., *Pamphlets,* 581–583, citing Max Beloff, *Public Order and Popular Disturbances, 1660–1714* (London, 1938), 38, 153, 155, calls Beloff "the historian of popular disturbances in pre-industrial England," thus bypassing at least one other candidate for the title, George Rudé, whom he describes as "an English historian of eighteenth-century crowd phenomena." Rudé has shown in *The Crowd in History* and elsewhere that the crowd was purposeful, disciplined, and discriminating, that "in the eighteenth century the typical and ever recurring form of social protest was the riot." Rudé finds in Beloff echoes of Burke and Paine. Thus, the European foundation for Bailyn's interpretation of the pre-1765 American crowd is somewhat one-sided. Compare with Bailyn R. S. Longley's extremely manipulative "Mob Activities in Revolutionary Massachusetts," *New Eng. Qtly.,* VI (1933), 108: "Up to 1765, the Massachusetts mob was not political. Even after this date, its political organization was gradual, but it began with the Stamp Act."

[8] For a further discussion see Lemisch, "American Revolution," in Bernstein, ed., *Towards a New Past, passim.* Bailyn, ed., *Pamphlets*, 581, is not entirely clear on the situation *after* 1765. He denies that "Revolutionary mobs" in America were in fact "revolutionary" and questions their "meliorist aspirations."

FIGURE 5. Parliament debating the colonial question.

Liberty, and chose their course and a new captain by voting? What shall we call the conduct of 150 seamen who demanded higher wages by marching along the streets of Philadelphia with clubs, unrigging vessels, and forcing workmen ashore? If "mutiny" is often the captain's name for what we have come to call a "strike," perhaps we might also detect some significance broader than mere criminality in the seamen's frequent assaults on captains and thefts from them. Is it not in some sense a political act for a seaman to tear off the mast a copy of a law which says that disobedient seamen will be punished as "seditious"?

Impressment meant the loss of freedom, both personal and economic, and, sometimes, the loss of life itself. The seaman who defended himself against impressment felt that he was fighting to defend his "liberty," and he justified his resistance on grounds of "right." It is in the concern for liberty and right that the seaman rises from vindictiveness to a somewhat more complex awareness that certain values larger than himself exist and that he is the victim not only of cruelty and hardship but also, in the light of those values, of injustice. The riots ashore, whether they be against impressment, the Stamp Act, or competition for work express that same sense of injustice. And here, thousands of men took positive and effective steps to demonstrate their opposition to both acts and policies.

Two of England's most exciting historians have immensely broadened our knowledge of past and present by examining phenomena strikingly like the conduct and thought of the seamen in America. These historians have described such manifestations as "sub-political" or "pre-political," and one of them has urged that such movements be "seriously considered not simply as an unconnected series of individual curiosities, as footnotes to history, but as a phenomenon of general importance and considerable weight in modern history." When Jack Tar went to sea in the American Revolution, he fought, as he had for many years before, quite literally, to protect his life, liberty, and property. It might be extravagant to call the seamen's conduct and the sense of injustice which underlay it in any fully developed sense ideological or political; on the other hand, it makes little sense to describe their ideological content as zero. There are many worlds and much of human history in that vast area between ideology and inertness.

IV IDEOLOGICAL ASPECTS OF THE REVOLUTIONARY MOVEMENT

Clinton Rossiter

THE AMERICAN CONSENSUS, 1765–1776

Clinton L. Rossiter, a political scientist at Cornell University, was the author of many works on American government and American political institutions. He is widely recognized as a leading spokesman of contemporary conservative political thought. The selection which follows is from Seedtime of the Republic, *a thorough and exhaustive examination of the political writings and political thought of America's formative years and of the events which produced them.*

On March 22, 1765, George III gave his royal assent to the Stamp Act, a stick of imperial dynamite so harmless in appearance that it had passed both houses of Parliament as effortlessly as "a common Turnpike Bill." Eleven years later, July 2, 1776, the Continental Congress resolved after "the greatest and most solemn debate":

> *That these United Colonies are, and, of right, ought to be, Free and Independent States; that they are absolved from all allegiance to the* British *crown, and that all political connexion between them, and the state of* Great Britain, *is, and ought to be totally dissolved.*

In the tumultuous years between these two fateful acts the American colonists, at least a sufficient number of them, stumbled and haggled their way to a heroic decision: to found a new nation upon political and social principles that were a standing reproach to almost every other nation in the world. Not for another seven years could they be certain that their decision had been sound as well as bold; only then would the mother country admit reluctantly that the new nation was a fact of life rather than an act of treason. The colonists were to learn at Brooklyn and Valley Forge that it was one thing to resolve for independence and another to achieve it.

Yet the resolution for independence, the decision to fight as a "separate and equal" people rather than as a loose association of remonstrating colonials, was as much the climax of a revolution as the formal beginning of one. The American Revolution, like most uprisings that are something more than a quick change of the palace guard, was a major event in intellectual as in political and social history. The Revolution in fact and law recognized by treaty in 1783 would never have taken place at all except for the revolution in mind and spirit between 1765 and 1776, and that revolution, as John Adams was later to point out, was made possible only by the great advances of the colonial period.

The intellectual history of the American Revolution is therefore largely confined to the years 1765–1776. In this period the colonists carried on their critical debates, proclaimed their central ideas, and reached their one truly revolutionary decision: to strike out for themselves as an independent republic. If the years under Washington were those that tried men's souls, the years under Samuel Adams were those that searched their minds. The intellectual history of this great event can be narrowed in subject matter as well as in time, for it is chiefly a history of political ideas. The announced purpose of the Americans was to dissolve the political bands that had connected them with England. The central problem for the decade was largely political in nature, and the search for solutions was pushed along political lines. Political theory rather than economic, religious, or social theory was the chief beneficiary of the outpouring of speeches, sermons, letters, resolves, and pamphlets that greeted each new move of the British ministry. . . .

The American Colonies, 1765–1776

Conditions in the continental colonies in the pre-Revolutionary decade were conducive to political thinking of a libertarian character. The colonies expanded noticeably in population, settled area, and wealth; they expanded even more noticeably in political, social, and religious liberty. Progress and freedom were the concerns of the time, and a political theory dedicated to progress and freedom was an inevitable result. . . .

Far more significant than this material progress was the quickened influence of . . . the "factors of freedom." The "forces behind the forces"—the English heritage, the ocean, the frontier, and imperial tension—never worked so positively for political liberty as in this decade of ferment. Until the last days before independence the colonists continued to argue as Englishmen demanding English rights. The more they acted like Americans, the more they talked like Englishmen. Heirs of a tradition that glorified resistance to tyranny, they moved into political combat as English Whigs rather than American democrats, reminding the world that "it is the peculiar Right of Englishmen to complain when injured." The other basic forces were no less conducive to liberty. In a situation that called desperately for accurate information, firm decisions, and resolute administration, the very distance between London and Boston frustrated the development of a viable imperial policy. In a situation that called no less desperately for colonial understanding of the financial and imperial difficulties facing Crown and Parliament, the push to the frontier weakened the bonds of loyalty to an already too-distant land. And the Stamp Act and Townshend Acts forced most articulate colonists to reduce the old conflict of English and American interests to the simplest possible terms. Since some Englishmen proposed to consign other Englishmen to perpetual inferiority, was it not simply a question of liberty or slavery?

Political factors of freedom enjoyed the sharpest increase in visible influence. The ancient struggle between royal governor and popular assembly took on new vigor and meaning. The depths of ill feeling were plumbed in the maneuvers and exchanges of Governors Bernard and Hutchinson and the Massachusetts legislature. The colonial press engaged in more political reporting and speculation in the single year between June 1765 and June 1766 than in all the sixty-odd years since the founding of the *Boston News-Letter.* In early 1765 there were twenty-three newspapers in the colonies, only two or three of which were politically conscious; in early 1775 there were thirty-eight, only two or three of which were not. The spirit of constitutionalism and the demand for written constitutions also quickened in the course of the great dispute over the undetermined boundaries of imperial power and colonial rights. The word "unconstitutional," an important adjunct of constitutionalism, became one of America's favorite words. Most important, the Stamp Act was a healthy spur to political awareness among all ranks of men. Wrote John Adams in 1766:

> *The people, even to the lowest ranks, have become more attentive to their liberties, more inquisitive about them, and more determined to defend them, than they were ever before known or had occasion to be; innumerable have been the monuments of wit, humor, sense, learning, spirit, patriotism, and heroism, erected in the several provinces in the*

course of this year. Their counties, towns, and even private clubs and sodalities have voted and determined; their merchants have agreed to sacrifice even their bread to the cause of liberty; their legislatures have resolved; the united colonies have remonstrated; the presses have everywhere groaned; and the pulpits have thundered.

The thundering pulpit, an old and faithful servant of American freedom, set out to demonstrate anew the affinity of religious and political liberty. Bumptious Protestantism vied with temperate rationalism as spurs to disestablishment and liberty of conscience. Conditions for the final triumph of unqualified religious liberty grew more favorable in this unsettled decade. So, too, did conditions of economic independence. The overall state of the American economy lent impressive support to radical claims that the colonies would get along just as well, if not better, outside the protecting confines of British mercantilism. In wealth, resources, production, ingenuity, and energy the Americans were fast approaching the end of the colonial line.

The broad social trends continued through the pre-Revolutionary decade. In every colony the middle class formed the nucleus of the patriot party, and in Boston it attained a position of commanding political influence. The aristocracy split into opposing camps, but the Lees of Virginia and the Livingstons of New York are reminders that a decisive share of patriotic leadership fell to the American aristocrat. The political storms of the decade, which deposited power in new hands in almost every colony, did much to stimulate social mobility and class conflict. The career of the Sons of Liberty attests the growing fluidity of colonial society; the uprisings of the "Paxton Boys" in Pennsylvania and the Regulators in North Carolina attest the heightened tensions of class and section.

Finally, the colonial mind took rapid strides forward in this period, not alone in the field of political thought. Deism, rationalism, and the scientific spirit claimed ever-increasing numbers of men in positions of leadership. The cult of virtue enjoyed a vogue even more intense than in the colonial period. The arts showed new signs of indigenous strength. The sharp increase in the number of newspapers was matched by an even sharper increase in the output of books and pamphlets. Three new colleges opened their doors to eager students, and King's and the Philadelphia Academy instituted the first American medical schools. Despite all the shouting about English rights and ways, the colonial mind was growing steadily less English and more American. By the standards of the Old World, it was a mind not especially attractive, not least because it was setting out at last to find standards of its own.

The American colonies moved fast and far between 1765 and 1776. While the king fumed, the ministry blundered, assemblies protested, mobs rioted, and Samuel Adams plotted, the people of the colonies, however calm or convulsed the political situation, pushed steadily ahead in numbers, wealth, self-reliance, and devotion to liberty. The political theory of the American Revolution can be understood only within this context of material and spiritual progress. It was a theory dedicated to ordered liberty, for liberty was something most Americans already enjoyed. . . .

The Problem of the American Spokesmen

American leaders . . . had two ends in view as they maneuvered their way through this confusing decade: one immediate, to resist and seek repeal of each oppressive act of Parliament or related policy of the ministry; and one long-range, to find the proper place for the colonies within the protecting pale of the rising British empire. In the first instance, the prime constitutional issue was the power of Parliament to tax the colonies; in the second, and ultimately more important and perplexing, it was the power of Crown and Parliament together to govern them, whether by taxation, legislation, supervision, inspection, royal veto, or other means. The chief constitutional problem was therefore to find the line, if such there was, between the general authority of Parliament and special authority of each assembly, between total submission and independence. We cannot investigate the political theory of the Revolution unless we first recall this great problem in constitutional theory, the organization of the British Empire, for at every stage of the imperial controversy the Americans appealed to first principles in support of their current constitutional stand. Political theory justified the first show of resistance; political theory was the final answer to the constitutional problem. Government by consent and the rights of man were the only theoretical foundation upon which independence could be based.

It is impossible to fix precisely the state of American opinion at any given time concerning the confused relationship between England and the colonies. Men who shared the same political views found themselves in clear if amiable disagreement over the central constitutional issue. Some shifted their opinions from one crisis to the next, driving one author to protest, "Shall we, Proteus-like, perpetually change our ground, assume every moment some new and strange shape, to defend, to evade?" Others, notably James Otis and Richard Bland, expressed two or three different interpretations in one pamphlet. Few Americans voiced their opinions in words that meant the same thing to all men. The problem of locating the line was a formidable one, principally because few men had ever tried to locate it before except in terms of subjection or independence. The result was a discouraging confusion of language and opinion. The most we can say is that all patriots began with a hazy belief in home rule quite opposed to the assumptions of the Stamp and Declaratory Acts, and moved at different speeds in the direction of a dominion theory of the British Empire. At least seven different solutions to the problem of imperial organization were brought forward at one time or another during this period.

Complete Subjection and Virtual Representation. The doctrine of the Declaratory Act—that the king in Parliament had "full power and authority to make laws and statutes of sufficient force and validity to bind the colonies and people of *America,* subjects of the Crown of *Great Britain,* in all cases whatsoever"—was apparently acceptable to only one leader of American thought, James Otis, and even he was not entirely convinced

> *that the Parliament of Great-Britain hath a just, clear, equitable and constitutional right, power and authority, to bind the colonies, by all acts wherein they are named.*

Nowhere else in patriot literature, certainly after 1765, was the Tory dogma of complete subjection treated with any attitude but contempt.

The chief historical interest of this dogma lies in the corollary through which ministerial supporters tried to make it palatable to colonial tastes: virtual representation. This argument was designed to silence the cry of "no taxation without representation" by reviving and extending the ancient fiction that all Englishmen, whether enfranchised or not, were virtually represented in Parliament. The colonies, asserted Tory writers, stood in the same constitutional and practical position as the cities of Manchester and Sheffield. That they elected no representatives did not mean they were unrepresented and therefore taxed without their consent, for each member of the House of Commons, whether from London or Old Sarum, represented the interests of all Englishmen.

> *Our nation is represented in parliament by an assembly as numerous as can well consist with order and dispatch, chosen by persons so differently qualified in different places, that the mode of choice seems to be, for the most part, formed by chance, and settled by custom. Of individuals far the greater part have no vote, and of the voters few have any personal knowledge of him to whom they intrust their liberty and fortune.*
>
> *Yet this representation has the whole effect expected or desired; that of spreading so wide the care of general interest, and the participation of publick counsels, that the advantage or corruption of particular men can seldom operate with much injury to the Publick.*
>
> *For this reason many populous and opulent towns neither enjoy nor desire particular representatives; they are included in the general scheme of public administration, and cannot suffer but with the rest of the empire.*
>
> *It is urged that the* Americans *have not the same security, and that a* British *legislator may wanton with their property; yet if it be true, that their wealth is our wealth, and that their ruin will be our ruin, the parliament has the same interest in attending to them, as to any other part of the nation. The reason why we place any confidence in our representatives is, that they must share in the good or evil which their counsels shall produce. Their share is indeed commonly consequential and remote; but it is not often possible that any immediate advantage can be extended to such numbers as may prevail against it. We are therefore as secure against intentional depravations of government as human wisdom can make us, and upon this security the* Americans *may venture to repose.*

The American answer to virtual representation was a mixture of irritation and contempt. "Our *privileges* are all *virtual*," shouted Arthur Lee, "our sufferings are *real*." Most writers rejected in just such a sentence or paragraph the sophistry of virtual representation, refusing to dignify it with lengthy rebuttal. James Otis spoke the colonial mind when he rattled off his famous retort:

> *To what purpose is it to ring everlasting changes to the colonists on the cases of Manchester, Birmingham and Sheffield, who return no members? If those now so considerable places are not represented, they ought to be. . . . It may perhaps sound strangely to some, but it is in my*

> *most humble opinion as good* law *and as good* sense *too, to affirm that all the plebeians of Great-Britain are in fact or virtually represented in the assembly of the Tuskaroras, as that all the colonists are in fact or virtually represented in the honourable house of Commons of Great-Britain.*

A few colonists took the doctrine of virtual representation seriously enough to refute it with a careful show of history and logic. The most convincing objector was Daniel Dulany the younger, later to become a loyalist, who devoted some of the best pages of his early pamphlet on taxation to demolishing virtual representation. This doctrine, he asserted, "consists of Facts not true, and of Conclusions inadmissible," and "is a mere Cobweb, spread to catch the unwary, and entangle the weak." The key paragraph of his argument was this.

> *There is not that intimate and inseparable Relation between the* Electors of Great-Britain *and the* Inhabitants of the Colonies, *which must inevitably involve both in the same Taxation; on the contrary, not a single* actual *Elector in* England, *might be immediately affected by a Taxation in* America, *imposed by a Statute which would have a general Operation and Effect, upon the Properties of the Inhabitants of the Colonies. The latter might be oppressed in a Thousand Shapes, without any Sympathy, or exciting any Alarm in the former. Moreover, even Acts, oppressive and injurious to the Colonies in an extreme Degree, might become popular in* England, *from the Promise or Expectation that the very Measures which depressed the Colonies, would give Ease to the Inhabitants of* Great-Britain. *It is indeed true, that the Interests of* England *and the Colonies are allied, and an Injury to the Colonies produced into all its Consequences, will eventually affect the Mother Country, yet these Consequences being generally remote, are not at once foreseen; they do not immediately alarm the Fears, and engage the Passions of the* English *Electors, the Connection between a Freeholder of* Great Britain, *and a* British American *being deducible only through a Train of Reasoning, which few will take the Trouble, or can have an Opportunity, if they have Capacity to investigate; wherefore the Relation between the* British Americans, *and the* English Electors, *is a Knot too infirm to be relied on as a competent Security, especially against the Force of a present, counteracting Expectation of Relief.*

Richard Bland, Maurice Moore of North Carolina, Edward Bancroft, John Dickinson, Arthur Lee, and an anonymous pamphleteer who may have been Samuel Cooper were other dissenters from this doctrine.

Representation in Parliament. One small band of patriots, for whom Otis and Franklin were spokesmen, proposed that the colonies be "represented in some proportion to their number and estates, in the grand legislature of the nation." In his *Right of the British Colonies* Otis wrote:

> *A representation in Parliament from the several Colonies, since they are become so large and numerous, as to be called on not to maintain provincial government, civil and military among themselves, for this they have chearfully done, but to contribute towards the support of a national standing army, by reason of the heavy national debt . . . can't be tho't an unreasonable thing, nor if asked, could it be called an immodest request. . . . Besides the equity of an American representation in parliament, a thousand advantages would result from it. It would be the most effectual means of giving those of both countries a thorough knowledge of each others interests; as well as that of the whole, which are inseparable.*

Neither Otis nor Franklin advanced this solution with any real show of conviction, for it proved equally distasteful to leaders and led on both sides of the ocean. The equity of American representation was not admitted by Parliament, the advantages were not at all clear to the colonists. The arguments of the Adamses were representative of an overwhelming colonial opinion. Samuel Adams wrote to the colony's agent in 1765:

> *We are far however from desiring any Representation there, because we think the Colonies cannot be equally and fully represented; and if not equally then in Effect not at all. A Representative should be, and continue to be well acquainted with the internal Circumstances of the People whom he represents. . . . Now the Colonies are at so great a Distance from the Place where the Parliament meets, from which they are separated by a wide Ocean; and their Circumstances are so often and continually varying, as is the Case in all Countries not fully settled, that it would not be possible for Men, tho' ever so well acquainted with them at the Beginning of a Parliament, to continue to have an adequate Knowledge of them during the Existence of that Parliament.*

And John Adams queried his readers in 1775:

> *Would not representatives in the house of commons, unless they were numerous in proportion to the numbers of people in America, be a snare rather than a blessing?*
>
> *Would Britain ever agree to a proportionable number of American members; and if she would, could America support the expense of them?*

> *Could American representatives possibly know the sense, the exigencies, &c. of their constituents, at such a distance, so perfectly as it is absolutely necessary legislators should know?*
>
> *Could Americans ever come to the knowledge of the behavior of their members, so as to dismiss the unworthy?*
>
> *Would Americans in general ever submit to septennial elections?*
>
> *Have we not sufficient evidence, in the general frailty and depravity of human nature . . . that a deep, treacherous, plausible, corrupt minister would be able to seduce our members to betray us as fast as we could send them?*

Imperial federation was unacceptable to colonial minds on historical, psychological, and practical grounds. To send a few representatives to England would serve only to legalize parliamentary taxation, not prevent it.

Internal and External Taxation. The threat and passage of the Stamp Act evoked the first unsuccessful attempt to locate a fixed line between parliamentary and provincial power: the distinction between excise taxes (internal taxation) and custom duties (external taxation). Although recent researches have demonstrated that this formula was neither so clear-cut nor popular as historians have hitherto assumed, many Americans did subscribe to the general notion that Parliament had the right to pass the Sugar Act but not the Stamp Act. The protests and pamphlets of 1765–1766 did not express this distinction so clearly as they might have, principally because the colonists saw no reason to approve a bad act in order to destroy an evil one. They talked a great deal about internal taxation, since that is what they were denying. They talked very little about external taxation, since to approve it positively was not essential to their arguments and to deny it flatly was not yet essential to their liberties. Therefore, while they resisted the Stamp Act, attacking it on grounds of unconstitutionality, they acquiesced in the Sugar Act, attacking it on grounds of inexpediency.

Actually, the distinction was quite untenable, and many leading Americans shunned it from the beginning. Otis, the lone wolf who argued against British policies while conceding their constitutionality, asserted flatly that "there is no foundation for the distinction some make in England, between an internal and an external tax on the colonies," and added "that the Parliament of Great-Britain has a just and equitable right, power and authority, to *impose taxes on the colonies, internal and external, on lands, as well as on trade.*" But English friends of America found this formula so useful that they converted it into a working principle of the imperial constitution. Enough had been said about "internal taxes" in official resolutions and in pamphlets like Dulany's *Considerations,* Bland's *Inquiry,* and Stephen Hopkins's *Grievances* to convince Pitt—and indeed Franklin—that the colonists had adopted the distinction as their own key to the imperial relationship. The implications of Dulany's widely read argument, which did not even use the phrase "external taxes," were good enough for Pitt. Having cut through Dulany's confusion to an interpretation that suited his own ends, he could blow down an obstreperous but also more perceptive member with the annoyed remark, "If the gentleman does not understand the difference between internal and external taxes, I cannot help it." Whether American or English in origin, the distinction was unworkable, as Charles Townshend was soon to demonstrate.

Taxation for Revenue and Taxation for Regulation of Trade. In the course of his examination before the House of Commons February 13, 1766, Franklin was asked if his countrymen had given much thought to the supposed distinction between internal and external taxation. "They never have hitherto," he answered, adding:

> *Many arguments have been used here to shew them, that there is no difference, and that, if you have no right to tax them internally, you have none to tax them externally, or make any other law to bind them. At present they do not reason so; but in time they may possibly be convinced by these arguments.*

Franklin, the public Franklin, was behind the onward surge of American opinion. Many colonists were already convinced that there was no distinction between these two forms of taxation. The Townshend duties, which were based squarely on the distinction, forced them now to deny it positively.

Townshend's error, of course, had been to announce in the legislation itself that the revenues from these duties would be used for a specific and highly unpopular purpose. Many Americans now raised a new distinction, already implicit in numerous resolves and pamphlets, between taxation for revenue (unconstitutional) and taxation as part of a scheme for regulating imperial trade (constitutional).

The area of unconstitutionality was expanded to include not only all internal taxes but those external taxes which were designed to produce revenue. The chief spokesman for this solution was John Dickinson. In his fantastically popular "Letters from a Farmer in Pennsylvania" he stated the new doctrine in these words:

> *The parliament unquestionably possesses a legal authority to* regulate *the trade of* Great-Britain, *and all her colonies. Such an authority is essential to the relation between a mother country and her colonies; and necessary for the common good of all. . . .*
>
> *I have looked over* every statute *relating to these colonies, from their settlement to this time; and I find every one of them founded on this principle, till the* Stamp-*Act administration.* All before, *are calculated to regulate trade, and preserve or promote a mutually beneficial intercourse between the several constituent parts of the empire; and though many of them imposed duties on trade, yet those duties were always imposed* with design *to restrain the commerce of one part, that was injurious to another, and thus to promote the general welfare. The raising a revenue thereby was never intended. Thus the King, by his judges in his courts of justice, imposes fines which all together amount to a very considerable sum, and contribute to the support of government. But this is merely a consequence arising from restrictions, that only meant to keep peace, and prevent confusion; and surely a man would argue very loosely, who should conclude from hence, that the King has a right to levy money in general upon his subjects. Never did the* British *parliament, till the period above mentioned, think of imposing duties in* America, *for the purpose of raising a revenue. . . .*
>
> *Here [in the Townshend Acts] we may observe an authority* expressly *claimed and exerted to impose duties on these colonies; not for the regulation of trade; not for the preservation or promotion of a mutually beneficial intercourse between the several constituent parts of the empire, heretofore the* sole objects *of parliamentary institutions;* but for the single purpose of levying money upon us.
>
> ***This I call an innovation; and a most dangerous innovation.***

The difficulty with this distinction, as critics on both sides of the ocean were quick to point out, could be framed in the simple question: What if a trade regulation should produce revenue? To this Dickinson answered:

> *The* nature *of any impositions laid by parliament on these colonies, must determine the* design *in laying them. It may not be easy in every instance to discover that design. Wherever it is doubtful, I think submission cannot be dangerous; nay, it must be right; for, in my opinion, there is no privilege these colonies claim, which they ought in* duty *and*

prudence *more earnestly to maintain and defend, than the authority of the* British parliament *to regulate the trade of all her dominions.*

The criterion of intent satisfied no one for long. Radical colonists were anxious to erect a constitutional barrier that left a good deal less scope to parliamentary discretion. Defenders of the English point of view asserted that it was "only a pretense under which to strip Parliament of all jurisdiction over the colonies." Dickinson's legalistic attempt to give precision to a vague boundary was doomed to failure. Yet until the end of the decade patriot writers made use of the distinction between taxation for revenue and "impositions" for regulation of trade.

Denial of Taxation; Home Rule. The next step beyond Dickinson, to which less cautious men had already pushed, was a doctrine of home rule that denied taxation of any description and admitted legislation only for concerns clearly imperial in nature. Clear-sighted men in both camps had already pointed to the absurdity of considering internal taxation and internal legislation as two different things, realizing that laws could do more than taxes to correct or impair the situation created by salutary neglect. Several tough-minded legislatures had seized upon the Stamp Act to voice constitutional objections to parliamentary legislation "respecting their internal Polity," and some movers of these resolutions had gone on to expand upon this point in the first searching pamphlets. This, for example, was the general if confused position taken by Richard Bland in his *Inquiry.* It was a position implicit in many later resolutions and pamphlets, especially after such shows of force as the act suspending the New York Assembly; it was the position finally adopted by conservative patriots like John Dickinson. His *Essay on the Constitutional Power,* published in July 1774, was the best and final statement of the doctrine of home rule, of exemption from Parliament's power to tax at all and to legislate on matters not clearly imperial in scope.

A Dominion Theory of the British Empire. By 1773 Governor Hutchinson of Massachusetts had lost both his good will and perspective. "I know of no line," he wrote to the Massachusetts legislature, "that can be drawn between the supreme authority of Parliament and the total independence of the colonies: it is impossible there should be two independent Legislatures in one and the same state." "If there be no such line," answered the lower house, with the help of John Adams, "the consequence is, either that the colonies are the vassals of the Parliament, or that they are totally independent." But there was yet a third possibility: the union of the colonies and England "in one head and common Sovereign." Thus, under pressure of events at home and abroad, the colonists arrived at a final theory of imperial organization that was still one step short of independence.

This dominion theory of the empire, which held simply and prophetically that the only tie between the colonies and England was a common sovereign, had been long in the making. As early as 1765 men were reaching out for this radical solution, and in 1768 Franklin could reflect:

> *The more I have thought and read on the subject, the more I find myself confirmed in opinion, that no middle doctrine can be well maintained, I mean not clearly with intelligible arguments. Something might be made of either of the extremes; that Parliament has a power to make* all laws *for us, or that it has a power to make* no laws *for us; and I think the arguments for the latter more numerous and weighty, than those for the former. Supposing that doctrine established, the colonies would then be so many separate states, only subject to the same king, as England and Scotland were before the union.*

By 1770 Franklin was no longer in doubt, nor, for that matter, were several other leaders of the American cause. Not until 1774, however, was the dominion theory put forward without apologies or qualifications. John Adams's "Novanglus," Jefferson's *Summary View,* Hamilton's *The Farmer Refuted,* and James Iredell's "To the Inhabitants of Great Britain" all arrived simultaneously at these conclusions: that the power of Parliament to lay taxes or pass laws for the colonies was "none at all"; that the colonies had voluntarily, by "free, cheerful consent," allowed Parliament the "power of regulating trade"; and that the "fealty and allegiance of Americans" was due only "to the person of King George III, whom God long preserve and prosper." The most brilliant statement of this radical position was James Wilson's *Considerations on the Nature and Extent of the Legislative Authority of the British Parliament.* The future justice of the Supreme Court rested the case for American equality not only on law and history, but on "natural right," "the principles of liberty," and "the happiness of the colonies" as well. Wilson's opening passage tells us graphically of the pains with which men like Wilson, Franklin, and John Adams groped in good faith for a line between parliamentary and provincial power:

> *The following sheets were written during the late non-importation agreement: but that agreement being dissolved before they were ready for the press, it was then judged unseasonable to publish them. Many will, perhaps, be surprised to see the legislative authority of the British parliament over the colonies denied* in every instance. *Those the writer informs, that, when he began this piece, he would probably have been surprised at such an opinion himself; for that it was the* result, *and not the* occasion, *of his disquisitions. He entered upon them with a view and expectation of being able to trace some constitutional line between those cases in which we ought, and those in which we ought not, to acknowledge the power of parliament over us. In the prosecution of his inquiries, he became fully convinced that such a line does not exist; and that there can be no medium between acknowledging and denying that power in* all *cases. Which of these two alternatives is most consistent with law, with the principles of liberty, and with the happiness of the colonies, let the publick determine.*

His closing paragraphs mark the abandonment of the attempt to admit Parliament to some sort of authority over the colonies. It was now considered "repugnant to the essential maxims of jurisprudence, to the ultimate end of all governments, to the genius of the British constitution, and to the liberty and happiness of the colonies, that they should be bound by the legislative authority of the parliament of Great Britain."

> *There is another, and a much more reasonable meaning, which may be intended by the dependence of the colonies on Great Britain. The phrase may be used to denote the obedience and loyalty, which the colonists owe to the* kings *of Great Britain. . . .*
>
> *Those who launched into the unknown deep, in quest of new countries and habitations, still considered themselves as subjects of the English monarchs, and behaved suitably to that character; but it no where appears, that they still considered themselves as represented in an English parliament, or that they thought the authority of the English parliament extended over them. They took possession of the country in the* king's *name: they treated, or made war with the Indians by* his *authority: they held the lands under* his *grants, and paid* him *the rents reserved upon them: they established governments under the sanction of* his *prerogative, or by virtue of* his *charters:—no application for those purposes was made*

to the parliament: no ratification of the charters or letters patent was solicited from that assembly, as is usual with England with regard to grants and franchises of much less importance. . . .

This is a dependence, which they have acknowledged hitherto; which they acknowledge now; and which, if it is reasonable to judge of the future by the past and the present, they will continue to acknowledge hereafter. . . .

From this dependence . . . arises a strict connexion between the inhabitants of Great Britain and those of America. They are fellow subjects; they are under allegiance to the same prince; and this union of allegiance naturally produces a union of hearts. It is also productive of a union of measures through the whole British dominions. To the king is intrusted the direction and management of the great machine of government. . . .

The connexion and harmony between Great Britain and us, which it is her interest and ours mutually to cultivate, and on which her prosperity, as well as ours, so materially depends, will be better preserved by the operation of the legal prerogatives of the crown, than by the exertion of an unlimited authority by parliament.

Even in this apparently clear-cut solution American spokesmen stood on confused ground, for in their anxiety to exclude Parliament from their affairs they had come dangerously near to a wholesale revival of the royal prerogative. Had this solution actually been given a trial, could they conceivably have been satisfied? The next step had to be independence.

Independence. From the dominion status of 1774 to independence in 1776 was an easy road in political and constitutional theory. If history and natural law justified immunity from the authority of Parliament, so, too, did they justify deposing a wicked king. Up to 1774 Americans had done little thinking in this vein. The authority of Parliament had been the bone of contention, and the participation of the king in the exercise of that authority had been studiously or carelessly ignored. The only independence the colonists sought was independence of Parliament. The publication of Jefferson's *Summary View* gave a brand-new twist to the imperial tie. At the same time that it reduced the imperial problem to a simple question of personal allegiance to a common sovereign, it made clear that colonists were learning to distinguish the actions of the sovereign from those of Parliament. The Virginia radical made separate listings of Parliament's usurpations and George III's "deviations from the line of duty," and warned the king that persistence in these deviations could lead to denunciation of the last bond of empire.

The final stage of American argument is, of course, most plainly read in the Declaration of Independence, in which the dominion theory and natural law were skillfully woven together to justify the bold decision to dissolve an empire. Thanks to the dominion theory of 1774, the Americans could ignore Parliament almost completely and concentrate their fire on George III. Having already proved, largely through their own reading of history, that they were totally outside the jurisdiction of Parliament and were subjects of the king by free choice, they had only to prove to a candid world that the latter, not the former, had played the tyrant. And it was exactly here, at the moment when they renounced a covenanted monarch, that the whole theory of natural law proved its worth to a people who prided themselves on their political morality. This theory had been extremely helpful at every stage of the struggle since 1765. In this final stage it was absolutely essential. . . .

The Conservatism of American Political Writing, 1765–1776

Perhaps the most remarkable feature of the political literature of this decade was its essential conservatism. If the Americans were the most successful revolutionaries of all time, they were revolutionaries by chance rather than choice. Until the last few months before independence the steady purpose of their resistance was to restore an old order rather than to build a new one, to get back to "the good days of George the second. There was no junto, no backstairs business then; a Whig King and Whig minister, speaking to a Whig people."

> *The British Parliament is violently usurping the powers of our colony governments, and rendering our legal Assemblies utterly useless; to prevent this, the necessity of our situation has obliged us to depart from the common forms, and to adopt measures which would be otherwise unjustifiable; but, in this departure, we have been influenced by an ardent desire to repeal innovations destructive to all good government among us, and fatal to the foundations of law, liberty, and justice: We have declared, in the most explicit terms, that we wish for nothing more, than a restoration to our ancient condition.*

The ingrained conservatism of even the most high-spirited sermons

GEORGE III. by the Grace of GOD, of GREAT-BRITAIN, FRANCE and IRELAND, King, Defender of the Faith.

In ev'ry Stroke, in ev'ry Line,
Does ſome exalted Virtue ſhine;
And *Albion*'s Happineſs we trace,
In every Feature of his Face.

FIGURE 6. Colonial loyalty: Woodcut frontispiece to Watt's *Speller*, a colonial schoolbook of 1770. (*The Granger Collection*)

and pamphlets is evident in four major themes that were chanted without pause: the invocation of the first settlers, appeal to the ancient charters, veneration of the British Constitution and British rights, and homage to the monarchy. There is no reason to believe that until the Coercive Acts or even later the American writers were not entirely sincere in their conservative wish to be "restored to their original standing." The ministry, not they, had changed the rules of the game. They stood fast in the great tradition, "Whigs in a Reign when Whiggism is out of Fashion."

Americans in 1776 like Americans today were fond of invoking the example of "Ancestors remarkable for their Zeal for true Religion & Liberty." "Let us read and recollect and impress upon our souls," wrote John Adams to the Boston public,

> *the views and ends of our own more immediate forefathers, in exchanging their native country for a dreary, inhospitable wilderness. Let us examine into the nature of that power, and the cruelty of that oppression, which drove them from their homes. Recollect their amazing fortitude, their bitter sufferings,—the hunger, the nakedness, the cold, which they patiently endured,—the severe labors of clearing their grounds, building their houses, raising their provisions, amidst dangers from wild beasts and savage men, before they had time or money or materials for commerce. Recollect the civil and religious principles and hopes and expectations which constantly supported and carried them through all hardships with patience and resignation. Let us recollect it was liberty, the hope of liberty for themselves and us and ours, which conquered all discouragements, dangers, and trials.*

"Look back, therefore," echoed Provost Smith of Philadelphia,

> *with reverence look back to the times of ancient virtue and renown. Look back to the mighty purposes which your fathers had in view, when they traversed a vast ocean, and planted this land. Recal to your minds their labours, their toils, their perseverance, and let their divine spirit animate you in all your actions.*

The Pilgrim Fathers were whirling in their graves 165 years before the founding of the American Liberty League: in 1769 a society was formed to commemorate annually the landing at Plymouth, and a good part of every celebration was devoted to a comparison of odious present with glorious past. Stephen Hopkins developed this theme in his account of the first settlers of Providence:

> *Nothing but extreme Diligence, and matchless Perseverance, could possibly have carried them through this Undertaking; could have procured them the scanty Morsels which supported a Life of Want and of Innocence. Too much have we their Descendants departed from the Diligence, Fortitude, Frugality, and Innocence of these our Fathers!*

For the most part, however, the colonists called upon their ancestors to inspire rather than to chastise. "The famous Tools of Power are holding up the picture of Want and Misery," wrote Samuel Adams from beleaguered Boston in 1774, "but in vain do they think to intimidate us; The Virtue of our Ancestors inspires—they were content with Clams & Muscles."

The appeal to the charter in defense of colonial rights, a usage popular even with residents of colonies without charters, was a second instance of the conservative orientation of the American mind. In law the charters were not much more sacred than medieval grants and were open to attack from Parliament, courts, and Crown. But in the eyes and arguments of the colonists, especially the men of New England, they were unassailable declarations of "the rights and privileges of natural freeborn subjects of Great Britain" and irrevocable recognitions of the authority of the assemblies to tax and govern without leave of Parliament. Actually, the charter-rights argument was extremely weak, at least in terms of home rule for all colonies. But so long as it made any sense, the New Englanders, for whom Otis was a typical spokesman, appealed repeatedly to their sacred charters.

> *It would indeed seem very hard and severe, for those of the colonists, who have charters, with peculiar privileges, to loose them. They were given to their ancestors, in consideration of their sufferings and merit, in discovering and settling America. Our fore-fathers were soon worn away in the toils of hard labour on their little plantations, and in war with the Savages. They thought they were earning a sure inheritance for their posterity. Could they imagine it would ever be tho't just to deprive them or theirs of their charter privileges!*

A much broader yet equally conservative footing on which to stand and resist oppressive acts of Parliament was the British Constitution and British rights—the former still that "glorious fabrick," "that noble constitution—the envy and terror of Europe," the latter still "the invaluable Rights of Englishmen. . . . Rights! which no Time, no Contract, no Climate can diminish!" Not until the end of the decade did Americans waver in their allegiance to the government and liberties they enjoyed as "descendants of freeborn Britons." Paine's open assault on "the so much boasted constitution of England" was perhaps the most radical section in *Common Sense.* Almost all other colonists were proud to live under governments that were "nearly copies of the happy British original," or of enjoying "the British constitution in greater purity and perfection than they do in England." Magna Charta, the Glorious Revolution, and other memorable documents or events in the story of English liberty were called upon for support. The Bill of Rights, the Habeas Corpus Act, and the Petition of Rights were reprinted widely for popular edification. Nowhere was the conservative temper of colonial polemics more evident than in this loyal, desperate veneration of a form of government and pattern of rights whose chief distinction was their undoubted antiquity. Whether conservative or radical, few Americans ever disagreed with John Witherspoon's judgment:

> *It is proper to observe, that the British settlements have been improved in a proportion far beyond the settlements of other European nations. To what can this be ascribed? Not to the climate, for they are of all climates; not to the people, for they are a mixture of all nations. It must therefore be resolved singly into the degree of British liberty which they brought from home, and which pervaded more or less their several constitutions.*

Finally, in their never-ending expression of "the warmest sentiments of affection and duty to his majesty's person and government" and attachment "to the present happy establishment of the protestant succession," the colonists revealed their deep-seated conservatism. Not until months after the shooting war had begun did they turn away sadly from their sincere conviction that the house of Hanover was "amongst the choicest of God's providential gifts to Great-Britain and the British Colonies." Rarely did a writer so much as hint that the oppressive acts of Parliament or coercions of the ministry could be laid at the king's door. In their anxiety to preserve the blessings of a cherished constitutional monarchy, the colonists ignored almost wilfully the plain fact of the king's eager association in the policy of tighter imperial control. Even after Lexington and Concord the Massachusetts Provincial Congress could declare:

> *These, brethren, are marks of ministerial vengeance against this colony, for refusing, with her sister colonies, a submission to slavery; but they have not yet detached us from our royal sovereign. We profess to be his loyal and dutiful subjects, and so hardly dealt with as we have been, are still ready, with our lives and fortunes, to defend his person, family, crown and dignity.*

Colonial propagandists contributed materially to the show of unanimity on this issue. Yet the propagandists themselves would have been the first to admit that the depth of American feeling for the monarchy and its incumbent made possible their fabrication of "the very model of a patriot king." Simple folk and propagandists alike were careful to maintain the crucial distinction between king and ministry:

> *Have we not repeatedly and solemnly professed an inviolable loyalty to the person, power, and dignity of our sovereign, and unanimously declared, that it is not with him we contend, but with an envious cloud of false witnesses, that surround his throne, and intercept the sunshine of his favor from our oppressed land?*

English Whigs were taken somewhat aback by the warmth of colonial fealty, especially when Hamilton, Wilson, and others seemed ready to grant the king wide powers of government. But Americans were Whigs, not Tories. They had no intention of blowing up the royal prerogative into a potential tyranny. The king so loved and exalted was a constitutional monarch. His chief business was to protect the Americans from parliamentary or ministerial oppression. His prerogative was a check on power rather than power itself. And if ever he should step out of his constitutional role, the remedy was that reserved for all tyrant kings:

> *Virginians, you have nothing to fear, for Centuries to come, while you continue under the Protection of the Crown. You are defended against its Encroachments by the Power you have derived from the People. Should the King of Britain ever invade your Rights, he ceases, according to the British Constitution, to be King of the Dominion of Virginia.*

Not until 1776 and *Common Sense* did Americans wake from their dream of a patriot king.

A conservatism in political speculation matched this conservatism in political debate. However radical revolutionary principles may have seemed to the rest of the world, in the minds of the colonists they were thoroughly preservative and respectful of the past. The explanation is, of course, that the American past—at least as Americans liked to read it—displayed a condition of human liberty and constitutional government that the rest of the world could only long for or detest. The political theory of this revolution was designed to preserve a world that had already been made over.

Sense of Destiny. Pamphleteers and orators had their eyes on the future as well as the past. Having called upon his listeners to "look back to times of ancient virtue and renown," Provost Smith reminded them that they were ancestors as well as descendants. It was entirely up to them whether they should be venerated, despised, or forgotten:

> *Look forward also to distant posterity. Figure to yourselves millions and millions to spring from your loins, who may be born* freemen *or* slaves, *as Heaven shall now approve or reject your councils. Think, that on you it may depend, whether this great country, in ages hence, shall be filled and adorned with a virtuous and inlightened people; enjoying* Liberty *and all its concomitant blessings, together with the* Religion *of Jesus, as it flows uncorrupted from his holy oracles; or covered with a race of men more contemptible than the savages that roam the wilderness.*

* * *

The American Mission was plainly a decisive factor in the shaping of revolutionary political thought, for it drove the colonists beyond charter and Constitution to claim sanction for their actions in the great principles of natural justice. The appeal to the universal doctrines of natural law and natural rights came easily to a people who believed words like these:

> *To anticipate the future glory of America from our present hopes and prospects is ravishing and transporting to the mind. In this light we behold our country, beyond the reach of all oppressors, under the great charter of independence, enjoying the purest liberty; beautiful and strong in its union; the envy of tyrants and devils, but the delight of God and all good men; a refuge to the oppressed; the joy of the earth; each state happy in a wise model of government, and abounding with wise men, patriots, and heroes; the strength and abilities of the whole continent, collected in a grave and venerable council, at the head of all, seeking and promoting the good of the present and future generations. Hail, my*

> *happy country, saved of the Lord! Happy land, emerged from the deluges of the Old World drowned in luxury and lewd excess! Hail, happy posterity, that shall reap the peaceful fruits of our sufferings, fatigues, and wars!*

This conviction of a higher destiny had much to do with the popularity of American political thought among liberty-minded men in England and France. America became an influential center of political speculation in the last three decades of the eighteenth century because American writers took the grand view of their country's past and future.

The Recourse to First Principles; The American Consensus

Occasional, propagandistic, legalistic, factual, conservative, conscious of destiny—these words catch the quality of political argument in the years that led to independence. One final characteristic, the most significant for our purposes, remains to be mentioned: the habit, in which most colonists indulged to excess, of "recurring to first principles," of appealing to basic doctrines of political theory to support legal, factual, and constitutional arguments. Few men were willing to argue about a specific issue—deny the wisdom of the Stamp Act, defend an editor against charges of libel, protest the landing of the tea, interpret the Massachusetts Charter, condemn the quartering of troops in New York—without first calling upon rules of justice that were considered to apply to all men everywhere. These rules, of course, were the ancient body of political assumptions known as natural law and natural rights. The great political philosophy of the Western world enjoyed one of its proudest seasons in this time of resistance and revolution. If the Americans added few novel twists of their own to this philosophy, they gave it a unique vogue among men of all ranks and callings. Few people in history have been so devoted to a "party line" that had no sanction other than its appeal to free minds; few people have made such effective use of the recourse to first principles. . . .

There were few deviationists from the American "party line." Some spokesmen for the patriot cause saluted natural law and natural rights only in passing; others demonstrated that the question was, after all, one of free choice by expressing irregular opinions of the nature of man or origin of government. But all American publicists—whether celebrated or anonymous, sophisticated or untutored, speculative or pedestrian—paid devotion of one sort or another to "revolution principles." Nowhere in patriot literature is there a single direct suggestion that the essentials of this political theory were unhistorical, illogical, or unsound. Even the Tories, except for bold spirits like Jonathan Boucher, refrained from attacking it frontally, and even Boucher, if the tactical situation demanded such talk, could speak of "consent," "constitutional right," and "the great Hampden." The warmest sort of enemy approval of the American consensus was expressed in Gentleman Johnny Burgoyne's famous letter to Charles Lee:

> *I am no stranger to the doctrines of Mr. Locke and other of the best advocates for the rights of mankind, upon the compact always implied between the governing and the governed, and the right of resistance in the latter, when the compact shall be so violated as to leave no other means of redress. I look with reverence, almost amounting to idolatry, upon those immortal whigs who adopted and applied such doctrine during part of the reign of Charles the 1st, and in that of James IId.*

In political theory, if not in devotion to the patriot cause, "nine tenths of the people" were, as John Adams remarked, "high whigs."

Elisha P. Douglass

THE CONFLICT OF IDEOLOGIES IN PRE-REVOLUTIONARY AMERICA

Besides the widely known work from which the selection offered here was taken, Elisha P. Douglass has written The Coming of Age of American Business *(1971), an analysis of three centuries' development following 1600, as well as articles on Fisher Ames, on the role played by German intellectuals in the American Revolution, and on other subjects concerning the colonial and revolutionary eras. He has taught for some years at the University of North Carolina.*

The groups who demanded equalitarian reform during the Revolution could find little support for their ideals in prevailing political philosophy. Since the time of Aristotle democracy had been recognized as a form of legitimate government, but it was usually considered so unstable as to be merely a prelude to anarchy. Yet outside of the politically active classes it had occasionally found advocates. The Levellers of the English Revolution, who resemble the American revolutionary democrats from the standpoint of social class and program for reform, demanded from the Puritan oligarchy the substance of democratic, constitutional government.[1] John Locke, as a defender of the existing social and political order, was certainly no advocate of democracy as a form of government, but his description of how the social compact was formed and his unqualified assertion of popular sovereignty constituted the framework of a democratic philosophy.[2]

Although the Puritan oligarchy of Massachusetts denounced democracy as a form of government, nevertheless their acceptance

Reprinted by permission from Elisha P. Douglass, *Rebels and Democrats* (Chapel Hill: University of North Carolina Press, 1955).

[1] Many fruitful comparisons can be made between the Levellers of 1645 to 1653 and American democrats of 1776 to 1783. See A. S. P. Woodhouse, *Puritanism and Liberty, being the Army Debates (1647–49) from the Clarke Manuscripts with Supplementary Documents Selected and Edited with an Introduction by A. S. P. Woodhouse; Foreword by A. D. Lindsay* (London, 1938); Theodore C. Pease, *The Leveller Movement* (Washington, 1916); William Haller (ed.), *The Leveller Tracts, 1647–1653* (New York, 1944); Don M. Wolfe, *Milton in the Puritan Revolution* (New York, 1941).

[2] John Locke, *An Essay Concerning the True Original, Extent and End of Civil Government,* § 19, 87, 89, 95, 99, 122, 124, 168, 240, 242.

of such equalitarian doctrines as Christian liberty and the priesthood of all believers and the existence of democratic procedures in Congregational polity made it possible for responsible men to advocate democratic principles in the political sphere. Thus John Wise, outspoken pastor of an Ipswich church from 1683 to 1725 and opponent of the Mathers' plan to introduce a semblance of Presbyterian polity into New England, made a spirited defense of democracy in his famous *Vindication of the Government of New England Churches.* According to Wise, democracy was ". . . a form of government which the light of nature does highly value, and often directs to as the most agreeable to the just and natural prerogatives of human beings." He felt that it gave the people a better guarantee against tyranny than any other political form.[3]

This tract, however, had little or no influence outside New England. Of more importance were the democratic implications in the writings of the Whig propagandists. Identifying their cause with universal principles of freedom, the Whigs often employed the language of democratic protest. This is particularly evident in the controversy over virtual representation. James Otis declared that absolute power "is *originally* and *ultimately* in the people" and can be reclaimed by them if not exercised for their welfare.[4] Moreover, "No good reason can be given in any country why every man of sound mind should not have his vote in the election of a representative. If a man has but little property to defend and protect, yet his life and liberty are things of some importance."[5] Samuel Adams agreed. "The Acts of Parliament and the Constitution, consider every individual in the Realm as present in the high Court of Parliament by his Representative upon his own free Election. This is his indisputable Privilege—It is founded in the eternal law of equity—It is an original Right of Nature."[6] These generous professions did not indicate, however, that Otis and Adams favored an extension of the suffrage for the colonial

[3] John Wise, *Vindication of the Government of New England Churches,* 3rd ed. (Boston, 1860), 54. For further details on Wise, see Paul S. McElroy, "John Wise: the Father of American Independence," Essex Institute Historical *Collections,* LXXXI (1945), 201–220; Clinton L. Rossiter, "John Wise: Colonial Democrat," *New England Quarterly,* XXII (1949), 3–32.

[4] Charles F. Mullett (ed.), *Some Political Writings of James Otis,* University of Missouri *Studies,* IV, 308–309.

[5] James Otis, "Considerations on behalf of the Colonists in a Letter to a Noble Lord," in *ibid.,* 366. See also "A Vindication of the British Colonies," *ibid.,* 398–399.

[6] Harry A. Cushing (ed.), *The Writings of Samuel Adams,* 4 Vols. (New York, 1904–1908), I, 46.

assemblies or a more equitable apportionment of representation. Identifying the cause of liberty with provincial autonomy within the empire, both men simply failed to see any inconsistency between their political principles and assembly government. The two actually proved later to be opponents of political equality and majority rule. "When the pot boils, the scum will rise" was Otis's pungent comment on the group of radicals who agitated for reform of the Massachusetts government in the fall of 1776.[7] Sam Adams lent his personal popularity to secure the ratification of the plainly aristocratic constitution of 1780.[8]

Although democrats might have derived some aid and comfort from Dickinson's *Farmer's Letters,* John Adams's *Novanglus,* and Jefferson's *Summary View of the Rights of British America,* it was Thomas Paine who first identified the Revolution with democracy. The only Whig propagandist who was not a member of the colonial ruling class, neither merchant, lawyer, nor planter, Paine spoke in the language of the common people. *Common Sense* was a breath of fresh air to a propaganda literature which was beginning to suffocate on legalisms. The educated might be impressed by Dickinson's and Dulany's briefs for an equitable division of taxing power between colonies and mother country and by Jefferson's and Wilson's theory that the alleged expatriation of the colonists justified their claim for autonomy,[9] but argument on this level could have little meaning for the man on the street or at the plow. Everyone, however, could understand Paine's contention that America was an independent continent temporarily held in subjection by a vicious despot who derived his authority from a no less vicious system of government.

Paine conceived the Revolution as the means of establishing a new society based on equal rights. The struggle would be the symbolic labor pains attending the birth of a new order which would realize the heritage of freedom withheld for countless generations. "We have it in our power to begin the world over again," he announced. "The birthday of a new world is at hand, and a race of men, perhaps as numerous as all Europe contains, are to receive their portion of freedom from the events of a few months. Every spot in the

[7] Elisha P. Douglass, *Rebels and Democrats* (Chapel Hill, N. C., 1955), pp. 156–157.
[8] *Ibid.,* p. 198.
[9] *Ibid.,* p. 291.

old world is overrun with oppression. Freedom hath been hunted round the globe. Asia and Africa have long expelled her. Europe regards her like a stranger, and England hath given her warning to depart. O! receive the fugitive and prepare in time an asylum for mankind."[10]

This strain of utopianism, this vision of a better world as the object of the Revolution, is stronger in Paine than in any of his contemporaries. Once the prerogative power had been suppressed and the royal officialdom overthrown, most of the revolutionary leaders were quite content to see a continuation of existing social and political relationships. For them the internal revolution was concluded by the summer of 1776. The task remaining was to insure the stability of society on its present basis; hence they turned for guidance in matters of government to colonial experience and to authorities who had already proved to be sound, such as Milton, Sidney, Bolingbroke, and Montesquieu. But Paine's conception of an adequate governmental framework owed nothing to authority or tradition. It represented only the minimum amount of machinery necessary to translate the will of majorities into legislation and insure unity among the colonies—unicameral assemblies in the states based on proportionate representation and subject to the Continental Congress.[11]

An anonymous Massachusetts pamphleteer who wrote about the same time and whose ideas were reflected later among democrats during constitutional struggles in that state, was more openly critical of the plans of government supported by the revolutionary leaders.[12]

[10] Phillip S. Foner (ed.), *The Complete Writings of Thomas Paine,* 2 Vols. (New York, 1945), I, 45, 31–32. Harry H. Clark argues that Paine's support of conservative fiscal policies in Pennsylvania during the early 1780s shows a basic conservatism which should be taken into account before labeling him a radical. See Clark (ed.), *Six New Letters of Paine* (Madison, 1939), introduction. It is true that Paine's economic ideas in this period are rather unexpected, but they in no way qualify his democratic political conceptions. His ideal government was always majoritarian democracy and he continually insisted on an equality of political rights. For illustrations of his thought, see his essays in defense of the Pennsylvania Constitution of 1776. *Writings,* II, 296–302. His democratic philosophy reached its fullest development during the period of his participation in the French Revolution, as evidenced by his "Dissertation on First Principles of Government," *ibid.,* 570–588, and *The Rights of Man*. Paine's importance as a democratic reformer has been emphasized by John C. Miller, *Origins of the American Revolution* (Boston, 1943), 504–505; *Triumph of Freedom* (Boston, 1948), 345.

[11] "Common Sense," in Foner (ed.), *Writings of Paine,* I, 28.

[12] *The People the Best Governors, or, a Plan of Government founded on the Just Principles of Natural Freedom* (1776), reprinted as an appendix in Frederick Chase, *History of Dartmouth College* (Cambridge, 1891). The pamphlet was probably printed either in Boston, Worcester, or Hartford. Although mentioned by name only twice

FIGURE 7. Thomas Paine. Portrait by John Wesley Jarvis. (*National Gallery of Art, Washington, D.C.*)

in 1776, nevertheless its spirit and specific recommendations reappear in scores of the political essays submitted by the Massachusetts towns to the General Court in reply to questions on constitutional issues. It summarizes the body of political thought which found expression in the instructions of Orange and Mecklenburg counties, North Carolina, to their delegates in the Provincial Congress, in the articles by democratic writers in Pennsylvania and Massachusetts newspapers, and in the public documents of the Pennsylvania Convention of 1776. The pamphlet is discussed briefly by Harry A. Cushing in *American Historical Review,* I (1895–1896), 284–287, and by William S. Carpenter in *The Development of American Political Thought* (Princeton, 1930), 66–68.

Asserting that the people "best know their wants and necessities and therefore are best able to govern themselves," he condemned upper houses armed with a veto and not directly responsible to the electorate as unworthy of a free state and declared that advocates of this type of bicameralism had designs against liberty. "The people are now contending for freedom; and would to God they might not only obtain, but likewise keep it in their own hands. There are many very noisy about liberty but are aiming at nothing more than personal power and grandeur. And are not many, under the delusive character of guardians of their country, collecting influence and honor only for oppression?"[13] He felt that representation should be in proportion to population, and that all adult free males should have the suffrage. Property qualifications for office he regarded as a source of corruption. "Social virtue and knowledge . . . is the best and only necessary qualification of [a representative]. So sure as we make interest necessary in this case, as sure we root out virtue. . . . The notion of an estate has the directest tendency to set up the avarisious [sic] over the heads of the poor. . . . Let it not be said in future generations that money was made by the founders of the American states an essential qualification in the rulers of a free people."[14] By his plan of government the executive and the judges would be selected by annual elections and the executive denied a veto. In a unique provision he stipulated that an appeal from superior court decisions would lie to the House of Representatives. "The judges, in many cases, are obliged . . . to put such a construction on matters as they think most agreeable to the spirit and reason of the law. Now so far as they are reduced to this necessity, they assume what is in fact the prerogative of the legislature, for those that made the laws ought to give them a meaning when they are doubtful."[15] The author apparently realized that legal interpretation by the courts was often a disguised form of legislation—a discovery usually attributed to the twentieth century. In recommending the principle of legislative authority over judicial decisions he anticipated modern critics of judicial review.

Common Sense and *The People the Best Governors* together illustrate the aspirations for a better world and the desire to equalize

[13] Chase, *History of Dartmouth College,* 662, 654.
[14] *Ibid.,* 659–660.
[15] *Ibid.,* 662.

political rights which characterized the democratic groups in the Revolution. For them the preamble of the Declaration of Independence was more than a collection of philosophical postulates; it was a set of principles to be incorporated into political institutions. Popular sovereignty and equality were to be realized by manhood suffrage, the abolition of property qualifications for officeholding, representation according to population, and a government directly responsible in all its branches to the people as a whole.

The Whig leaders in the spring of 1776 were not slow to realize the threat to the established order in the confusion accompanying the Revolution. Wrote Paine, "I have heard some men say . . . that they dreaded an independence, fearing that it would produce civil wars: . . ."[16] John Adams was one of these. "From the beginning," he declared, "I always expected we should have more difficulty and danger in our attempts to govern ourselves and in our negotiations and connections with foreign powers than from all the fleets and armies of Great Britain."[17] His kinsman, Sam Adams, found in 1776 that many Whig leaders felt the establishment of new governments would serve as a cloak for licentiousness.[18] Thus many representatives from colonies not already committed to war by the turn of events became almost desperate in their attempts to bring about a reconciliation with Britain.[19]

Before the suppression of royal government brought confusion to the colonies many Whigs had belittled the dangers to be anticipated from mob violence—at least in public. John Dickinson, replying to Tories who denounced the Stamp Act riots, had declared, "It was indeed a very improper way of acting, but may *not the agonies of minds not quite so polished as your own* be in some measure ex-

[16] Foner (ed.), "Common Sense," *Writings of Paine,* I, 27.

[17] Charles F. Adams (ed.), *The Works of John Adams,* 10 Vols. (Boston, 1850–1856), III, 13. Adams wrote his wife in the spring of 1776, "Such mighty revolutions make a deep impression on the minds of men and set many violent passions to work. Hope, fear, joy, sorrow, love, hatred, malice, envy, revenge, jealousy, ambition, avarice, resentment, gratitude, . . . were never in more lively exercise than they are now from Florida to Canada." Charles F. Adams (ed.), *Familiar Letters of John Adams and his Wife . . .* (Boston and New York, 1875), 168.

[18] Cushing (ed.), *Writings of Samuel Adams,* III, 244.

[19] The reluctance of the colonial ruling class as a whole to declare independence has been often noted. See Merrill Jensen, *The Articles of Confederation* (Madison, 1940), chs. 2 and 3; Arthur M. Schlesinger, *The Colonial Merchants and the American Revolution, 1763–1776* (New York, 1918), 593–606; Miller, *Origins of the American Revolution,* chs. 20 and 21.

cused?"[20] Sam Adams, although exhibiting proper disapproval of the sacking of Lieutenant Governor Hutchinson's house in 1765, in 1769 described effigy burnings and riots as "joys of the Evening among the lower Sort, which, however innocent, are sometimes noisy."[21] When the Tory, Daniel Leonard, accused the Whigs of establishing a democratic despotism, John Adams, as "Novanglus," had replied magisterially, "The two ideas are incompatible with each other. A democratical despotism is a contradiction in terms,"[22]—a position he was to reverse in a very short time.

But by 1776 the tolerant Whig attitude toward lawlessness underwent a transformation. The responsibilities of government gave them a new appreciation of the necessity for order, authority, and subordination. The rascals had been turned out; therefore good patriots should settle down and show a proper respect for authority. "How much soever I may heretofore have found fault with the powers that were I suppose I shall be well pleased now to hear submission inculcated to the powers that are," wrote John Adams.[23] Elbridge Gerry complained from Massachusetts that the people were feeling too strongly their new importance and needed a curb,[24] and James Warren, speaker of the Massachusetts House, dreaded the consequences of "the levelling spirit, encouraged and drove to such lengths as it is."[25] Sam Adams, to whom *vox populi* had been *vox Dei* when Hutchinson was in office, felt that there was "danger of errors on the side of the people" after the Whig leaders had seized control in Massachusetts. James Allen, a Pennsylvania Whig and a member of a wealthy family which had been a constant recipient of the proprietors' patronage, retired to his country seat in 1776 because the "mobility is triumphant."[26]

The Whig leaders were particularly alarmed at the popular re-

[20] John Dickinson, *Political Writings,* 2 Vols. (Wilmington, 1801), I, 128.

[21] Cushing, *Writings of Samuel Adams,* I, 406. Young Josiah Quincy, Jr., observed philosophically, "It is much easier to restrain liberty from running into licentiousness, than power from swelling into tyranny and oppression." *Memoir of the Life of Josiah Quincy, Jr., by his Son* (Boston, 1874), 304.

[22] *Novanglus and Massachusettsensis* (Boston, 1819), 61.

[23] Adams, *Works,* IX, 391.

[24] James T. Austin, *The Life of Elbridge Gerry,* 2 Vols. (Boston, 1828–1829), I, 78.

[25] *Warren-Adams Letters,* 2 Vols. (Boston, 1917, 1925), Massachusetts Historical Society, *Collections,* LXXII, LXXIII, Vol. I, 219.

[26] "Diary of James Allen," *Pennsylvania Magazine of History and Biography,* IX (1885), 186. He added that "The madness of the multitude is but one degree better than submission to Britain."

sistance to their plans to reopen the courts. As patriots they had been eager to drive royal judges off the benches, but as responsible administrators they were equally desirous to reestablish the judicial process as soon as possible.[27] The commissioning of courts, however, would amount to an assertion of sovereignty, a *de facto* declaration of independence. Thus the Whig leaders were placed in an uncomfortable dilemma: to continue without tribunals and legal government would be to invite chaos, but to establish authority equal to the exigencies of the hour would be open treason. It became apparent in some localities that debtors were using the glorious state of nature to prevent collection of their obligations. John Adams tells in his diary that a former client, whom he described contemptuously as a "horse jockey," exclaimed to him with an enthusiasm which Adams could hardly share: "Oh, Mr. Adams, what great things you and your colleagues have done for us. We can never be grateful enough to you. There are no courts of justice in this province, and I hope there never will be another."[28] John Winthrop of Harvard, a pioneer American mathematician, physicist, and astronomer, informed Adams that the basic cause of opposition to the revolutionary government of Massachusetts was "an unwillingness to submit to law and pay debts."[29]

When the course of events in the various colonies made it clear that there was no middle ground between capitulation to British demands and independence, the radical section of the Whig party firmly, if with misgivings, moved to seize the sovereign power. Thus Massachusetts established government under the provincial charter in order, among other things, to counter "the alarming symptoms of the abatement in the minds of the people of the sacredness of private property."[30] Edmund Pendleton, accepting the presidency of the Virginia Convention, observed, "It will become us to reflect whether we can longer sustain the great struggle we are making in this situation."[31] In Pennsylvania, many of the radical Whigs who had in 1774 done their best to discredit the proprietary government rallied

27 See Fletcher M. Green, *Constitutional Development in the South Atlantic States, 1776–1860; A Study in the Evolution of Democracy* (Chapel Hill, 1930), 56–58.
28 Adams, *Works,* II, 420.
29 Massachusetts Historical Society, *Collections,* 5th Ser., IV, 307.
30 *American Archives* (Washington, 1837–1853), 4th Ser., II, 955.
31 *Ibid.,* VI, 1511.

to its support when the threat of internal revolution appeared imminent.

Lack of plans and procedures for the formation of succession governments as well as the gravity of seizing the sovereignty embarrassed the Whig leaders. Although *Common Sense* had received enthusiastic approval from radicals because of its castigation of Britain, its suggestions on government elicited at best silence and at worst active opposition. Conservatives denounced the pamphlet in unmeasured terms. Landon Carter, a Virginia planter, could hardly restrain his rage. *Common Sense,* he asserted, was "repleat with art and contradiction . . . rascally and nonsensical . . . a sophisticated attempt to throw all men out of Principles . . . which has drove all who espouse it from the justice of their contest."[32] Samuel Johnston of North Carolina called it "specious and dangerous," and Henry Laurens condemned "those indecent expressions with which the pages abound."[33] The North Carolina delegation to the Continental Congress at first refused to send copies home and only changed their minds at the insistence of the third delegate who had known democratic leanings.[34] Paine's *chef-d'oeuvre* started a pamphlet war in Philadelphia—a type of slaughter not new to the city of brotherly love and one in which personal reputations and the English language had in the past been the chief sufferers. In Massachusetts the pamphlet was received enthusiastically by the radicals because of the tremendous assistance it afforded in drawing the other colonies into war. Nevertheless, some leaders realized the danger of its democratic ideas. "Don't be displeased with me," wrote Sam Adams to James Warren in a letter recommending the piece, "if you find the Spirit of it totally repugnant to your Ideas of Government."[35]

One of the most important effects of *Common Sense* was that in large part it stirred John Adams to write his famous *Thoughts on Government,* a pamphlet of almost equal importance in American history. Whereas *Common Sense* was the inspiration for indepen-

32 "The Diary of Landon Carter," *William and Mary Quarterly,* XVI (1907), 149–155.

33 Johnston to Hewes, March 3, 1776. Hayes Collection, North Carolina Department of History and Archives. David D. Wallace, *The Life of Henry Laurens* (New York and London, 1915), 22.

34 Hewes to Johnston, Feb. 20, 1776. North Carolina Letters from the Emmet Collection, North Carolina Department of History and Archives.

35 *Warren-Adams Letters,* I, 204.

dence and a new equalitarian society, *Thoughts on Government* erected the framework of American republicanism out of the solid materials of traditional institutions. The two stand as symbols of the democratic and conservative programs, the thesis and antithesis of the Revolution. Tom Paine, devastating as he was in his attack on hereditary government, had little of a practical nature to put in its place. Adams could never have matched Paine's fire and commonsense logic in presenting the case for independence, but his intellectual background made him much more able to construct a stable and practical government which would appeal to the ruling class.

Adams has given two versions of the circumstances surrounding the writing of *Thoughts on Government.* In a letter of April 20, 1776, he explained to Warren that the writer (the pamphlet was published anonymously) had been asked by two of the North Carolina delegates —William Hooper and John Penn—to put his ideas on paper for the benefit of their Provincial Congress, which would shortly draft a constitution. Adams complied, then on request made copies for other delegates whose colonies were on the point of establishing permanent governments—George Wythe, of Virginia, and Jonathan Dickinson Sergeant, of New Jersey. When still more copies were requested he gave permission to have one of the drafts printed.[36] In his autobiography however—written many years after the event—Adams claimed that he wrote the pamphlet to counteract the pernicious influence of Paine's political ideas. He "dreaded the effect so popular a pamphlet might have among the people, and determined to do all in his power to counteract the effect of it."[37]

Although Adams's later statement of his motives in writing *Thoughts on Government* was undoubtedly influenced by his controversy with Paine during the era of the French Revolution, it is nevertheless plain that he regarded this "disastrous meteor" with some suspicion in the spring of 1776. "Sensible men think there are some whims, some sophisms, some artful addresses to superstitious

[36] *Ibid.,* 230–231.

[37] Adams, *Works,* II, 507. He considered Paine's ideas of government "as flowing from simple ignorance and a desire to please the democratic party in Philadelphia . . . ." In the autobiography he mentions no solicitation from fellow delegates to write *Thoughts on Government* but stated that it was printed in response to a request from Richard Henry Lee.

notions, some keen attempts upon the passions [in *Common Sense*]," he wrote to his wife in March. Then noting that it had been bruited about that he was the author, he declared with candor, "although I could not have written anything in so manly and striking a style, I flatter myself I should have made a more respectable figure as an architect if I had undertaken such a work. This writer seems to have very inadequate ideas of what is proper and necessary to be done in order to form constitutions for single colonies as well as a great model of union for the whole."[38] Although Adams's account in later life exaggerates his antipathy for Paine in 1776, it is nevertheless clear that an important object of *Thoughts on Government* was to correct what he regarded as the dangerous heresies to be found in *Common Sense.*

The central theme of Adams's political architecture was the separation of powers, a device which he thought would check the drift toward social revolution. Since the separation of powers has had such a tremendous influence on American political thought and has been such a mainstay of conservatism, it will be necessary to examine its assumptions, processes, and objectives.

Like Locke's theory of compact and natural law, separation of powers was a very old idea, even in the eighteenth century. It was discussed by Aristotle and was perhaps even known to Herodotus.[39] It may be defined as a political device designed to maintain stability in constitutional government by so balancing governmental organs and functions that power-seeking individuals and groups would automatically check each other before they could endanger the state. If democracy has always rested on an assumption that man is essentially cooperative, the theory of separation of powers in the eighteenth century was based on the premise that man is essentially unsocial, devoted exclusively to his own interests, and prepared to make war on his fellows at any time when advantage outweighed risk. According to the theory, government should not try to repress disruptive forces, for if it was strong enough to accomplish this it would be an oppressive force in itself. Rather it should direct these forces in such a way that they would neutralize each other. Like the

38 Adams (ed.), *Familiar Letters of John Adams,* 146.

39 M. P. Sharpe, "The Classical American Doctrine of Separation of Powers," 2 *Chicago Law Review* (1935), 386.

balance of power in international affairs, the separation of powers was considered the only way to maintain stability and the moral order in an essentially unstable and immoral world.

There were three conceptions, or variants, of separation of powers in the eighteenth century. The first, and most primitive, was "balanced government" or "mixed monarchy." By this interpretation the medieval estates of the realm—crown, clergy, nobles, and commons—symbolized and represented the principal classes in society, and a balanced government kept them in equilibrium. Each estate was identified with a certain form of government—the king, monarchy; the nobles, aristocracy; the people, democracy. Each form had certain advantages and disadvantages. When it stood alone as a "simple" government, the disadvantages—or "weaknesses," as contemporary theorists preferred to call them—were greater than the advantages; but when the three forms were mixed together as in the British Constitution, the disadvantages cancelled each other out by some mysterious metaphysical process never explained but never doubted.[40] The second conception of separation of powers was the separation of the organs or departments of government. This interpretation was partially a functional abstraction of balanced government and partially an attempt empirically to analyze the processes of government as a whole. Prior to 1776 colonial leaders thought of the separation of powers as mixed monarchy; when monarchical institutions became discredited they viewed crown, nobles, and commons functionally as executive, senate, and house of representatives. The third conception of the separation of powers was the equal distribution of the multitude of political functions performed by any government. This view predominated in the Federal Convention of 1787. Nomination, veto, appropriation, impeachment, trial of impeachment, judgment, treaty making, and the like were assigned to the different departments in such a way that each department would have equal weight. This was the most effective application of separation of powers, for only the proper distribution of functions

[40] The two best treatments of balanced government are: Stanley Pargellis, "The Theory of Balanced Government," in Conyers Read (ed.), *The Constitution Reconsidered* (New York, 1938), 37–50; Leonard W. Labaree, "A Balanced Government," *Conservatism in Early American History* (New York, 1948), ch. 5. Pargellis traces the idea through English history of the seventeenth and eighteenth centuries. Labaree discusses the views of colonial conservatives concerning it.

could give the balance which was the object of separation.[41] Separation without the balance of power would be of little help in maintaining stability.

The separation of powers derives its essential character from the type of institutions it is designed to protect. Applied to a democratic government it brings stability and efficiency without loss of responsiveness to the people, but applied to the essentially hierarchical institutions of the eighteenth century it became a means of blocking popular expression and insuring the continuance of classified citizenship. Both the democrats and the conservatives of the Revolution, appreciating its value, included it in their programs, but in somewhat different forms and with quite different objectives. Democrats, viewing it primarily as a safeguard against a monopoly of political power by the upper classes, made it the basis of their demands for the abolition of plural officeholding; conservatives, conceiving it as a safeguard against arbitrary rule by mob or despot, gave it institutional expression in their plans for bicameral legislatures.

It is entirely understandable, therefore, that Adams, in combating what he felt to be the drift toward social revolution, should seize on the separation of powers institutionalized in bicameralism as the best hope for maintaining stability, human rights, and the leadership of the Whig revolutionaries in the succession governments. And in so doing he made Montesquieu, not Locke, the chief luminary among political philosophers, for Montesquieu had conceived—wrongly, of course—that separation of powers was the guiding principle of the eighteenth-century British Constitution and the only way to avert tyranny from either mob or despot.[42] With the revolutionary con-

[41] Separation of powers as separation of organs and distribution of functions is discussed by Sharpe, "The Classical Doctrine of Separation of Powers" in *Chicago Law Review,* and by B. F. Wright Jr., "The Origins of the Separation of Powers in America," *Economica,* XIII (1933), 169–185, but the distinction between the two variants is not made clear by either author.

[42] Locke, as well as Montesquieu, had advocated separation of powers, but the two philosophers had different views of the device which in some ways resembled those of the Revolutionary democrats and conservatives respectively. For Locke, separation of powers was primarily a means of promoting efficiency in government. The ultimate guarantee of liberty was popular sovereignty. *Second Essay,* § 242, 240, 168. Montesquieu, whose essential aim was to strengthen the power of the nobility against the capricious authoritarianism of the Bourbon monarchy, saw it as the sole guarantee of liberty. "The liberty he preached was the liberty of the aristocracy. His *Spirit of the Laws,* from this point of view can be considered a handbook of aristocratic belief," writes Georges Lefebvre. *The Coming of the*

gresses, conventions, and committees in mind, Adams declared that single assemblies were capricious, avaricious, and ambitious. They "would make arbitrary laws for their own interest, execute all laws arbitrarily for their own interest, and adjudge all controversies in their own favor."[43] In order to secure stability and the rule of justice, therefore, Adams would create a second house, independent alike of the people and their representatives, to act as a check upon the lower. The executive power he would place in the hands of a governor assisted by a council, and, as a further check upon the legislature, he suggested for the executive an absolute veto. In later writings Adams treated the two houses as representative of the democratic and aristocratic elements in society. They would be perpetually in conflict, he felt; a victory of either would bring despotism. Therefore the governor occupied a key position in maintaining a balance. In this tripartite system Adams recreated the elements of mixed monarchy in the form of a "regal republic."[44]

If the common people were to have only a one-third interest in government under the Adams scheme, the lower house at least was to be their very own. "It should be in miniature an exact portrait of the people at large. It should think, feel, reason, and act like them."[45] But Adams did not implement this logic by advocating manhood suffrage for the lower house. Instead he called on the states "to agree on the number and qualifications of persons who shall have the benefit of choosing . . . representatives." In his view, the propertyless should be classified with women and children as inherently

French Revolution, 1789 (Princeton, 1947, tr. by R. R. Palmer), 20. For a concise statement of Montesquieu's aims, see E. Carcasonne, *Montesquieu et le problème de la constitution française au XVIIIe siècle* (Paris, n. d.), 84–85.

[43] Adams, *Works,* IV, 196.

[44] This apt phrase was apparently coined by Joseph Dorfman in his article, "The Regal Republic of John Adams," *Political Science Quarterly,* LIX (1944), 227–248. In his *Defense of the Constitutions . . . of the United States . . .* (1787), Adams laid great stress on the need for an independent executive because he felt that bicameralism alone had proved unequal to protecting conservative interests. Lower houses of the legislatures often dominated senates in the same manner as colonial assemblies sometimes dominated royal councils. Governors, almost devoid of power under the terms of most state constitutions, were unable to maintain a balance. Adams never departed from the basic rule of three laid down in *Thoughts on Government.* Subsequent changes in his ideas were only ones of emphasis. For an extended analysis of Adams's thought, see Correa M. Walsh, *The Political Science of John Adams* (New York and London, 1915). Edward S. Corwin discusses the general problem to which Adams addressed himself in "The Progress of Political Theory from the Declaration of Independence to the Federal Convention," *American Historical Review,* XXX (1924–1925), 511–536.

[45] Adams, *Works,* IV, 195.

unfit to vote. "Is it not true," he wrote to James Sullivan, "that men in general, in every society, who are wholly destitute of property, are also too little acquainted with public affairs to form a right judgment and too dependent on other men to have a will of their own? If this is a fact, if you give to every man who has no property a vote, will you not make a fine encouraging provision for corruption by your fundamental law? Such is the frailty of the human heart that very few men who have no property have any judgment of their own."[46]

Adams's fear of manhood suffrage was based primarily on English rather than American experience. In Parliamentary elections, tenant farmers had proved to be very susceptible to bribery and corruption, primarily because they did not have the economic security to afford independent judgment. Therefore eighteenth-century conservatives perhaps had some justification for fearing that if the suffrage were broadened under similar circumstances, impecunious voters might become the willing tools of demagogues. Quite possibly infatuated majorities might demand a redistribution of wealth or an overthrow of the constitution. General Ireton had put it bluntly in the Army debates of 1647. If suffrage were given to all adult males, as the Levellers demanded, ". . . we shall plainly go to take away all property and interest that a man hath either in land or by inheritance, or in estate by possession or anything else. . . . All the main thing I speak for, is because I would have an eye to property."[47] James Wilson, much admired by Lord Bryce and often considered a democrat because of his advocacy in the Federal Convention of a popularly elected senate and executive, expressed the prevailing justification for limitations on the right to vote when he wrote in his *Considerations on the Nature and Extent of the Legislative Authority of the British Parliament:*

> *In Britain, all those are excluded from voting whose poverty is such that they cannot live independent, and therefore must be subject to the undue influence of their superiors. Such are supposed to have no will of their own; and it is judged improper that they should vote in the representation of a free state. . . . Thus is the freedom of elections secured from the* servility, *the* ignorance, *and the* corruption *of electors; and from the*

[46] *Ibid.*, IX, 376.

[47] Woodhouse, *Puritanism and Liberty*, 55, 57. The argument over the extent of the suffrage between Ireton and Rainborough during the Putney debates of October 29, 1647, is one of the most revealing illustrations in print of the perennial clash between conservatives and democrats on majority rule. *Ibid.*, 52–86.

interpositions of officers depending immediately upon the crown. But this is not all. Provisions, equally salutary, have been made concerning the qualifications of those who shall be elected. All imaginable care has been taken that the Commons of Great Britain may be neither awed, nor allured, *nor* deceived *into any nomination inconsistent with their liberties.*[48]

Forecasts of the consequences of manhood suffrage and the abolition of property qualifications for office varied. Some conservatives—like Ireton—were particularly anxious for the safety of property. Others—like Adams—while not ignoring this threat felt that the danger of dictatorship and the loss of constitutional liberties was greater. But few, if any, of the Whig leaders evidenced any awareness of the basic contradiction between a limited suffrage and their equalitarian philosophy. Hence a double paradox: to preserve their own liberty, the unprivileged masses must be prevented from infringing on the privileged few; to maintain a government based on consent, a large proportion of the people must be deprived of the ability to extend or withhold consent.

The effect of Adams's pamphlet, *Thoughts on Government,* can hardly be overestimated. Most Whig leaders, although worried by the growing anarchy and disregard for private property exhibited by their more humble followers, had not yet realized that permanent stability could be reached only by abolishing the dictatorship of the revolutionary congresses and committees.[49] Regarding royal governors and councils as the greatest threat to freedom, they were determined above all else to avoid a reestablishment of anything which resembled the prerogative. So strong was the obsessive fear of executive power that even in 1787 it constituted the greatest obstacle which the Federalists had to face in their drive for a balanced government. But if Adams could not persuade the Whig leaders to establish strong governors, he at least convinced them of the need

[48] Randolph G. Adams (ed.), *Selected Political Essays of James Wilson* (New York, 1930), 51–53.

[49] In 1775 Adams had decided against urging the Continental Congress to recommend a form of government for all the colonies because "all those who were most zealous for assuming governments, had at that time no idea of any other government but a contemptible legislature in one assembly with committees for executive magistrates and judges." Adams, *Works,* III, 22. Even Sam Adams and Thomas Cushing "were inclined to the most democratical forms." Their inclination was only temporary, however. Cushing later became a mainstay of the conservatives and Adams used his personal popularity to insure the ratification of the obviously antidemocratic Massachusetts Constitution of 1780.

for bicameral legislatures. Only Pennsylvania, Georgia, and Vermont stubbornly adhered to democratic unicameralism. *Thoughts on Government* was not only discussed in the committee drafting the North Carolina constitution but was written verbatim into the executive letter book.[50] Arriving in Virginia at the moment the constitution was under discussion, it was enthusiastically received by Patrick Henry.[51] Jonathan Dickinson Sergeant adopted some of its provisions for the constitution of New Jersey,[52] and—according to Adams—the constitution of New York was modeled on his plan.[53] Finally, he was able literally to translate *Thoughts on Government* into political reality when he drafted the Massachusetts Constitution of 1780. Thus in five states his proposals were possibly the paramount guide in composing the first instruments of government, and, when it is considered that the state constitutions—particularly that of Massachusetts—were the greatest single influence on the Federal Constitution, the full importance of the pamphlet should be evident. In the words of one authority, "Adams' ideas, more than those of any other single person, guided and pervaded the movement which established republican government in America, and therefore in the modern world."[54]

Common Sense, The People the Best Governors, and *Thoughts on Government* made clear in 1776 what the issues were to be in the forthcoming struggle between democrats and conservatives to write their political ideas into the first state constitutions. Although the necessity for compromise made both groups relinquish their extreme demands, the democratic ideal continued to be a simple government with a sovereign legislature—preferably unicameral—directly dependent upon an electorate which included all adult, free

50 Walter Clark (ed.), *The State Records of North Carolina,* Vols. 11 to 26 (Winston, Goldsboro, Charlotte, 1895–1905), XI, 321.

51 "I have two reasons for liking the book," wrote Henry. "The sentiments are precisely the same I have long since taken up, and they come recommended by you." Adams, *Works,* IV, 201.

52 Adams and Sergeant were close friends. For a discussion of their relations and the influence of *Thoughts on Government* on the New Jersey constitution, see Charles R. Erdman, Jr., *The New Jersey Constitution of 1776* (Princeton, 1929), 36, 50, 57.

53 Adams to Mercy Warren, July 11, 1807. Massachusetts Historical Society, *Collections,* 5th Ser., IV, 326.

54 George M. Dutcher, "The Rise of Republican Government in the United States," *Political Science Quarterly,* LV (1940), 211.

males. In contrast to this equalitarianism, the revolutionary leaders were to press for complex governments based on the separation of powers and traditional institutions which would preserve the existing social system, guard the existing distribution of wealth, preserve human rights, and secure the dominance of the revolutionary party in the new regimes.

Bernard Bailyn

POLITICAL EXPERIENCE AND ENLIGHTENMENT IDEAS IN EIGHTEENTH-CENTURY AMERICA

*Bernard Bailyn, professor of history at Harvard University and winner of the George E. Bancroft and Pulitzer prizes for history in 1968, is the best known proponent of the essentially ideological and doctrinal character of the revolutionary movement. In addition to major works propounding this thesis—*The Ideological Origins of the American Revolution *(1967) and* The Origins of American Politics *(1968)—he has written important books about James Wilson and John Adams.*

A basic, organizing assumption of the group of ideas that dominated the earlier interpretation of eighteenth-century American history is the belief that previous to the Revolution the political experience of the colonial Americans had been roughly analogous to that of the English. Control of public authority had been firmly held by a native aristocracy—merchants and landlords in the North, planters in the South—allied, commonly, with British officialdom. By restricting representation in the provincial assemblies, limiting the franchise, and invoking the restrictive power of the English state, this aristocracy had dominated the governmental machinery of the mainland colonies. Their political control, together with legal devices such as primogeniture and entail, had allowed them to dominate the economy as well. Not only were they successful in engrossing landed estates

Reprinted by permission of the author from *American Historical Review* 67 (January 1962): 339–351. Abridged.

and mercantile fortunes, but they were for the most part able to fight off the clamor of yeoman debtors for cheap paper currency, and of depressed tenants for freehold property. But the control of this colonial counterpart of a traditional aristocracy, with its Old World ideas of privilege and hierarchy, orthodoxy in religious establishment, and economic inequality, was progressively threatened by the growing strength of a native, frontier-bred democracy that expressed itself most forcefully in the lower houses of the "rising" provincial assemblies. A conflict between the two groups and ways of life was building up, and it broke out in fury after 1765.

The outbreak of the Revolution, the argument runs, fundamentally altered the old regime. The Revolution destroyed the power of this traditional aristocracy, for the movement of opposition to parliamentary taxation, 1760–1776, originally controlled by conservative elements, had been taken over by extremists nourished on Enlightenment radicalism, and the once dominant conservative groups had gradually been alienated. The break with England over the question of home rule was part of a general struggle, as Carl Becker put it, over who shall rule at home. Independence gave control to the radicals, who, imposing their advanced doctrines on a traditional society, transformed a rebellious secession into a social revolution. They created a new regime, a reformed society, based on enlightened political and social theory.

But that is not the end of the story; the sequel is important. The success of the enlightened radicals during the early years of the Revolution was notable; but, the argument continues, it was not wholly unqualified. The remnants of the earlier aristocracy, though defeated, had not been eliminated: they were able to reassert themselves in the postwar years. In the 1780s they gradually regained power until, in what amounted to a counterrevolution, they impressed their views indelibly on history in the new Federal Constitution, in the revocation of some of the more enthusiastic actions of the earlier revolutionary period, and in the Hamiltonian program for the new government. This was not, of course, merely the old regime resurrected. In a new age whose institutions and ideals had been born of revolutionary radicalism, the old conservative elements made adjustments and concessions by which to survive and periodically to flourish as a force in American life.

The importance of this formulation derived not merely from its usefulness in interpreting eighteenth-century history. It provided a key also for understanding the entire course of American politics. By its light, politics in America, from the very beginning, could be seen to have been a dialectical process in which an aristocracy of wealth and power struggled with the People, who, ordinarily ill-organized and inarticulate, rose upon provocation armed with powerful institutional and ideological weapons, to reform a periodically corrupt and oppressive policy.

In all of this the underlying assumption is the belief that Enlightenment thought—the reforming ideas of advanced thinkers in eighteenth-century England and on the Continent—had been the effective lever by which native American radicals had turned a dispute on imperial relations into a sweeping reformation of public institutions and thereby laid the basis for American democracy.

For some time now, and particularly during the last decade, this interpretation has been fundamentally weakened by the work of many scholars working from different approaches and on different problems. Almost every important point has been challenged in one way or another.[1] All arguments concerning politics during the pre-Revolutionary years have been affected by an exhaustive demonstration for

[1] Recent revisionist writings on eighteenth-century America are voluminous. The main points of reinterpretation will be found in the following books and articles, to which specific reference is made in the paragraphs that follow: Robert E. Brown, *Middle-Class Democracy and the Revolution in Massachusetts, 1691–1780* (Ithaca, N. Y., 1955); E. James Ferguson, "Currency Finance: An Interpretation of Colonial Monetary Practices," *William and Mary Quarterly,* X (Apr. 1953), 153–80; Theodore Thayer, "The Land Bank System in the American Colonies," *Journal of Economic History,* XIII (Spring 1953), 145–59; Bray Hammond, *Banks and Politics in America from the Revolution to the Civil War* (Princeton, N. J., 1957); George A. Billias, *The Massachusetts Land Bankers of 1740* (Orono, Me., 1959); Milton M. Klein, "Democracy and Politics in Colonial New York," *New York History,* XL (July 1959), 221–46; Oscar and Mary F. Handlin, "Radicals and Conservatives in Massachusetts after Independence," *New England Quarterly,* XVII (Sept. 1944), 343–55; Bernard Bailyn, "The Blount Papers: Notes on the Merchant 'Class' in the Revolutionary Period," *William and Mary Quarterly,* XI (Jan. 1954), 98–104; Frederick B. Tolles, "The American Revolution Considered as a Social Movement: A Re-Evaluation," *American Historical Review,* LX (Oct. 1954), 1–12; Robert E. Brown, *Charles Beard and the Constitution: A Critical Analysis of "An Economic Interpretation of the Constitution"* (Princeton, N. J., 1956); Forrest McDonald, *We the People: The Economic Origins of the Constitution* (Chicago, 1958); Daniel J. Boorstin, *The Genius of American Politics* (Chicago, 1953); and *The Americans: The Colonial Experience* (New York, 1958). References to other writings and other viewpoints will be found in Edmund S. Morgan, "The American Revolution: Revisions in Need of Revising," *William and Mary Quarterly,* XIV (Jan. 1957), 3–15; and Richard B. Morris, "The Confederation Period and the American Historian," *ibid.,* XIII (Apr. 1956), 139–56.

one colony, which might well be duplicated for others, that the franchise, far from having been restricted in behalf of a borough-mongering aristocracy, was widely available for popular use. Indeed, it was more widespread than the desire to use it—a fact which in itself calls into question a whole range of traditional arguments and assumptions. Similarly, the Populist terms in which economic elements of pre-Revolutionary history have most often been discussed may no longer be used with the same confidence. For it has been shown that paper money, long believed to have been the inflationary instrument of a depressed and desperate debtor yeomanry, was in general a fiscally sound and successful means—whether issued directly by the governments or through land banks—not only of providing a medium of exchange but also of creating sources of credit necessary for the growth of an underdeveloped economy and a stable system of public finance for otherwise resourceless governments. Merchants and creditors commonly supported the issuance of paper, and many of the debtors who did so turn out to have been substantial property owners.

Equally, the key writings extending the interpretation into the revolutionary years have come under question. The first and still classic monograph detailing the inner social struggle of the decade before 1776—Carl Becker's *History of Political Parties in the Province of New York, 1760–1776* (1909)—has been subjected to sharp criticism on points of validation and consistency. And, because Becker's book, like other studies of the movement toward revolution, rests upon a belief in the continuity of "radical" and "conservative" groupings, it has been weakened by an analysis proving such terminology to be deceptive in that it fails to define consistently identifiable groups of people. Similarly, the "class" characteristic of the merchant group in the northern colonies, a presupposition of important studies of the merchants in the revolutionary movement, has been questioned, and along with it the belief that there was an economic or occupational basis for positions taken on the revolutionary controversy. More important, a recent survey of the writings following up J. F. Jameson's classic essay, *The American Revolution Considered as a Social Movement* (1926), has shown how little has been written in the last twenty-five years to substantiate that famous statement of the Revolution as a movement of social reform. Most dramatic of all has been the demolition of Charles Beard's *Economic*

Interpretation of the Constitution (1913), which stood solidly for over forty years as the central pillar of the counterrevolution argument: the idea, that is, that the Constitution was a "conservative" document, the polar opposite of the "radical" Articles of Confederation, embodying the interests and desires of public creditors and other moneyed conservatives, and marking the Thermidorian conclusion to the enlightened radicalism of the early revolutionary years.

Finally, there are arguments of another sort, assertions to the effect that not only did Enlightenment ideas not provoke native American radicals to undertake serious reform during the Revolution, but that ideas have never played an important role in American public life, in the eighteenth century or after, and that the political "genius" of the American people, during the Revolution as later, has lain in their brute pragmatism, their successful resistance to the "distant example and teachings of the European Enlightenment," the maunderings of "garret-spawned European illuminati."

Thus from several directions at once have come evidence and arguments that cloud if they do not totally obscure the picture of eighteenth-century American history composed by a generation of scholars. These recent critical writings are of course of unequal weight and validity; but few of them are totally unsubstantiated, almost all of them have some point and substance, and taken together they are sufficient to raise serious doubts about the organization of thought within which we have become accustomed to view the eighteenth century. A full reconsideration of the problems raised by these findings and ideas would of course be out of the question here even if sufficient facts were now available. But one might make at least an approach to the task and a first approximation to some answers to the problems by isolating the central premise concerning the relationship between Enlightenment ideas and political experience and reconsidering it in view of the evidence that is now available.

Considering the material at hand, old and new, that bears on this question, one discovers an apparent paradox. There appear to be two primary and contradictory sets of facts. The first and more obvious is the undeniable evidence of the seriousness with which colonial and revolutionary leaders took ideas, and the deliberateness of their efforts during the Revolution to reshape institutions in their pattern. The more we know about these American provincials the clearer it is that among them were remarkably well informed students of contemporary social and political theory. There never was a dark age that destroyed the cultural contacts between Europe and America. The sources of transmission had been numerous in the seventeenth century; they increased in the eighteenth. There were not only the impersonal agencies of newspapers, books, and pamphlets, but also continuous personal contact through travel and correspondence. Above all, there were Pan-Atlantic, mainly Anglo-American, interest groups that occasioned a continuous flow of fresh information and ideas between Europe and the mainland colonies in America. Of these, the most important were the English dissenters and their numerous codenominationalists in America. Located perforce on the left of the English political spectrum, acutely alive to ideas of reform that might increase their security in England, they were, for the almost endemically nonconformist colonists, a rich source of political and social theory. It was largely through nonconformist connections, as Caroline Robbins's recent book, *The Eighteenth-Century Commonwealthman* (1959), suggests, that the commonwealth radicalism of seventeenth-century England continued to flow to the colonists, blending, ultimately, with other strains of thought to form a common body of advanced theory.

In every colony and in every legislature there were people who knew Locke and Beccaria, Montesquieu and Voltaire; but perhaps more important, there was in every village of every colony someone who knew such transmitters of English nonconformist thought as Watts, Neal, and Burgh; later Priestley and Price—lesser writers, no doubt, but staunch opponents of traditional authority, and they spoke in a familiar idiom. In the bitterly contentious pamphlet literature of mid-eighteenth-century American politics, the most frequently cited authority on matters of principle and theory was not Locke or Montesquieu but *Cato's Letters,* a series of radically libertarian essays written in London in 1720–1723 by two supporters of the dissenting interest, John Trenchard and Thomas Gordon. Through such writers, as well as through the major authors, leading colonists kept contact with a powerful tradition of enlightened thought.

This body of doctrine fell naturally into play in the controversy over the power of the imperial government. For the revolutionary leaders it supplied a common vocabulary and a common pattern of thought, and, when the time came, common principles of political reform. That reform was sought and seriously if unevenly undertaken, there can be no doubt. Institutions were remodeled, laws altered, practices questioned all in accordance with advanced doctrine on the nature of liberty and of the institutions needed to achieve it. The Americans were acutely aware of being innovators, of bringing mankind a long step forward. They believed that they had so far succeeded in their effort to reshape circumstances to conform to enlightened ideas and ideals that they had introduced a new era in human affairs. And they were supported in this by the opinion of informed thinkers in Europe. The contemporary image of the American Revolution at home and abroad was complex; but no one doubted that a revolution that threatened the existing order and portended new social and political arrangements had been made, and made in the name of reason.

Thus, throughout the eighteenth century there were prominent, politically active Americans who were well aware of the development of European thinking, took ideas seriously, and during the Revolution deliberately used them in an effort to reform the institutional basis of society. This much seems obvious. But, paradoxically, and less obviously, it is equally true that many, indeed most, of what these leaders considered to be their greatest achievements during the Revolution—reforms that made America seem to half the world like the veritable heavenly city of the eighteenth-century philosophers—had been matters of fact before they were matters of theory and revolutionary doctrine.

No reform in the entire Revolution appeared of greater importance to Jefferson than the Virginia acts abolishing primogeniture and entail. This action, he later wrote, was part of "a system by which every fibre would be eradicated of antient or future aristocracy; and a foundation laid for a government truly republican." But primogeniture and entail had never taken deep roots in America, not even in tidewater Virginia. Where land was cheap and easily available such legal restrictions proved to be encumbrances profiting few. Often they tended to threaten rather than secure the survival of the family, as Jefferson himself realized when in 1774 he petitioned the Assembly to break an entail on his wife's estate on the very practical, untheoretical, and common ground that to do so would be "greatly to their [the petitioners'] Interest and that of their Families." The legal abolition of primogeniture and entail during and after the

Revolution was of little material consequence. Their demise had been effectively decreed years before by the circumstancs of life in a wilderness environment.

Similarly, the disestablishment of religion—a major goal of revolutionary reform—was carried out, to the extent that it was, in circumstances so favorable to it that one wonders not how it was done but why it was not done more thoroughly. There is no more eloquent, moving testimony to revolutionary idealism than the Virginia Act for Establishing Religious Freedom: it is the essence of Enlightenment faith. But what did it, and the disestablishment legislation that had preceded it, reform? What had the establishment of religion meant in pre-Revolutionary Virginia? The Church of England was the state church, but dissent was tolerated well beyond the limits of the English Acts of Toleration. The law required nonconformist organizations to be licensed by the government, but dissenters were not barred from their own worship nor penalized for failure to attend the Anglican communion, and they were commonly exempted from parish taxes. Nonconformity excluded no one from voting and only the very few Catholics from enjoying public office. And when the itineracy of revivalist preachers led the establishment to contemplate more restrictive measures, the Baptists and Presbyterians advanced to the point of arguing publicly, and pragmatically, that the toleration they had so far enjoyed was an encumbrance, and that the only proper solution was total liberty: in effect, disestablishment.

Virginia was if anything more conservative than most colonies. The legal establishment of the Church of England was in fact no more rigorous in South Carolina and Georgia: it was considerably weaker in North Carolina. It hardly existed at all in the middle colonies (there was of course no vestige of it in Pennsylvania), and where it did, as in four counties of New York, it was either ignored or had become embattled by violent opposition well before the Revolution. And in Massachusetts and Connecticut, where the establishment, being nonconformist according to English law, was legally tenuous to begin with, tolerance in worship and relief from taxation had been extended to the major dissenting groups early in the century, resulting well before the Revolution in what was, in effect if not in law, a multiple establishment. And this had been further weakened by the splintering effect of the Great Awakening. Almost everywhere the Church of England, the established church of the highest state authority, was embattled and defensive—driven to rely more and more on its missionary arm, the Society for the Propagation of the Gospel, to sustain it against the cohorts of dissent.

None of this had resulted from Enlightenment theory. It had been created by the mundane exigencies of the situation: by the distance that separated Americans from ecclesiastical centers in England and the Continent; by the never-ending need to encourage immigration to the colonies; by the variety, the mere numbers, of religious groups, each by itself a minority, forced to live together; and by the weakness of the coercive powers of the state, its inability to control the social forces within it.

Even more gradual and less contested had been the process by which government in the colonies had become government by the consent of the governed. What has been proved about the franchise in early Massachusetts—that it was open for practically the entire free adult male population—can be proved to a lesser or greater extent for all the colonies. But the extraordinary breadth of the franchise in the American colonies had not resulted from popular demands: there had been no cries for universal manhood suffrage, nor were there popular theories claiming, or even justifying, general participation in politics. Nowhere in eighteenth-century America was there "democracy"—middle-class or otherwise—as we use the term. The main reason for the wide franchise was that the traditional English laws limiting suffrage to freeholders of certain competences proved in the colonies, where freehold property was almost universal, to be not restrictive but widely permissive.

Representation would seem to be different, since before the Revolution complaints had been voiced against the inequity of its apportioning, especially in the Pennsylvania and North Carolina assemblies. But these complaints were based on an assumption that would have seemed natural and reasonable almost nowhere else in the Western world: the assumption that representation in governing assemblages was a proper and rightful attribute of people as such —of regular units of population, or of populated land—rather than the privilege of particular groups, institutions, or regions. Complaints there were, bitter ones. But they were complaints claiming injury and deprivation, not abstract ideals or unfamiliar desires. They assumed from common experience the normalcy of regular and systematic representation. And how should it have been otherwise? The colonial assemblies had not, like ancient parliaments, grown to satisfy a monarch's need for the support of particular groups or individuals or to protect the interests of a social order, and they had not developed insensibly from precedent to precedent. They had been created at a stroke, and they were in their composition necessarily regular and systematic. Nor did the process, the character, of representation as it was known in the colonies derive from theory. For colonial Americans, representation had none of the symbolic and little of the purely deliberative qualities which, as a result of the revolutionary debates and of Burke's speeches, would become celebrated as "virtual." To the colonists it was direct and actual: it was, most often, a kind of agency, a delegation of powers, to individuals commonly required to be residents of their constituencies and, often, bound by instructions from them—with the result that eighteenth-century American legislatures frequently resembled, in spirit if not otherwise, those "ancient assemblies" of New York, composed, the contemporary historian William Smith wrote, "of plain, illiterate husbandmen, whose views seldom extended farther than to the regulation of highways, the destruction of wolves, wild cats, and foxes, and the advancement of the other little interests of the particular counties which they were chosen to represent." There was no theoretical basis for such direct and actual representation. It had been created and was continuously reinforced by the pressure of local politics in the colonies and by the political circumstances in England, to which the colonists had found it necessary to send closely instructed, paid representatives—agents, so called—from the very beginning.

But franchise and representation are mere mechanisms of government by consent. At its heart lies freedom from executive power, from the independent action of state authority, and the concentration of power in representative bodies and elected officials. The greatest achievement of the Revolution was of course the repudiation of just such state authority and the transfer of power to popular legislatures. No one will deny that this action was taken in accordance with the highest principles of Enlightenment theory. But the way had been paved by fifty years of grinding factionalism in colonial politics. In the details of pre-Revolutionary American politics, in the complicated maneuverings of provincial politicians seeking the benefits of government, in the patterns of local patronage and the forms of factional groupings, there lies a history of progressive alienation from the state which resulted, at least by the 1750s, in what Professor Robert Palmer has lucidly described as a revolutionary situation: a condition

> *. . . in which confidence in the justice or reasonableness of existing authority is undermined; where old loyalties fade, obligations are felt as impositions, law seems arbitrary, and respect for superiors is felt as a form of humiliation; where existing sources of prestige seem undeserved . . . and government is sensed as distant, apart from the governed and not really "representing" them.*

Such a situation had developed in mid-eighteenth-century America, not from theories of government or Enlightenment ideas but from the factional opposition that had grown up against a succession of legally powerful, but often cynically self-seeking, inept, and above all politically weak officers of state.

Surrounding all of these circumstances and in various ways controlling them is the fact that that great goal of the European revolutions of the late eighteenth century, equality of status before the law—the abolition of legal privilege—had been reached almost everywhere in the American colonies at least by the early years of the eighteenth century. Analogies between the upper strata of colonial society and the European aristocracies are misleading. Social stratification existed, of course; but the differences between aristocracies in eighteenth-century Europe and in America are more important than the similarities. So far was legal privilege, or even distinction, absent in the colonies that where it existed it was an open sore of festering discontent, leading not merely, as in the case of the Penn family's hereditary claims to tax exemption, to formal protests, but, as in the case of the powers enjoyed by the Hudson River land magnates, to violent opposition as well. More important, the colonial aristocracy, such as it was, had no formal, institutional role in government. No public office or function was legally a prerogative of birth. As there were no social orders in the eyes of the law, so there were no governmental bodies to represent them. The only claim that has been made to the contrary is that, in effect, the governors' Councils constituted political institutions in the service of the aristocracy. But this claim—of dubious value in any case because of the steadily declining political importance of the Councils in the eighteenth century—cannot be substantiated. It is true that certain families tended to dominate the Councils, but they had less legal claim to places in those bodies than certain royal officials who, though hardly members of an American aristocracy, sat on the Councils by virtue of their office. Councillors could be and were removed by simple political maneuver. Council seats were filled either by appointment or election: when appointive, they were vulnerable to political pressure in England; when elective, to the vagaries of public opinion at home. Thus on the one hand it took William Byrd II three years of maneuvering in London to get himself appointed to the seat on the Virginia Council vacated by his father's death in 1704, and on the other, when in 1766 the Hutchinson faction's control of the Massachusetts Council proved unpopular, it was simply removed wholesale by being voted out of office at the next election. As there were no special privileges, no peculiar group possessions, manners, or attitudes to distinguish councillors from other affluent Americans, so there were no separate political interests expressed in the Councils as such. Councillors joined as directly as others in the factional disputes of the time, associating with groups of all sorts, from minute and transient American opposition parties to massive English-centered political syndicates. A century before the Revolution and not as the result of antiaristocratic ideas, the colonial aristocracy had become a vaguely defined, fluid group whose power—in no way guaranteed, buttressed, or even recognized in law—was competitively maintained and dependent on continuous, popular support.

Other examples could be given. Were written constitutions felt to be particular guarantees of liberty in enlightened states? Americans had known them in the form of colonial charters and governors' instructions for a century before the Revolution; and after 1763, seeking a basis for their claims against the constitutionality of specific acts of Parliament, they had been driven, out of sheer logical necessity and not out of principle, to generalize that experience. But the point is perhaps clear enough. Major attributes of enlightened politics had developed naturally, spontaneously, early in the history of the American colonies, and they existed as simple matters of social and political fact on the eve of the Revolution.

But if all this is true, what did the Revolution accomplish? Of what real significance were the ideals and ideas? What was the bearing of Enlightenment thought on the political experience of eighteenth-century Americans?

Perhaps this much may be said. What had evolved spontaneously from the demands of place and time was not self-justifying, nor was it universally welcomed. New developments, however gradual, were suspect by some, resisted in part, and confined in their effects. If it was true that the establishment of religion was everywhere weak in the colonies and that in some places it was even difficult to know what was orthodoxy and what was not, it was nevertheless also true that faith in the idea of orthodoxy persisted and with it belief in the propriety of a privileged state religion. If, as a matter of fact, the spread of freehold tenure qualified large populations for voting, it did not create new reasons for using that power nor make the victims of its use content with what, in terms of the dominant ideal of balance in the state, seemed a disproportionate influence of "the democracy." If many colonists came naturally to assume that representation should be direct and actual, growing with the population and bearing some relation to its distribution, crown officials did not, and they had the weight of precedent and theory as well as of authority with them and hence justification for resistance. If state authority was seen increasingly as alien and hostile and was forced to fight for survival within an abrasive, kaleidoscopic factionalism, the traditional idea nevertheless persisted that the common good was somehow defined by the state and that political parties or factions —organized opposition to established government—were seditious. A traditional aristocracy did not in fact exist; but the assumption that superiority was indivisible, that social eminence and political influence had a natural affinity to each other, did. The colonists instinctively conceded to the claims of the well-born and rich to exercise public office, and in this sense politics remained aristocratic. Behavior had changed—had had to change—with the circumstances of everyday life; but habits of mind and the sense of rightness lagged behind. Many felt the changes to be *away from,* not *toward,* something: that they represented deviance; that they lacked, in a word, legitimacy.

This divergence between habits of mind and belief on the one hand and experience and behavior on the other was ended at the Revolution. A rebellion that destroyed the traditional sources of public authority called forth the full range of advanced ideas. Long-settled attitudes were jolted and loosened. The grounds of legitimacy suddenly shifted. What had happened was seen to have been good and proper, steps in the right direction. The glass was half full, not half empty; and to complete the work of fate and nature, further thought must be taken, theories tested, ideas applied. Precisely because so many social and institutional reforms had already taken place in America, the revolutionary movement there, more than elsewhere, was a matter of doctrine, ideas, and comprehension.

And so it remained. Social change and social conflict of course took place during the revolutionary years; but the essential developments of the period lay elsewhere, in the effort to think through and to apply under the most favorable, permissive, circumstances enlightened ideas of government and society. The problems were many, often unexpected and difficult; some were only gradually perceived. Social and personal privilege, for example, could easily be eliminated—it hardly existed; but what of the impersonal privileges of corporate bodies? Legal orders and ranks within society could be outlawed without creating the slightest tremor, and executive power with equal ease subordinated to the legislative: but how was balance within a polity to be achieved? What were the elements to be balanced and how were they to be separated? It was not even necessary formally to abolish the interest of state as a symbol and determinant of the common good; it was simply dissolved: but what was left to keep clashing factions from tearing a government apart? The problems were pressing, and the efforts to solve them mark the stages of revolutionary history.

In behalf of Enlightenment liberalism the revolutionary leaders undertook to complete, formalize, systematize, and symbolize what previously had been only partially realized, confused, and disputed matters of fact. Enlightenment ideas were not instruments of a particular social group, nor did they destroy a social order. They did not create new social and political forces in America. They released those that had long existed, and vastly increased their power. This completion, this rationalization, this symbolization, this lifting into consciousness and endowing with high moral purpose inchoate, confused elements of social and political change—this was the American Revolution.

Jesse Lemisch

WHAT MADE OUR REVOLUTION?

This second selection by Professor Lemisch, clashing head-on with the theses and outlook of Bernard Bailyn, states also Lemisch's belief that most interpretations of the causes and consequences of the American Revolution reflect a distinctly anti-lower-class bias on the part of historians. He has argued this point more generally in his article, "The American Revolution Seen from the Bottom Up," which appeared in Towards a New Past: Dissenting Essays in American History *(1968), edited by Barton J. Bernstein.*

Bernard Bailyn sees the American Revolution as an event in the history of ideas. He shows how the disparity between American political realities and the English experience from which certain political ideas derived, finally led to revolution. Much of what he says is novel and persuasive. But it misleads us about the nature of the American Revolution, and it also is representative of certain glaring blind spots of recent American historiography.

Social conditions in eighteenth-century England seem a natural starting point for an exploration of the revolutionary ideology which emerged there. Bailyn quotes J. H. Plumb, who describes a savage and violent society of slums, starvation, epidemic, "rick burnings, machine-smashing, hunger-riots"; the poor "herded" into jails and workhouses which "resembled concentration camps"; ten-year-olds hanged for petty thefts. But this is the last we are to hear of the poor. Bailyn shifts from this Hogarthian reality to the world of Gainsborough so abruptly that the brief appearance of the poor becomes inexplicable; everything which follows seems to deny their existence: "England was rich, and getting richer." (Bailyn omits Plumb's suggestion that things were getting worse for the poor.) But once he has let the poor out of the bag, they remain with the reader, who has a right to be puzzled by "eighteenth-century Britons' sense of their multifarious accomplishments . . . and their distinctiveness in the achievement of liberty." How can Bailyn speak of an era of "harmony and political stability" in the face of widespread riot and protest? How could the English pride themselves on having "eliminated . . . arbitrary power" from government when, to take one instance, the press gang was omnipresent, abusive of human liberty, and—according to learned jurists—legal?

Although Bailyn repeatedly describes the self-congratulatory mood as simply "English," it turns out that these beliefs were "universally shared by all *informed* Englishmen" (emphasis added). How universal is that? Not very, Bailyn suggests a few footnotes later: "the uninformed and credulous of all classes . . . were the majority." He views British society from the vantage point of a minority, an "informed" elite. Not the entire elite; Bailyn's focus is on Walpole's opposition: Bolingbroke on the "far right" and, on the "far left," a group of "left-wing" writers and "coffehouse radicals" of whom the "most effective" were John Trenchard and Thomas Gordon. Left and right merge on "fundamental points," and somehow, with a mathematics which the contemporary left might well envy, it all adds up to an ideology which Bailyn describes variously as "radical," "democratic," and "popular."

The opposition as a whole was in fact part of the mainstream on "major points of doctrine." Bailyn's radicals saw their task as the preservation of a proper balance within government, lest magistrates become "plunderers and murderers." But magistrates *were* plunderers and murderers. Edward Thompson has described the politics of a slightly later period as a game in which the king was the croupier; the opposition seems to have wanted simply to have the croupier play by the rules, not to end the game.

Trenchard and Gordon thought a commonwealth or republic the ideal government, but they rejected it in practice, since it could be brought about only through "bloodshed and upheaval" (of which, Bailyn seems to have forgotten, there was a great deal in England, much of it official). The *Dictionary of National Biography* tersely describes Trenchard as "a Whig with popular sympathies, but by no means a republican, as his opponents wished to consider him." Elsewhere, Bailyn belatedly but temporarily notes that his radicals did not seek "to recast the social order" or to deal with "problems of economic inequality and the injustices of stratified societies."

When Bailyn says that the views of the English opposition were determinative of American views, we want to know, *which* Americans? By Americans, he means "informed" ones, especially certain pamphleteers whose work he collected and analyzed in his *Pamphlets of the American Revolution.* It should come as no surprise that Bailyn's study of such sources "confirmed [his] rather old-fashioned view that the American Revolution was above all else an ideological-constitutional struggle" and convinced him that "in no obvious sense was the American Revolution undertaken as a social revolution." These conclusions arose directly out of his choice of sources, not necessarily out of reality. Did he expect to find an attack on elitism in the thought of the colonial elite? What assumptions led him to suppose that study of the pamphlets gave him an "interior" view of the "revolutionary movement"? In what sense are the "informed" closer to reality than the "uninformed"? Whose definition of the Revolution shall we accept, John Adams's or that of the men who fought in it? Why not *both*?

Bailyn describes political practices in the colonial legislatures. Where there was harmony in England, there was strife in America: strife between and among executive and legislature. Legally the executive had more power in America than in England. But the "private" constitution through which the executive maintained control in England—e.g., patronage and an easily manipulated electoral system—scarcely existed here. Thus American politics was a matter of "swollen claims and shrunken powers." Colonials applied the view of politics acquired from the English opposition: the mixed constitution was the ideal, and the colonial executives seemed to threaten a proper balance. That threat seemed deliberate and conspiratorial and, in the 1760s and 1770s, overt. Americans went to war to maintain the Glorious Revolution, to oppose arbitrary power.

Bailyn has made a major contribution in making sense of the legislatures' fears; it seems very clear that they did indeed see the actions of the governors through lenses acquired from Trenchard and Gordon. But is it correct to see the struggle of the legislatures as one in which they are "radical," stand for "popular interests," "popular forces," and "an over-great democracy"? Bailyn's account of the conflicts of colonial politics is to an extraordinary extent a story of economic interests competing to divide the treasure of America: rarely has a scholar arguing for an "ideological" interpretation presented so much evidence to delight economic determinists. Conflicts occur among "ambitious merchant farmers," "merchants and landowners," a governor who came to America "to recoup his dwindling fortune." Traders struggle with traders and are supported by a syndicate of London export merchants; a governor is supported by merchants whose interests in military contracting he favors: he is accused of "profiteering." Colonial politics presents "an almost unchartable chaos of competing groups." Although economic groups sought political expression, there were no "classes," only "stratified 'dignities'." (Bailyn earlier found a similar diversity among seventeenth-century New England merchants—who "formed not a singular social entity, but a spectrum; not a clearly defined bloc"—and in seventeenth-century Virginia, although in the latter case he was able to detect what he called a "ruling class.")

The conduct of the legislators among themselves, or even in conflict with the governors, really tells us next to nothing about democracy. The only way in which we can even approach valid judgments on such matters as class and democracy is to examine the smaller group as it relates to the larger; in the case of colonial America, we must look to those outside of and below the legislature.

Another way of putting the issue is to ask: Were there, with regard to the populace at large, matters on which the contentious legislators agreed and thus did not *have* to argue? As in England, both administration and opposition accepted the necessity of the tripartite constitutional balance. They did not argue about the social structure because they did not wish to change it; their silence on this matter makes them more partisan than neutral. They all agreed that effective power should not be given to the people; dispute as they might over who was to get what share in America, the legislators and the governors agreed that that was a matter to be decided *for* the people, not *by* them.

The consensus was not total: Bailyn has not in fact explored here what he calls "the full range of advanced ideas." The existence of Tom Paine and a few other political thinkers . . . indicates that it was possible to conceive *more* advanced ideas. There was an alternative body of political thought, majoritarian and democratic, rejecting checks and balances, which were seen, correctly, as a means of shackling the popular will. The quality of the mainstream "democratic" consensus is better defined by its response to these deviant doctrines than by its quarrels with the governors. John Adams "dreaded the Effect so popular a pamphlet" as Paine's *Common Sense* might have, with its proposals which he thought "so democratical, without any restraint or even an attempt at any Equilibrium or Counterpoise, that it must produce confusion and every Evil work."

When we view the colonial legislatures from below, it is immediately evident that the underlying ingredient of the consensus which held the elite together was anti-Populism. Did Trenchard and Gordon's American followers believe in freedom of speech and press? For themselves, yes, but certainly not for those outside the legislature. What Bailyn seems uncritically to accept as libertarianism has been more accurately described by Leonard Levy as a "legacy of suppression," much of it done by the legislatures.

Although he seems to accept the dubious idea that government in eighteenth-century England did not "act on society," Bailyn sees the colonial legislatures as being led, "willy-nilly . . . to exercise creative powers." A large part of that creativity was economic. "Out of the necessity of the situation," writes Bailyn there devolved upon colonial legislatures the power of distributing land. "Social institutions too had to be created, or legalized." But the content of colonial legislation reveals a forthright expression of class interest; its execution shows a pattern of class justice. If the colonial governors found themselves largely powerless against the economic onslaught of the legislatures, what of the people? Why do we acknowledge a conflict of economic interest in the former instance and ignore it in the latter?

For Bailyn, political representation in the colonies was either "remarkably equitable" or well on its way there, because it was "dynamic, growing": "freehold tenure was almost universal among the white population." (That universality is almost immediately halved when he says that "fifty to seventy-five percent of the adult male white population was entitled to vote.") His argument for universality is based in part on acceptance of the work of Robert Brown. Since 1955, when Brown advanced this idea, there has been over a decade of critical scholarship, some of it attacking Brown's statistical methods and suggesting that the truth might be the opposite of what he contended, but for Bailyn, it is as if this decade never existed. Not only have historians challenged the universality of suffrage in the colonies; they have carried the debate to a higher level, pointing out that voting may have nothing to do with political power.

Bailyn's contention that representation in the colonies was equitable reduces to the argument that apportionment kept pace with geography. This seems a narrow measure of equitability. If every new town was represented, we still want to know something of the dynamics of control in small towns: *Which* townspeople were represented? Who gets elected when balloting is open? A town meeting may be one of the most easily controlled institutions in a democracy.

There is another sense in which representation in the colonies was anything but equitable, dynamic, or "well adjusted to the growth . . . of population." In this book [*The Origins of American Politics*] Bailyn focuses on the "openness" of the colonial economy. In his other work he has shown that the long-term trend in colonial society was towards increasing social stratification; "mobility was slowing down." Others have revealed that this was happening on all levels. The open economy was closing down: seamen earned a decreasing share of the rising productivity of shipping; the propertyless multiplied. Thus when we consider representation in terms not of geography but of class we find that the trend is the reverse of dynamic. One wants to reexamine the meaning of America as a land of opportunity in the light of declining opportunity. One wants to consider the meaning of the slogan, "no taxation without representation" for those who had nothing to be taxed.

Bailyn has successfully depicted the ideology of the American ruling class. Yet this gives us hardly an inkling of what the Revolution meant to 3 million Americans. That revolution was led by men who defined their own privilege as synonymous with "liberty"; Bailyn accepts them on their own terms and ignores what they chose to ignore.

In an ironic sense, he has described the origins of American politics. For some time now our historians have been telling us that our politics has been one of consensus: although there have been disagreements among Americans, there has been agreement about fundamentals. In fact there have been real divisions in American life, together with pain, suffering, atrocity, and genocide. Our politics has not reflected this; politics has achieved consensus by the simple device of being a politics of exclusion. Daniel Bell blundered onto this when he defined democratic politics as "bargaining between *legitimate* groups and the search for consensus" (emphasis added). Thus those academic boosters who have reveled in the nonideological nature of American politics and the lack of substantial differences within it have been defining what is essentially a one-party politics. To find the other party we must move outside the political structure, beyond the "mainstream." . . .

V INTERPRETATION OF HISTORICAL REALITY: IDEAS, MOTIVES, INTERESTS

Page Smith

DAVID RAMSAY AND THE CAUSES OF THE AMERICAN REVOLUTION

Author of a biography of James Wilson, one of the "Founding Fathers," Page Smith is a specialist in American history of the revolutionary period. The article from which the following selection is taken urges the merit of David Ramsay's eighteenth-century interpretation of the Revolution and surveys the various schools of thought that have, since Ramsay's day, interpreted and reinterpreted the Revolution.

Much attention has been given recently to the changes that have taken place since the late eighteenth century in historians' interpretations of the causes of the American Revolution.[1]

. . . The thesis of this essay is that the best interpretation of the causes of the Revolution was made in the decade following the treaty of peace in 1783 and that thereafter, as we moved further in time from the dramatic events of the Revolution and brought to bear on the problem all the vast resources of modern scholarship, we moved further and further from the truth about our revolutionary beginnings.

Among the generation of historians who themselves lived through the era of the American Revolution, David Ramsay is preeminent, though by no means atypical. Ramsay (1749–1815) was born in Pennsylvania of Scottish Presbyterian parents and attended the College of New Jersey where his friend Benjamin Rush said of him that he was "far superior to any person we ever graduated at our college . . . I can promise more for him, in every thing, than I could for myself."[2] After graduating from Princeton, Ramsay moved to Charleston, South Carolina, where he began the practice of medicine. He was a prominent patriot, serving in the Continental Congress and taking an active part in the political life of his state.

By all reasonable standards Ramsay, as an actor in those violent

Reprinted from the *William and Mary Quarterly: A Magazine of Early American History* 17 (1960): 50–77.

1 Edmund S. Morgan, "The American Revolution: Revisions in Need of Revising," *William and Mary Quarterly,* 3d Ser., XIV (1957), 3–15.

2 *Letters of Benjamin Rush,* ed. Lyman Butterfield (Princeton, 1951), I, 220.

times, should have written in an extreme and partisan spirit: caught up in the excitement and emotionalism of the revolutionary crisis in which England appeared as tyrant and oppressor, he had none of that perspective in time supposedly requisite for an objective and impartial treatment; he had no training as a historian and made no boast of impartiality; the passions which the war aroused had had little time to cool when he began his work; his *History of the American Revolution,* moreover, had a frankly didactic purpose—completed just as the delegates to the Federal Convention finished their work on the Federal Constitution, it was designed to awaken Americans to their responsibilities as citizens under the new government. Finally, he, like many of his fellow eighteenth-century historians, drew heavily and without specific citation from the *Annual Register.* Yet, with all these handicaps (from the viewpoint of orthodox historiography), Ramsay's history is a remarkable achievement. In his analysis and interpretation of the events culminating in the Revolution he showed unusual insight and a keen sense of proportion.

In considering the causes of the conflict between Great Britain and the colonists, Ramsay went back to examine the Puritan attitudes toward church and state, finding in Puritan theology a tradition of opposition to tyranny, which was considered to be contrary "to nature, reason, and revelation."[3] More important in nourishing a spirit of independence in the American colonies, however, was the fact that "the prerogatives of royalty and dependence on the Mother Country, were but feebly impressed on the colonial forms of government." In charter and proprietary colonies the Crown delegated broad powers, and even in the royal provinces the king exercised no more control over the colonists "than over their fellow subjects in England." Thus, "from the acquiescence of the parent state [in the growth of self-government], the spirit of her constitution, and daily experience, the Colonists grew up in a belief, that their local assemblies stood in the same relation to them, as the Parliament of Great Britain to the inhabitants of that island. The benefits of legislation were conferred on both, only through these constitutional channels." In this situation, the colonists claimed as part of their birthright all the benefits of the British Constitution, chief among which was that "the people could not be compelled to pay any taxes,

[3] David Ramsay, *History of the American Revolution,* 1st ed. (Philadelphia, 1789), (London, 1793), I, 8–9. The latter edition is cited throughout this essay.

nor be bound by any laws, but such as had been granted or enacted by the consent of themselves, or of their representatives."[4]

England had not markedly interfered with the colonists' economic welfare either. Indeed, "the wise and liberal policy of England towards her Colonies, during the first century and a half after their settlement" had exalted them to the preeminence they enjoyed at the beginning of the crisis with the mother country. England had given the Americans "full liberty to govern themselves by such laws as the local legislatures thought necessary, and left their trade open to every individual in her dominions. She also gave them the amplest permission to pursue their respective interests in such manner as they thought proper, and reserved little for herself, but the benefit of their trade, and that of political union under the same head."[5] Great Britain, Ramsay added, "without charging herself with the care of their internal police, or seeking a revenue from [the colonies], . . . contented herself with a monopoly of their trade. She treated them as a judicious mother does her dutiful children. They shared in every privilege belonging to her native sons, and but slightly felt the inconveniences of subordination. Small was the catalogue of grievances, with which even democratical jealousy charged the Parent State" prior to the revolutionary crisis. It was Ramsay's conviction that "The good resulting to the Colonies, from their connection with Great Britain, infinitely outweighed the evil."[6]

Among the causes contributing to the breach with Great Britain were such subtle factors as "the distance of America from Great-Britain [which] generated ideas in the minds of the Colonists favourable to liberty." Moreover, the religion of the great majority of the colonists "nurtured a love for liberty. They were chiefly Protestants, and all Protestantism is founded on a strong claim to natural liberty, and the right of private judgment." There were, in addition, intellectual currents in the age which encouraged libertarian ideals. "The reading of those Colonists who were inclined to books, generally favoured the cause of liberty. . . . Their books were generally small in size, and few in number: a great part of them consisted of those fashionable authors, who have defended the cause of liberty. Cato's letters, the Independent Whig, and such productions, were

[4] *Ibid.*, I, 20.
[5] *Ibid.*, I, 17–18.
[6] *Ibid.*, I, 42, 43.

common in one extreme of the Colonies, while in the other, histories of the Puritans kept alive the remembrance of the sufferings of their forefathers, and inspired a warm attachment, both to the civil and the religious rights of human nature."[7]

The social development of the colonies was likewise, in Ramsay's view, congenial to "a spirit of liberty and independence. Their inhabitants were all of one rank . . . from their first settlements, the English Provinces received impressions favourable to democratic forms of government. . . . A sameness of circumstances and occupations created a great sense of equality, and disposed them to union in any common cause from the success of which, they might expect to partake of equal advantages."[8] The vast majority of the colonists were farmers. "The merchants, mechanics, and manufacturers, taken collectively, did not amount to one fifteenth of the whole number of inhabitants," Ramsay pointed out, adding in characteristically Jeffersonian terms that while "the cultivators of the soil depend on nothing but Heaven and their own industry, other classes of men contract more or less of severity, from depending on the caprice of their customers."[9]

Against this background of maturing colonies, constitutional usage, libertarian ideas, and social equality, the British ministers undertook to tighten the lead strings by which the colonists had heretofore been so loosely guided. The decision of Parliament and the ministers of the Crown to attempt to raise a revenue in the American colonies destroyed at one blow "the guards which the constitution had placed round property, and the fences, which the ancestors of both countries had erected against arbitrary power."[10]

The reaction of the colonists to the Stamp Act was prompt, if unexpected. While the tax worked no considerable hardship on the colonists, public resistance was widespread and apparently spontaneous. The issue was not primarily an economic one, but one of principle—the principle of no taxation without representation for which the Revolution would eventually be fought. The Stamp Act aroused the sentiment for liberty among the Americans as no other pre-Revolutionary issue, and, in Ramsay's words, it became "evident,

[7] *Ibid.*, I, 29, 30.
[8] *Ibid.*, I, 31, 32–33.
[9] *Ibid.*, I, 33.
[10] *Ibid.*, I, 47.

from the determined opposition of the Colonies, that it could not be enforced without a civil war. . . ."[11]

With the repeal of the Stamp Act, the colonies, "instead of feeling themselves dependent on Great Britain, . . . conceived that, in respect to commerce, she was dependent on them." They were thus "inspired with such high ideas of the importance of their trade, that they considered the Mother Country to be brought under greater obligations to them, for purchasing her manufactures, than they were to her for protection and the administration of civil government." The upshot of repeal was that "the freemen of British America, . . . conceived it to be within their power, by future combinations, at any time to convulse, if not to bankrupt, the nation from which they sprung."[12]

In America, the revolutionary stage was set. What of England after the Stamp Act? In Ramsay we do not find what we have every reason to expect—a devil theory of the Revolution in which George III and his ministers appear as the malevolent instruments of tyranny and oppression. Pride and inflexibility were the principal shortcomings of the British. " 'What,' said they, 'shall we, who have so lately humbled France and Spain, be dictated to by our own Colonists? Shall our subjects, educated by our care, and defended by our arms, presume to question the rights of Parliament, to which we are obliged to submit?' . . . The love of power and of property on the one side of the Atlantic were opposed to the same powerful passions on the other."[13]

The British task was, at best, not an easy one. "Great and flourishing Colonies . . . already grown to the magnitude of a nation, planted at an immense distance, and governed by constitutions resembling that of the country from which they sprung, were novelties in the history of the world," Ramsay pointed out. "To combine Colonies, so circumstanced, in one uniform system of government with the Parent State, required a great knowledge of mankind, and an extensive comprehension of things. It was an arduous business, far beyond the grasp of ordinary state[smen], whose minds were narrowed by the formalities of laws, or the trammels of office. An original

[11] *Ibid.*, I, 71.
[12] *Ibid.*, I, 74–75.
[13] *Ibid.*, I, 52–53.

genius, unfettered with precedents, and exalted with just ideas of the rights of human nature, and the obligations of universal benevolence, might have struck out a middle line, which would have secured as much liberty to the Colonies, and as great a degree of supremacy to the Parent State, as their common good required: But the helm of Great Britain was not in such hands."[14]

Ramsay here offers us no evil George III, no tyrannical ministers, no demons and oppressors, but simply well-meaning men caught in a situation too complex and demanding for their very average talents. His wise and temperate assessment of the British failure has not been improved on. Ramsay here demonstrated not vast research labors but an unusual sense of proportion and capacity for analysis.

Remarkably sensitive to all currents in the tide of revolutionary agitation, Ramsay paid due attention to the economic motif. Many Americans, he pointed out, especially among the merchant class, found it profitable to oppose British measures. The reaction of the merchants to the threatened importation of East India tea was, in his view, motivated by their fear of losing a profitable trade in smuggled tea. "They doubtless conceived themselves to be supporting the rights of their country, by refusing to purchase tea from Britain," Ramsay wrote, "but they also reflected that if they could bring the same commodity to market, free from duty, their profits would be proportionately greater." Hence the merchants took the lead in denouncing the dutied tea. But "though the opposition originated in the selfishness of the merchants, it did not end there." When the Tea Act of 1773 was passed, the majority of colonists opposed Great Britain on the ground of "principle." They saw it as a scheme "calculated to seduce them into an acquiescence with the views of Parliament for raising an American revenue."[15] In accepting the cheaper tea, they would be accepting the tea tax.

The South Carolina doctor knew likewise that the motives of the patriots, like the motives of all men, were mixed. He offered no picture of a united country rushing to arms in defense of its liberties. "The inhabitants of the Colonies . . . with regard to political opinions," he wrote, "might be divided into three classes; of these, one was for rushing precipitately into extremities. They were for immediately stopping all trade, and could not even brook the delay of waiting

[14] *Ibid.*, I, 54–55.
[15] *Ibid.*, I, 95, 97.

till the proposed Continental Congress should meet. Another party, equally respectable, both as to character, property, and patriotism, was more moderate, but not less firm. These were averse to the adoption of any violent resolutions till all others were ineffectually tried. They wished that a clear statement of their rights, claims, and grievances, should precede every other measure. A third class disapproved of what was generally going on. A few from principle, and a persuasion that they ought to submit to the Mother Country; some from the love of ease, others from self-interest, but the bulk from fear of the mischievous consequences likely to follow. All these latter classes, for the most part, lay still, while the friends of liberty acted with spirit. If they, or any of them, ventured to oppose popular measures, they were not supported, and therefore declined farther efforts. The resentment of the people was so strong against them, that they sought for peace by remaining quiet. . . . The spirited part of the community being on the side of liberty, the patriots had the appearance of unanimity. . . ."[16]

To his summary analysis of the temper of these three classes, Ramsay added a detailed accounting on the basis of section and interest. That 3 million loyal subjects "should break through all former attachments, and unanimously adopt new ones, could not reasonably be expected. The Revolution had its enemies, as well as its friends, in every period of the war. Country, religion, local policy, as well as private views, operated in disposing the inhabitants to take different sides. The New-England provinces being mostly settled by one sort of people, were nearly of one sentiment. The influence of placemen in Boston, together with the connections which they had formed by marriages, had attached sundry influential characters in that capital to the British interest, but these were but as the dust in the balance, when compared with the numerous independent Whig yeomanry of the country."[17] The Quakers of Pennsylvania and the Tory farmers of the Carolina frontier were treated by Ramsay with as much sympathy and understanding as the independent yeoman of New England or the gentlemen planters of the Southern colonies.[18]

"The age and temperament of individuals [Ramsay continued]

16 *Ibid.*, I, 125–126.
17 *Ibid.*, II, 310.
18 *Ibid.*, II, 312–313.

had often an influence in fixing their political character. Old men were seldom warm Whigs; they could not relish the changes which were daily taking place; attached to ancient forms and habits, they could not readily accommodate themselves to new systems. Few of the very rich were active in forwarding the revolution. This was remarkably the case in the eastern and middle States; but the reverse took place in the southern extreme of the confederacy. There were in no part of America more determined Whigs than the opulent slave-holders in Virginia, the Carolinas, and Georgia. The active and spirited part of the community, who felt themselves possessed of talents that would raise them to eminence in a free government, longed for the establishment of independent constitutions: but those who were in possession or expectation of royal favour, or of promotion from Great Britain, wished that the connection between the Parent State and the Colonies might be preserved. The young, the ardent, the ambitious, and the enterprising, were mostly Whigs; but the phlegmatic, the timid, the interested, and those who wanted decision were, in general, favourers of Great Britain, or at least only the lukewarm, inactive friends of independence."[19]

Again economic factors exerted a strong influence: "The Whigs received a great reinforcement from the operation of continental money. In the years 1775, 1776, and in the first months of 1777, while the bills of Congress were in good credit, the effects of them were the same as if a foreign power had made the United States a present of 20 million of silver dollars. The circulation of so large a sum of money, and the employment given to great numbers in providing for the American army, increased the numbers and invigorated the zeal of the friends to the revolution."[20]

Even after Lexington, Ramsay pointed out, the colonial leaders, like the great mass of people everywhere, showed the greatest reluctance to take the decisive step toward independence. It was Thomas Paine's *Common Sense* which, more than anything else, nerved the colonies to declare themselves independent of the mother country. In an excellent analysis of Paine's pamphlet as propaganda, Ramsay concluded that "in union with the feelings and sentiments of the people, it produced surprising effects. Many thousands were convinced, and were led to approve and long for a separation from

[19] *Ibid.*, II, 314.
[20] *Ibid.*

the Mother Country. Though that measure, a few months before, was not only foreign from their wishes, but the object of their abhorrence, a current suddenly became so strong in its favour, that it bore down all opposition."[21]

Despite his sensitivity to the more subtle problems of colonial psychology, to self-interest, chance, and the inflexibility of the British government as elements in the revolutionary crisis, Ramsay grasped firmly, as lying at the heart of the conflict, the constitutional principle. "This was the very hinge of the controversy. The absolute unlimited supremacy of the British Parliament, both in legislation and taxation, was contended for on one side; while on the other, no farther authority was conceded than such a limited legislation, with regard to external commerce, as would combine the interests of the whole empire." "In government," Ramsay added, "as well as in religion, there are mysteries from the close investigation of which little advantage can be expected. From the unity of empire it was necessary, that some acts should extend over the whole. From the local situation of the Colonies it was equally reasonable that their legislatures should at least in some matters be independent. Where the supremacy of the first ended and the independency of the last began, was to the best informed a puzzling question."[22]

David Ramsay's *History of the American Revolution* has been treated at some length in order to provide a base point of interpretation against which the views of later historians may be measured. In addition, Ramsay can be considered an excellent representative of the first generation of Revolutionary War historians. If he outstrips his contemporaries in the depth and perception of his analyses, he stands with them in the main outlines of his interpretation.

The absence of rancor against Great Britain that characterized the histories of Ramsay and William Gordon was apparent in most first generation histories of the Revolution. Many were journeymen jobs, but the authors, almost without exception, presented fair and balanced narratives of the events leading to the Revolution. One looks in vain for mention of the "long train of abuses and usurpa-

[21] *Ibid.*, I, 336–337.

[22] *Ibid.*, I, 136; see also I, 48: "As the claim of taxation on one side, and the refusal of it on the other, was the very hinge on which the revolution turned, it merits a particular discussion."

tions," or the dark designs "to reduce [the colonies] under absolute despotism" referred to in the Declaration of Independence.[23]

The ablest representative of the second generation of American historians who dealt with the Revolution was George Bancroft. Bancroft allowed his Jacksonian principles to color his interpretation. In him, we find an openly polemical tone. To Bancroft the era of the Revolution was the golden age, the time of giants, the opening act of the extraordinary drama of American democracy. There is thus in his mammoth history much of what appears to modern eyes as rhetorical embellishment. Where his predecessors had been content to describe the events they had observed, Bancroft was an unconscious mythmaker. . . .

History, for Bancroft, was the working of Divine Wisdom, and God's eternal principles were discoverable through its study. History traced "the vestiges of moral law through the practice of the nations in every age . . . and confirms by induction the intuitions of reason."[24] Seen in this light, the Revolution appeared as part of God's plan: it was intended for the edification of man and the improvement of society; it ushered in a new and brighter age of human progress.

What in earlier histories had been presented as essentially a misunderstanding between two power systems became, by Bancroft's interpretation, a conscious plan to subvert liberty. George III, in the perspective of a triumphant Whig tradition, was a relentless authoritarian with a "hatred of reform, and an antipathy to philosophical freedom and to popular power."[25] Under his leadership, "Great Britain, allured by a phantom of absolute authority over the colonies, made war on human freedom." If the British Parliament

[23] Some of Ramsay's contemporaries who, like the Carolinian, wrote Revolutionary history of unusual breadth and balance are William Gordon, *History of the Rise, Progress and Establishment of the Independence of the United States of America . . .* (London, 1788); Charles Stedman, *History of the American War* (London, 1794); John Marshall, *Life of George Washington,* 5 vols. (Philadelphia, 1804–07). At the end of the nineteenth century, Orin Grant Libby attacked Gordon and Ramsay as plagiarists, discrediting them as reliable sources on the Revolution: "A Critical Examination of William Gordon's History of the American Revolution," American Historical Association, *Annual Report, 1899* (Washington, 1900), I, 367–388; and "Ramsay as a Plagiarist," *American Historical Review,* VII (1901–02), 697–703. See also William A. Foran, "John Marshall as a Historian," *ibid.,* XLIII (1937–38), 51–64; R. Kent Newmyer, "Charles Stedman's *History of the American War,*" *ibid.,* LXIII (1957–58), 924–934.

[24] George Bancroft, *History of the United States* (Boston, 1876), V, 70.

[25] *Ibid.,* IV, 197–198.

had succeeded "in establishing by force of arms its 'boundless' authority over America," where would "humanity find an asylum?"[26] The struggle was thus a contest between progress and reaction for the soul of man. The Revolution sounded the death knell of "the ages of servitude and inequality," and rang in "those of equality and brotherhood." America's feet were, thereby, set on a "never-ending career of reform and progress."[27]

If Bancroft fixed the image of a wicked king that was to have a long life in American historiography, his political ideals led him into what became in time another classic error. His own free-trade sentiments induced him to count the Acts of Trade and Navigation, some of which dated from the middle of the seventeenth century, as one of the principal causes of the revolutionary crisis. As a good Democrat and a low-tariff man, he concluded that mercantilism, as expressed in Parliamentary statutes, must have been a bitter grievance to the American colonists. This interpretation became, in the years that followed, one of the most persistently stated "causes" of the Revolution. . . .

By the turn of the century the ideals of "scientific" history had penetrated the historical profession. Nurtured in the German seminars of Leopold von Ranke and Barthold Niebuhr, the champions of the new history cast a cold eye on the patriotic effusions of a Bancroft. The task of the historian was to recount with dispassionate objectivity "what had happened," ruthlessly suppressing personal prejudices and loyalties wherever possible, leaving the facts to speak for themselves.

Sydney George Fisher's *The Struggle for American Independence* (1908) was the first detailed treatment of the Revolution since Bancroft's history and the first, as Fisher was at some pains to make clear, written under the new scholarly dispensation. Previous historians, he wrote, had never made "any attempt to describe, from the original records, England's exact position with regard to ourselves at the outbreak of the Revolution, except the usual assumption that the Tory statesmen who were in power were either ignorantly stupid, and blind to their own interests, or desperately corrupt and wicked, and that the Whig minority were angels of light who would

[26] *Ibid.*, IV, 308.
[27] *Ibid.*, IV, 311, 308.

have saved the colonies for the British empire."[28] Fisher directed his fire primarily at Bancroft and John Fiske, but such a Rhadamanthine judgment was certainly not fair to Bancroft and missed the mark entirely with the first generation of revolutionary historians.

In attempting to correct what he considered the anti-British prejudices of his predecessors, Fisher stressed the "mildness" of Great Britain and her "spirit of concilliation." "Modern readers of history," he wrote, knew nothing of "the conciliatory measures Great Britain adopted" or "her gentle and mild efforts to persuade us to remain in the empire."[29] The Revolution was "not a contest between a dragon and a fairy," not "a mere accidental mistake on the part of England" resulting in a war brought on "by the king alone against the wishes of the English people." It was, on the contrary, a path "entered upon by the English nation as deliberately and intelligently as any other imperial expansion they have undertaken and upon principles which for them are still unchangeable."[30]

In explaining the Revolution, Fisher's emphasis was primarily on the character of colonial life which had shaped the New World settlers and in so doing had made independence inevitable. He thus shifted his focus from the immediate causes, such as the Stamp Act, to underlying changes in outlook and ideology. If England was to be exonerated, it was necessary to neutralize the moral and political conflict and to stress, in place of the traditionally offered explanations of the revolutionary crisis, the "*characterological* divergence" that had developed between England and her colonies. Forces thus take the place of issues. The action of individuals is of little significance, except as a response to these forces, and it is obviously pointless to try to apportion praise or blame for events which move onward, ineluctable and impersonal as the slow passage of a glacier.[31]

While the story of the Revolution lost, by such treatment, much of the drama with which Bancroft had invested it, and perhaps more important, lost its didactic quality—its ability to teach patriotism to the young by inspiring examples—it gained a greater breadth, a wider tolerance, and an insight into the fact that "forces" did indeed exert great influence upon the behavior of individuals and the course

28 Sydney George Fisher, *The Struggle for American Independence* (Philadelphia, 1908), I, vii.
29 *Ibid.*
30 *Ibid.*, I, xiii.
31 *Ibid.*, I. 104.

of history. If the individual thereby lost in dignity and significance, the recapturing of a deeper awareness of the complexity of historical events was partial compensation. . . .

What had been implicit in Fisher—that the underlying causes of the Revolution were primarily economic—was boldly stated by a young historian, Arthur M. Schlesinger, in *The Colonial Merchants and the American Revolution, 1763–1776,* where he spelled out in impressive detail his thesis that the colonial merchants brought on the revolutionary crisis, albeit unwittingly. Two rival systems of capitalist enterprise, England's and America's, developed inevitable conflicts of interest which precipitated the war for independence. Schlesinger stated this thesis boldly in 1919 in an article summarizing his views on the causes of the Revolution. "In the first years of the republic," he noted, "the tendency of the popular histories and text-books was to dwell almost exclusively upon the spectacular developments of the struggle and to dramatize the heroism of the patriots."[32] The real explanation for independence, however, was to be found in "the clashing of economic interests and the interplay of mutual prejudices, opposing ideals and personal antagonisms—whether in England or America." These "made inevitable in 1776 what was unthinkable in 1760. . . ."[33]

His conclusions were that the merchants, hit in the pocketbook by the tightening of England's imperial policy, promoted the early agitation against Great Britain. It was they who encouraged the radicals' leaders to whip up mobs of angry patriots. Their purpose was to exert, thereby, countervailing pressure against their English rivals and thus win relief from measures which placed their trade under crippling inhibitions. "As a class they [the merchants] entertained neither earlier nor later the idea of independence, for withdrawal from the British empire meant for them the loss of vital business advantages. . . ."[34]

At each stage of the colonial resistance, the merchants stood in the background manipulating the Sons of Liberty. The rhetoric of

[32] Arthur M. Schlesinger, "The American Revolution Reconsidered," *Political Science Quarterly,* XXXIV (1919), 61. Schlesinger's *The Colonial Merchants and the American Revolution, 1763–1776* (New York, 1917), like Charles A. Beard's *An Economic Interpretation of the Constitution of the United States* (New York, 1913), made historians aware of the importance of economic factors in the Revolutionary era.
[33] Schlesinger, "The American Revolution Reconsidered," p. 63.
[34] *Ibid.,* p. 66.

the radical leaders meant nothing to them; their concern was with profits not principles. But they had calculated without the ambitions of patriot champions and the ardor of the people. The agitation against Great Britain gathered a momentum that swept it onward with a force of its own. Too late the merchants realized that they had summoned up a whirlwind they could not ride. They found it impossible "to reassert their earlier control and to stop a movement that had lost all significance for hard-headed men of business."[35]

The talk of "no taxation without representation," the appeals to Magna Charta, the heated debate over the authority of Parliament—all this was simply flotsam which showed where deeper currents were flowing. "The popular view of the Revolution as a great forensic controversy over abstract governmental rights," Schlesinger wrote, "will not bear close scrutiny."[36]

In a historiography which disclaimed heroes and villains in the name of scientific objectivity, heroes and villains nonetheless crept in. To Schlesinger, as a liberal idealist, those without ideals, that is, the colonial merchants, were the villains. It was not coincidence that the colonial merchants appeared in Schlesinger's book as narrow, self-seeking men, who, in their blind devotion to pounds and shillings, rent the fabric of the British Empire, at the same time that modern-day American captains of industry were testifying before Congressional committees as to their ruthless repression of labor and their callous exploitation of the public. Even George III appears in his familiar role of wicked tyrant. With all his professions of scientific objectivity, Schlesinger, like Bancroft, charges the king with trying to convert the British government to "a personal autocracy."

Having identified the villains, we do not need to look far for the heroes. They are the "proletarian element," the workers in the colonial towns, who were "for the most part unenfranchised," and the sturdy frontiersmen, who "brought to the controversy a moral conviction and bold philosophy which gave great impetus to the agitation for independence"—presumably more moral conviction than could be found among the self-interested elite of the seacoast towns. In Schlesinger's work, tidewater radicals and back-country farmers march side by side toward independence. Exploited by the cunning merchants, they finally seize control and the revolutionary initiative

[35] *Ibid.,* p. 71.
[36] *Ibid.,* pp. 76–77.

passes "into the hands of the democratic mechanic class," in other words—the workers.

In this formula of Schlesinger's we have a significant union between Turner's frontier thesis, which credited the frontier with all that was liberal, progressive, and uniquely American, and the twentieth-century liberals' idealization of the industrial worker whose spiritual ancestor they perceived in the mechanic class of colonial towns. Here was a "modern" analysis of the causes of the Revolution which for the first time stated the case explicitly for an "economic interpretation," which swept away the argument from "principle," which freed Great Britain from any taint, and which, above all, carried the imprimatur of "scientific" history, self-stamped to be sure, but hardly the less impressive for that.

Arthur Schlesinger's liberal formulary was carried further by Claude Van Tyne in his book, *The Causes of the War of Independence,* published in 1922. Like Schlesinger, Van Tyne saw himself as one of a company of courageous historians, guided by scientific principles and bent on presenting the facts about the Revolution to a people long misled by the distorted accounts of men who put patriotism ahead of the search for objective truth. . . .

[In] Van Tyne's history . . . we find a strong emphasis on the frontier thesis adapted from Turner. For on the frontier "the English race" experienced "a rebirth, the first of these destined to occur perennially as the race marched westward toward the setting sun."[37] In the raw environment of a new continent, "townbred men became denizens of the wilds." Van Tyne accepted without question Schlesinger's picture of the merchants guiding the early stages of colonial resistance and then dropping out, as "radicals everywhere, from Samuel Adams at the North to Christopher Gadsden in the South, seized the moment of high feeling to carry America beyond the point where there could be any going back." The conflict became a class struggle. In Massachusetts as in Pennsylvania "the masses [were] pitted against the great merchants." "Thus, in 1776, came the climax in the struggle between rich and poor, East and West, those with a vote and those who were voteless, between privilege and the welfare of the common man."[38]

The terms have shifted but we find, nonetheless, familiar echoes

37 Van Tyne, *The Causes of the War of Independence* (Boston, 1922), p. 15.
38 *Ibid.,* pp. 416, 421, 425.

of Bancroft in Van Tyne's insistence that the Revolution was "one of the glories of British history," since the colonists, as heirs of all the political accomplishments of England, were simply carrying forward the fight for democracy and political liberty which "England had fostered beyond any other country of the world."[39] And, as in Bancroft, we find an unscrupulous George III drawing on "an inexhaustible treasure of corruption" to obliterate the liberties of the colonists, despite the warnings of Burke, Pitt, Fox, and Camden. The cast has changed somewhat but the final curtain rings down on the same stirring patriotic note.

Two years aften Van Tyne's book appeared, Charles McLean Andrews surveyed *The Colonial Background of the American Revolution* in a notable collection of essays. Andrews accepted what had by now become the general view of the revolutionary crisis: that the basis of the dispute lay in a conflict of interests. The question of colonial rights was "a subject of more or less legal and metaphysical speculation. . . . There is nothing to show," he wrote, "that the somewhat precise and finely spun reasoning of these intellectual leaders had any marked influence on the popular mind."[40] Andrews, like Van Tyne, emphasized the role of the frontier which encouraged individualism and independence, but the conflict remained in its broader outlines a struggle over trade and commerce. We find in Andrews, it must be said, in addition to the residues of many earlier interpretations, a tentativeness and absence of the doctrinaire.

Under the surface of historical investigation the economic interpretation of history had been moving like a subterranean current, influencing individuals in many areas of American history. It was discernible in Arthur Schlesinger's study of the colonial merchants, and in the works of a number of his contemporaries. As applied to the Revolution, however, it was persistently modified in the works we have been concerned with by the naturalistic and romantic gloss of the frontier thesis, and by the fact that even skeptical historians of the scientific school found it extremely difficult to disengage themselves from the mythic elements of the Revolution. However resolutely they started out demolishing, as they boasted, the biased and

[39] *Ibid.*, p. 478.
[40] Charles McLean Andrews, *The Colonial Background of the American Revolution* (New Haven, 1924), p. 135.

partisan accounts of earlier historians, they all ended up sounding remarkably like George Bancroft.

In 1954, Lawrence Henry Gipson's *The Coming of the Revolution, 1763–1775,* was published in *The New American Nation Series. . . .* It is Gipson's argument "that the causes of the Revolution stem first from the effort of the British government, faced with vast territorial acquisitions in North America at the end of the Great War for Empire, along with an unprecedented war debt, to organize a more efficient administration on that continent and to make the colonies contribute directly to the support of the enlarged Empire. . . . Secondly, the causes of the breach can be traced to the radically altered situation of the colonies after 1760, by which date they were at long last relieved of the intense pressure previously exerted along their borders by hostile nations."[41] The heart of the issue was a clash of "interests."

From the time of Sydney George Fisher to that of Lawrence Gipson an interpretation of the causes of the American Revolution had slowly taken form. By the early 1950s its outlines seemed, generally speaking, clear and stable and satisfyingly impersonal. The Revolution was the outcome of forces rather than "the result of the actions of wicked men—neither of the King or Lord North, on the one hand, nor of American radicals on the other." The forces were primarily economic and social—the clash between rival systems of mercantilism and the differentiation of the colonists from citizens of the mother country through the influence of an agricultural frontier. The problem of dealing with human motivations, decisions, aspirations, and illusions was thus solved by submerging them in the larger currents of history.[42]

41 Lawrence Henry Gipson, *The Coming of the Revolution, 1763–1775,* in *The New American Nation Series,* ed. Henry Steele Commager and Richard B. Morris (New York, 1954), pp. ix, xii.

42 Nineteenth-century historians who dealt with the Revolution such as George Washington Greene, *Historical View of the American Revolution* (Cambridge, 1876), and John Fiske, *The American Revolution* (Cambridge, 1896), wrote in the tradition of George Bancroft. For the twentieth century, no mention has been made of John C. Miller's excellent narrative history, *The Origins of the American Revolution* (Boston, 1943), because it failed to cast new light on the causes of the Revolution. Max Savelle's *Seeds of Liberty: The Genesis of the American Mind* (New York, 1948), in my view, simply applies a cultural-social veneer to older interpretations. Limitations of space have also compelled me to omit consideration of the influence of Sir Lewis Namier and his revisionist school. The Namierists, by rehabilitating

Onto this settled and orderly scene burst Edmund and Helen Morgan's *The Stamp Act Crisis: Prologue to Revolution.*[43] Their argument, like that of David Ramsay 165 years earlier, hinged on the decisive character of the Stamp Act and threatened at once to undermine the whole painstaking, if jerry-built, structure of interpretation that had been erected by a dozen twentieth-century historians. The Morgans reminded their readers that the Stamp Act aroused an instant and entirely unexpected wave of protest and of determined resistance in the colonies—resistance which could have led to revolution. Never again were the colonists to be so united in opposition to a British measure. The actual cost of the stamp tax to the colonists would have been relatively light. In most places it was never even put into effect so that the colonists had no opportunity to experience it as a material hardship. The opposition was thus almost entirely on the grounds of abstract principle—the constitutional principle of no taxation without representation.

Moreover, the leaders who came forward at the time of the act to direct colonial resistance were the individuals who in most instances carried through to the Revolution and beyond. Of the twenty-six members of the Stamp Act Congress, "only two . . . are known to have become loyalists in 1776. . . . Others who took no part in the congress but led the resistance to the Stamp Act within their own colonies were likewise conspicuous in the revolutionary movement. It seems particularly significant that the parties which brought on the revolution in the two leading colonies, Massachusetts and Virginia, gained their ascendancy at the time of the Stamp Act."[44]

But even more important than the appearance, at the very outset of the controversy, of able and aggressive leaders who continued to lead was "the emergence . . . of well-defined constitutional principles." The colonial assemblies in 1765 "laid down the line on which Americans stood until they cut their connections with England. Consistently from 1765 to 1776 they denied the authority of Parliament to tax them externally or internally; consistently they affirmed their

George III, reinforced the view of the Revolution as a clash of "forces" or "interests." See Morgan, "American Revolution" for an excellent discussion of the Namier position and some effective counterarguments.

[43] Edmund S. Morgan and Helen M. Morgan, *The Stamp Act Crisis: Prologue to Revolution* (Chapel Hill, 1953).

[44] *Ibid.*, p. 293.

willingness to submit to whatever legislation Parliament should enact for the supervision of the empire as a whole."[45]

In the Morgans' view far too much had been made of the shifts in the colonial position in regard to the powers of Parliament. Historians of the Schlesinger school had pointed to these shifts—from no power to impose internal taxes, to no external taxes for revenue, to no internal or external taxes of any kind, to no right to legislate for the colonies in any case whatever—as an indication that material self-interest rather than principle motivated the colonial actions. On the contrary, the Morgans argued, the colonists did not advance from one position to another under the pressure of Parliamentary enactments. In actual fact the Stamp Act brought at once a denial of the right of Parliament to tax the colonies "without representation." All official statements such as the resolves of the Stamp Act Congress asserted this principle, conceding nothing but a willingness to acquiesce in the Acts of Trade and Navigation in force in 1763. Moreover, a number of colonial leaders at the time of the Stamp Act crisis or soon afterwards came to the conclusion that Parliament had no constitutional authority to legislate for the colonies. But understanding that to press such a view would rouse the deepest suspicions of Parliament and its supporters and alarm all colonial moderates, they kept their peace.

Like Ramsay, the Morgans express the conviction that the growing conflict "was not irretrievable, but that to retrieve it would have required an understanding on each side of the exact limits of the other's claims." While "the English thought that they saw the Americans inching their way toward independence, the Americans thought that they saw a sinister party in England seeking by gradual degree to enslave them."[46] So the crisis moved to its denouement.

If the Morgans' argument in its main outlines is granted, it of course modifies those interpretations which see the Revolution as the more or less inevitable result of a slow process of economic, social, cultural, and political differentiation between the colonies and the mother country. The Schlesinger thesis that the merchants used the radical leaders and the mobs simply to gain redress of specific grievances becomes likewise untenable, and the frontier

[45] *Ibid.*, p. 295.
[46] *Ibid.*, pp. 291, 290.

thesis loses much of its force. The Morgans' position, in addition, diminishes the importance of class conflict as an element in the revolutionary crisis. While class and sectional frictions undoubtedly existed in some of the colonies, they did not become sharply defined until the later years of the war and the postwar period, and they were, in no sense, determinants in the development of the revolutionary crisis.

In the Morgans' book we have come, in full circle, back to the position of Ramsay and the historians of the first generation. After a century and a half of progress in historical scholarship, in research techniques, in tools and methods, we have found our way to the interpretation held, substantially, by those historians who themselves participated in, or lived through the era of, the Revolution. If it is undoubtedly true that, as Morgan suggests, "George Bancroft may not have been so far from the mark as we have often assumed," it is equally true that Ramsay was closer still. . . .

In justice to later historians, it should, of course, be pointed out that the historian's task in interpreting the American Revolution has been more than ordinarily difficult. The America that emerged from the War of Independence was a nation without prehistory in the traditional sense. Having won their independence, the rather loosely knit United States had to find myths and symbols to reinforce and give substance to that national unity which for the first eighty years was so precariously maintained. Myths had, perforce, to be created around the moment of birth. What Homer and the siege of Troy had been to the Greek states of the Periclean Age, George Washington and the campaigns of the Revolution were to nineteenth-century Americans. What Romulus and Remus and the Twelve Tables of the Law had been for Imperial Rome, the Founding Fathers and the Federal Constitution were for a United States searching in the midst of extraordinary social and economic transformations for unifying symbols.

The American Revolution has, thus, been encrusted with mythic elements and residues which have vastly complicated the task of the historian who wishes to state the truth of the events that took place in that era. The historian, being human and ineluctably partaking of the ideals and values of his own day, has been under the strongest pressure to make the events of the Revolution conform to the particular time spirit of which he himself has been a self-conscious and articulate representative. He has been, therefore, not simply the enemy of the myths, as he would like to see himself, but quite as often the victim, in the sense that he has seldom escaped the temptation to make the Revolution prove something about his own society or about the society which he wishes to see evolve in the future. . . .

Whatever imperfections there may be in Ramsay's facts (and his detractors have not indeed argued that they were at fault but that, in a number of instances, they were taken from the *Annual Register*), it was a poor bargain to get in the place of his work histories which were factually impeccable but which lost their grip on the essential meaning of the revolutionary experience.

On the basis of this brief survey of interpretations of the Revolution it would be very difficult to demonstrate clear and consistent progress in the interpretation of historical events primarily as the result of the longer time-perspectives of successive historians dealing with them. Nor, again, will we find that the opening up of new archives and the discovery of new documents (beyond a certain point, of course) result in notably improved or more acceptable (in any final sense) interpretations.[47]

Indeed, in regard to the Revolution, the most extreme distortions appeared in the work of those historians who made the loudest claims to be "scientific" in their approach. Perhaps these men, believing implicitly in the authority of the data, the "facts" as disclosed by their researches, have been less sensitive to the nature and extent of their own prejudices. The older "prescientific" historians realized that there was no way of evading judgments and were thus quite conscious of the distortion produced by their own personal loyalties and allegiances. The scientific historian, comforted by the illusion of a vast amount of supporting data, might (and obviously in many instances did) have his own predispositions come upon him disguised as the objective results of research. . . .

The story of successive interpretations of the American Revolution seems then to bear this moral: There is, or has been so far, no

[47] Herbert Butterfield in an essay entitled, "The Reconstruction of an Historical Episode; the History of an Inquiry into the Origins of the Seven Years' War," *Man on His Past* (Cambridge, Eng., 1955), pp. 143–167, has shown how Leopold von Ranke, writing not many years after that war, gave a better analysis of its causes than those made with a longer perspective in time and far greater access to documentary materials.

panacea (like scientific method) which can perform for the historian the functions of judgment and analysis. Whatever the historian gains in time-perspective or new materials or specialized monographs, he may well lose through distortions that are the result of his own *Zeitgeist.* He thus fails to approach in any orderly, systematic way the truth in the form of some final, or often, some better interpretation or understanding of the events he is concerned with. We would do well, therefore, to show more respect for the best contemporary history and abandon some of those professional pieties with which we have solaced ourselves in the past. In the struggle for historical understanding there are no final triumphs. Insights once gained will not automatically sustain themselves but must be rediscovered time and again. We cannot solve problems of historical interpretation and then, having reduced the solutions to formulas, pass on to new problems, for the "solved" problems are remarkably full of life, tenacious and enduring.

This being the case, the responsibility is clearly placed where it belongs—on the individual historian. He cannot take refuge from judgments in techniques. His judgments, on the other hand, will be no better than his own capacity for wise insight and human understanding. . . .

Gordon S. Wood

RHETORIC AND REALITY IN THE AMERICAN REVOLUTION

Professor Wood taught history at the University of Michigan and at Harvard before going to Brown University in 1969. In addition to The Creation of the American Republic, 1776–1787 *(1969) and* The Rising Glory of America, 1760–1870 *(1971), he has written a monograph on* Representation in the American Revolution *(1969). In the selection which follows, assessing the way historians have analyzed the problems surveyed in this volume since the beginning of historical writing on the subject, he shows how writers even down to the present day have not merely taken sides on academic, historiographical issues, but, how in so doing, they have become partisans on one side or another of those cleavages which divided revolutionists, loyalists, and Englishmen participating in the events themselves.*

Any intellectually satisfying explanation of the Revolution must encompass the Tory perspective as well as the Whig, for if we are compelled to take sides and choose between opposing motives—unconscious or avowed, passion or principle, greed or liberty—we will be endlessly caught up in the polemics of the participants themselves. We must, in other words, eventually dissolve the distinction between conscious and unconscious motives, between the revolutionaries' stated intentions and their supposedly hidden needs and desires, a dissolution that involves somehow relating beliefs and ideas to the social world in which they operate. If we are to understand the causes of the Revolution we must therefore ultimately transcend this problem of motivation. But this we can never do as long as we attempt to explain the Revolution mainly in terms of the intentions of the participants. It is not that men's motives are unimportant; they indeed make events, including revolutions. But the purposes of men, especially in a revolution, are so numerous, so varied, and so contradictory that their complex interaction produces results that no one intended or could even foresee. It is this interaction and these results that recent historians are referring to when they speak so disparagingly of those "underlying determinants" and "impersonal and inexorable forces" bringing on the Revolution. His-

Reprinted by permission of the author from *William and Mary Quarterly,* 3d ser. 23 (January, 1966): 3–32. Abridged.

torical explanation which does not account for these "forces," which, in other words, relies simply on understanding the conscious intentions of the actors, will thus be limited. This preoccupation with men's purposes was what restricted the perspectives of the contemporaneous Whig and Tory interpretations; and it is still the weakness of the neo-Whig histories, and indeed of any interpretation which attempts to explain the events of the Revolution by discovering the calculations from which individuals supposed themselves to have acted.

No explanation of the American Revolution in terms of the intentions and designs of particular individuals could have been more crudely put than that offered by the revolutionaries themselves. American Whigs, like men of the eighteenth century generally, were fascinated with what seemed to the age to be the newly appreciated problem of human motivation and causation in the affairs of the world. In the decade before independence the Americans sought endlessly to discover the supposed calculations and purposes of individuals or groups that lay behind the otherwise incomprehensible rush of events. More than anything else perhaps, it was this obsession with motives that led to the prevalence in the eighteenth century of beliefs in conspiracies to account for the confusing happenings in which men found themselves caught up. Bailyn has suggested that this common fear of conspiracy was "deeply rooted in the political awareness of eighteenth-century Britons, involved in the very structure of their political life"; it "reflected so clearly the realities of life in an age in which monarchical autocracy flourished, [and] in which the stability and freedom of England's 'mixed' constitution was a recent and remarkable achievement."[1] Yet it might also be argued that the tendency to see conspiracy behind what happened reflected as well the very enlightenment of the age. To attribute events to the designs and purposes of human agents seemed after all to be an enlightened advance over older beliefs in blind chance, providence, or God's interventions. It was rational and scientific, a product of both the popularization of politics and the secularization of knowledge. It was obvious to Americans that the series of events in the years after 1763, those "unheard of intolerable calamities, spring not of the dust, come not causeless." "Ought not

[1] Bailyn, *Revolutionary Pamphlets,* I, 87, ix.

the PEOPLE therefore," asked John Dickinson, "to watch? to observe facts? to search into causes? to investigate designs?"[2] And these causes and designs could be traced to individuals in high places, to ministers, to royal governors, and their lackeys. The belief in conspiracy grew naturally out of the enlightened need to find the human purposes behind the multitude of phenomena, to find the causes for what happened in the social world just as the natural scientist was discovering the causes for what happened in the physical world.[3] It was a necessary consequence of the search for connections and patterns in events. The various acts of the British government, the Americans knew, should not be "regarded according to the simple force of each, but as parts of a system of oppression."[4] The Whigs' intense search for the human purposes behind events was in fact an example of the beginnings of modern history.

In attempting to rebut those interpretations disparaging the colonists' cause, the present neo-Whig historians have been drawn into writing as partisans of the revolutionaries. And they have thus found themselves entangled in the same kind of explanation used by the original antagonists, an explanation, despite obvious refinements, still involved with the discovery of motives and its corollary, the assessing of a personal sort of responsibility for what happened. While most of the neo-Whig historians have not gone so far as to

[2] [Moses Mather], *America's Appeal to the Impartial World . . .* (Hartford, 1775), 59; [John Dickinson], *Letters from a Farmer in Pennsylvania to the Inhabitants of the British Colonies* (1768), in Paul L. Ford, ed., *The Life and Writings of John Dickinson* (Historical Society of Pennsylvania, *Memoirs,* XIV [Philadelphia, 1895]), II, 348. Dickinson hinged his entire argument on the ability of the Americans to decipher the "intention" of parliamentary legislation, whether for revenue or for commercial regulation. *Ibid.,* 348, 364.

[3] See Herbert Davis, "The Augustan Conception of History," in J. A. Mazzeo, ed., *Reason and the Imagination: Studies in the History of Ideas, 1600–1800* (New York, 1962), 226–228; W. H. Greenleaf, *Order, Empiricism and Politics: Two Traditions of English Political Thought, 1500–1700* (New York, 1964), 166; R. N. Stromberg, "History in the Eighteenth Century," *Journal of the History of Ideas,* XII (1951), 300. It was against this "dominant characteristic of the historical thought of the age," this "tendency to explain events in terms of conscious action by individuals," that the brilliant group of Scottish social scientists writing at the end of the eighteenth century directed much of their work. Duncan Forbes, "'Scientific' Whiggism: Adam Smith and John Millar," *Cambridge Journal,* VII (1954), 651, 653–654. While we have had recently several good studies of historical thinking in seventeenth-century England, virtually nothing has been done on the eighteenth century. See, however, J. G. A. Pocock, "Burke and the Ancient Constitution—A Problem in the History of Ideas," *The Historical Journal,* III (1960), 125–143; and Stow Persons, "The Cyclical Theory of History in Eighteenth Century America," *American Quarterly,* VI (1954), 147–163.

[4] [Dickinson], *Letters from a Farmer,* in Ford, ed., *Writings of Dickinson*, 388.

FIGURE 8. "The Bostonians paying the exciseman; or, tarring and feathering." A London cartoon showing what happened to John Malcomb, a Tory exciseman who collected the Tea Tax in Boston in 1774. (*Library of Congress*)

see conspiracy in British actions (although some have come close),[5] they have tended to point up the blundering and stupidity of British officials in contrast to "the breadth of vision" that moved the Americans. If George III was in a position of central responsibility in the British government, as English historians have recently said, then, according to Edmund S. Morgan, "he must bear most of the praise or blame for the series of measures that alienated and lost the colonies, and it is hard to see how there can be much praise." By seeking "to define issues, fix responsibilities," and thereby to shift the "burden of proof" onto those who say the Americans were narrow and selfish and the empire was basically just and beneficent, the neo-Whigs have attempted to redress what they felt was an unfair neo-Tory bias of previous explanations of the Revolution;[6] they have not, however, challenged the terms of the argument. They are still obsessed with why men said they acted and with who was right and who was wrong. Viewing the history of the Revolution in this judicatory manner has therefore restricted the issues over which historians have disagreed to those of motivation and responsibility, the very issues with which the participants themselves were concerned.

The neo-Whig "conviction that the colonists' attachment to principle was genuine"[7] has undoubtedly been refreshing, and indeed necessary, given the Tory slant of earlier twentieth-century interpretations. It now seems clearer that the Progressive historians, with their naive and crude reflex conception of human behavior, had too long treated the ideas of the Revolution superficially if not superciliously. Psychologists and sociologists are now willing to grant a more determining role to beliefs, particularly in revolutionary situations. It is now accepted that men act not simply in response to some kind of objective reality but to the meaning they give to that reality. Since men's beliefs are as much a part of the given stimuli as the objective environment, the beliefs must be understood and taken seriously if men's behavior is to be fully explained. The American revolutionary ideas were more than cooked up pieces of

5 Bailyn has noted that Oliver M. Dickerson, in chap. 7 of his *The Navigation Acts and the American Revolution* (Philadelphia, 1951), "adopts wholesale the contemporary Whig interpretation of the Revolution as the result of a conspiracy of 'King's Friends.' " Bailyn, *Revolutionary Pamphlets,* I, 724.

6 Morgan, "Revisions in Need of Revising," 7, 13, 8; Greene, "Flight From Determinism," 237.

7 Edmund S. Morgan, *The Birth of the Republic, 1763–89* (Chicago, 1959), 51.

thought served by an aggressive and interested minority to a gullible and unsuspecting populace. The concept of propaganda permitted the Progressive historians to account for the presence of ideas but it prevented them from recognizing ideas as an important determinant of the Americans' behavior. The weight attributed to ideas and constitutional principles by the neo-Whig historians was thus an essential corrective to the propagandist studies.

Yet in its laudable effort to resurrect the importance of ideas in historical explanation much of the writing of the neo-Whigs has tended to return to the simple nineteenth-century intellectualist assumption that history is the consequence of a rational calculation of ends and means, that what happened was what was consciously desired and planned. By supposing "that individual actions and immediate issues are more important than underlying determinants in explaining particular events," by emphasizing conscious and articulated motives, the neo-Whig historians have selected and presented that evidence which is most directly and clearly expressive of the intentions of the Whigs, that is, the most well defined, the most constitutional, the most reasonable of the Whig beliefs, those found in their public documents, their several declarations of grievances and causes. It is not surprising that for the neo-Whigs the history of the American Revolution should be more than anything else "the history of the Americans' search for principles."[8] Not only, then, did nothing in the Americans' economic and social structure really determine their behavior, but the colonists in fact acted from the most rational and calculated of motives: they fought, as they said they would, simply to defend their ancient liberties against British provocation.

By implying that certain declared rational purposes are by themselves an adequate explanation for the Americans' revolt, in other words that the Revolution was really nothing more than a contest over constitutional principles, the neo-Whig historians have not only threatened to deny what we have learned of human psychology in the twentieth century, but they have also in fact failed to exploit fully the terms of their own idealist approach by not taking into account all of what the Americans believed and said. Whatever the deficiencies and misunderstandings of the role of ideas in human behavior present

[8] Greene, "Flight From Determinism," 258; Morgan, *Birth of the Republic*, 3.

in the propagandist studies of the 1930s, these studies did for the first time attempt to deal with the entirety and complexity of American revolutionary thought—to explain not only all the well-reasoned notions of law and liberty that were so familiar but, more important, all the irrational and hysterical beliefs that had been so long neglected. Indeed, it was the patent absurdity and implausibility of much of what the Americans said that lent credence and persuasiveness to their mistrustful approach to the ideas. Once this exaggerated and fanatical rhetoric was uncovered by the Progressive historians, it should not have subsequently been ignored—no matter how much it may have impugned the reasonableness of the American response. No widely expressed ideas can be dismissed out of hand by the historian.

In his recent analysis of revolutionary thinking Bernard Bailyn has avoided the neo-Whig tendency to distort the historical reconstruction of the American mind. By comprehending "the assumptions, beliefs, and ideas that lay behind the manifest events of the time," Bailyn has attempted to get inside the Whigs' mind, and to experience vicariously all of what they thought and felt, both their rational constitutional beliefs and their hysterical and emotional ideas as well. The inflammatory phrases, "slavery," "corruption," "conspiracy," that most historians had either ignored or readily dismissed as propaganda, took on a new significance for Bailyn. He came "to suspect that they meant something very real to both the writers and their readers: that there were real fears, real anxieties, a sense of real danger behind these phrases, and not merely the desire to influence by rhetoric and propaganda the inert minds of an otherwise passive populace."[9] No part of American thinking, Bailyn suggests—not the widespread belief in a ministerial conspiracy, not the hostile and vicious indictments of individuals, not the fear of corruption and the hope for regeneration, not any of the violent seemingly absurd distortions and falsifications of what we now believe to be true, in short, none of the frenzied rhetoric—can be safely ignored by the historian seeking to understand the causes of the Revolution.

Bailyn's study, however, represents something other than a more complete and uncorrupted version of the common idealist interpretations of the Revolution. By viewing from the "interior" the revolu-

[9] Bailyn, *Revolutionary Pamphlets,* I, vii, ix.

tionary pamphlets, which were "to an unusual degree, *explanatory*," revealing "not merely positions taken but the reasons why positions were taken," Bailyn like any idealist historian has sought to discover the motives the participants themselves gave for their actions, to reenact their thinking at crucial moments, and thereby to recapture some of the "unpredictable reality" of the Revolution.[10] But for Bailyn the very unpredictability of the reality he has disclosed has undermined the idealist obsession with explaining why, in the participants' own estimation, they acted as they did. Ideas emerge as more than explanatory devices, as more than indicators of motives. They become as well objects for analysis in and for themselves, historical events in their own right to be treated as other historical events are treated. Although Bailyn has examined the revolutionary ideas subjectively from the inside, he has also analyzed them objectively from the outside. Thus, in addition to a contemporary Whig perspective, he presents us with a retrospective view of the ideas—their complexity, their development, and their consequences—that the actual participants did not have. In effect his essay represents what has been called "a Namierism of the history of ideas,"[11] a structural analysis of thought that suggests a conclusion about the movement of history not very different from Sir Lewis Namier's, where history becomes something "started in ridiculous beginnings, while small men did things both infinitely smaller and infinitely greater than they knew."[12]

In his *England in the Age of the American Revolution* Namier attacked the Whig tendency to overrate "the importance of the conscious will and purpose in individuals." Above all he urged us "to ascertain and recognize the deeper irrelevancies and incoherence of human actions, which are not so much directed by reason, as invested by it *ex post facto* with the appearances of logic and rationality," to discover the unpredictable reality, where men's motives and intentions were lost in the accumulation and momentum of interacting events. The whole force of Namier's approach tended to squeeze the intellectual content out of what men did. Ideas setting

[10] *Ibid.,* vii, viii, 17.

[11] J. G. A. Pocock, "Machiavelli, Harrington, and English Political Ideologies in the Eighteenth Century," *Wm. and Mary Qtly.,* 3d Ser., XXII (1965), 550.

[12] Sir Lewis Namier, *England in the Age of the American Revolution,* 2d ed. (London, 1961), 131.

forth principles and purposes for action, said Namier, did not count for much in the movement of history.[13]

In his study of the revolutionary ideas Bailyn has come to an opposite conclusion: ideas counted for a great deal, not only being responsible for the Revolution but also for transforming the character of American society. Yet in his hands ideas lose that static quality they have commonly had for the Whig historians, the simple statements of intention that so exasperated Namier. For Bailyn the ideas of the revolutionaries take on an elusive and unmanageable quality, a dynamic self-intensifying character that transcended the intentions and desires of any of the historical participants. By emphasizing how the thought of the colonists was "strangely reshaped, turned in unfamiliar directions," by describing how the Americans "indeliberately, half-knowingly" groped toward "conclusions they could not themselves clearly perceive," by demonstrating how new beliefs and hence new actions were the responses not to desire but to the logic of developing situations, Bailyn has wrested the explanation of the Revolution out of the realm of motivation in which the neo-Whig historians had confined it.

With this kind of approach to ideas, the degree of consistency and devotion to principles become less important, and indeed the major issues of motivation and responsibility over which historians have disagreed become largely irrelevant. Action becomes not the product of rational and conscious calculation but of dimly perceived and rapidly changing thoughts and situations, "where the familiar meaning of ideas and words faded away into confusion, and leaders felt themselves peering into a haze, seeking to bring shifting conceptions somehow into focus." Men become more the victims than the manipulators of their ideas, as their thought unfolds in ways few anticipated, "rapid, irreversible, and irresistible," creating new problems, new considerations, new ideas, which have their own unforeseen implications. In this kind of atmosphere the Revolution, not at first desired by the Americans, takes on something of an inevitable character, moving through a process of escalation into levels few had intended or perceived. It no longer makes sense to assign motives or responsibility to particular individuals for the totality of what happened. Men were involved in a complicated web of phe-

[13] *Ibid.,* 129.

nomena, ideas, and situations, from which in retrospect escape seems impossible.[14]

By seeking to uncover the motives of the Americans expressed in the revolutionary pamphlets, Bailyn has ended by demonstrating the autonomy of ideas as phenomena, where the ideas operate, as it were, over the heads of the participants, taking them in directions no one could have foreseen. His discussion of revolutionary thought thus represents a move back to a deterministic approach to the Revolution, a determinism, however, which is different from that which the neo-Whig historians have so recently and self-consciously abandoned. Yet while the suggested determinism is thoroughly idealist—indeed never before has the force of ideas in bringing on the Revolution been so emphatically put—its implications are not. By helping to purge our writing about the Revolution of its concentration on constitutional principles and its stifling judicial-like preoccupation with motivation and responsibility, the study serves to open the way for new questions and new appraisals. In fact, it is out of the very completeness of his idealist interpretation, out of his exposition of the extraordinary nature—the very dynamism and emotionalism—of the Americans' thought that we have the evidence for an entirely different, a behaviorist, perspective on the causes of the American Revolution. Bailyn's book-length introduction to his edition of revolutionary pamphlets is therefore not only a point of fulfillment for the idealist approach to the Revolution, it is also a point of departure for a new look at the social sources of the Revolution.

It seems clear that historians of eighteenth-century America and the Revolution cannot ignore the force of ideas in history to the extent that Namier and his students have done in their investigations of eighteenth-century English politics. This is not to say, however, that the Namier approach to English politics has been crucially limiting and distorting. Rather it may suggest that the Namier denigration of ideas and principles is inapplicable for American politics because the American social situation in which ideas operated was very different from that of eighteenth-century England. It may be that

[14] Bailyn, *Revolutionary Pamphlets,* I, 90, x, 169, 140. See Hannah Arendt, *On Revolution* (New York, 1963), 173: "American experience had taught the men of the Revolution that action, though it may be started in isolation and decided upon by single individuals for very different motives, can be accomplished only by some joint effort in which the motivation of single individuals . . . no longer counts. . . ."

ideas are less meaningful to a people in a socially stable situation. Only when ideas have become stereotyped reflexes do evasion and hypocrisy and the Namier mistrust of what men believe become significant. Only in a relatively settled society does ideology become a kind of habit, a bundle of widely shared and instinctive conventions, offering ready-made explanations for men who are not being compelled to ask any serious questions. Conversely, it is perhaps only in a relatively unsettled, disordered society, where the questions come faster than men's answers, that ideas become truly vital and creative.[15]

Paradoxically it may be the very vitality of the Americans' ideas, then, that suggests the need to examine the circumstances in which they flourished. Since ideas and beliefs are ways of perceiving and explaining the world, the nature of the ideas expressed is determined as much by the character of the world being confronted as by the internal development of inherited and borrowed conceptions. Out of the multitude of inherited and transmitted ideas available in the eighteenth century, Americans selected and emphasized those which seemed to make meaningful what was happening to them. In the colonists' use of classical literature, for example, "their detailed knowledge and engaged interest covered only one era and one small group of writers," Plutarch, Livy, Cicero, Sallust, and Tacitus—those who "had hated and feared the trends of their own time, and in their writing had contrasted the present with a better past, which they endowed with qualities absent from their own, corrupt era."[16] There was always, in Max Weber's term, some sort of elective affinity between the Americans' interests and their beliefs, and without that affinity their ideas would not have possessed the peculiar character and persuasiveness they did. Only the most revolutionary social needs and circumstances could have sustained such revolutionary ideas.[17]

[15] See Sir Lewis Namier, *The Structure of Politics at the Accession of George III*, 2d ed. (London, 1961), 16; Sir Lewis Namier, "Human Nature in Politics," in *Personalities and Power: Selected Essays* (New York, 1965), 5–6.

[16] Bailyn, *Revolutionary Pamphlets*, I, 22. The French Revolutionaries were using the same group of classical writings to express their estrangement from the *ancien régime* and their hope for the new order. Harold T. Parker, *The Cult of Antiquity and the French Revolutionaries: A Study in the Development of the Revolutionary Spirit* (Chicago, 1937), 22–23.

[17] The relation of ideas to social structure is one of the most perplexing and intriguing in the social sciences. For an extensive bibliography on the subject see

When the ideas of the Americans are examined comprehensively, when all of the Whig rhetoric, irrational as well as rational, is taken into account, one cannot but be struck by the predominant characteristics of fear and frenzy, the exaggerations and the enthusiasm, the general sense of social corruption and disorder out of which would be born a new world of benevolence and harmony where Americans would become the "eminent examples of every divine and social virtue."[18] As Bailyn and the propaganda studies have amply shown, there is simply too much fanatical and millennial thinking even by the best minds that must be explained before we can characterize the Americans' ideas as peculiarly rational and legalistic and thus view the Revolution as merely a conservative defense of constitutional liberties. To isolate refined and nicely reasoned arguments from the writings of John Adams and Jefferson is not only to disregard the more inflamed expressions of the rest of the Whigs but also to overlook the enthusiastic extravagance—the paranoiac obsession with a diabolical Crown conspiracy and the dream of a restored Saxon era—in the thinking of Adams and Jefferson themselves.

The ideas of the Americans seem, in fact, to form what can only be called a revolutionary syndrome. If we were to confine ourselves to examining the revolutionary rhetoric alone, apart from what happened politically or socially, it would be virtually impossible to distinguish the American Revolution from any other revolution in modern Western history. In the kinds of ideas expressed the American Revolution is remarkably similar to the seventeenth-century Puritan Revolution and to the eighteenth-century French Revolution: the same general disgust with a chaotic and corrupt world, the same anxious and angry bombast, the same excited fears of conspiracies by depraved men, the same utopian hopes for the construction of a new and virtuous order.[19] It was not that this syndrome of ideas was

Norman Birnbaum, "The Sociological Study of Ideology (1940–60)," *Current Sociology,* IX (1960).

[18] Jacob Duché, *The American Vine, A Sermon, Preached . . . Before the Honourable Continental Congress, July 20th, 1775 . . .* (Philadelphia, 1775), 29.

[19] For recent discussions of French and Puritan revolutionary rhetoric see Peter Gay, "Rhetoric and Politics in the French Revolution," *Amer. Hist. Rev.,* LXVI (1960–61), 664–676; Michael Walzer, "Puritanism as a Revolutionary Ideology," *History and Theory,* III (1963), 59–90. This entire issue of *History and Theory* is devoted to a symposium on the uses of theory in the study of history. In addition to the Walzer article, I have found the papers by Samuel H. Beer, "Causal Explana-

simply transmitted from one generation or from one people to another. It was rather perhaps that similar, though hardly identical, social situations called forth within the limitations of inherited and available conceptions similar modes of expression. Although we need to know much more about the sociology of revolutions and collective movements, it does seem possible that particular patterns of thought, particular forms of expression, correspond to certain basic social experiences. There may be, in other words, typical modes of expression, typical kinds of beliefs and values, characterizing a revolutionary situation, at least within roughly similar Western societies. Indeed, the types of ideas manifested may be the best way of identifying a collective movement as a revolution. As one student of revolutions writes, "It is on the basis of a knowledge of men's beliefs that we can distinguish their behaviour from riot, rebellion or insanity."[20]

It is thus the very nature of the Americans' rhetoric—its obsession with corruption and disorder, its hostile and conspiratorial outlook, and its millennial vision of a regenerated society—that reveals as nothing else apparently can the American Revolution as a true revolution with its sources lying deep in the social structure. For this kind of frenzied rhetoric could spring only from the most severe sorts of social strain. The grandiose and feverish language of the Americans was indeed the natural, even the inevitable, expression of a people caught up in a revolutionary situation, deeply alienated from the existing sources of authority and vehemently involved in a basic reconstruction of their political and social order. The hysteria of the Americans' thinking was but a measure of the intensity of their revolutionary passions. Undoubtedly the growing American alienation from British authority contributed greatly to this revolutionary situation. Yet the very weakness of the British imperial system and the accumulating ferocity of American antagonism to it suggests that other sources of social strain were being fed into the revolutionary movement. It may be that the Progressive historians in their preoccupation with internal social problems were more right than we have recently been willing to grant. It would be repeating their

tion and Imaginative Re-enactment," and Charles Tilly, "The Analysis of a Counter-Revolution," very stimulating and helpful.

[20] Bryan A. Wilson, "Millennialism in Comparative Perspective," *Comparative Studies in Society and History,* VI (1963–64), 108. See also Neil J. Smelser, *Theory of Collective Behaviour* (London, 1962), 83, 120, 383.

mistake, however, to expect this internal social strain necessarily to take the form of coherent class conflict or overt social disruption. The sources of revolutionary social stress may have been much more subtle but no less severe.

Of all of the colonies in the mid-eighteenth century, Virginia seems the most settled, the most lacking in obvious social tensions. Therefore, as it has been recently argued, since conspicuous social issues were nonexistent, the only plausible remaining explanation for the Virginians' energetic and almost unanimous commitment to the Revolution must have been their devotion to constitutional principles.[21] Yet it may be that we have been looking for the wrong kind of social issues, for organized conflicts, for conscious divisions, within the society. It seems clear that Virginia's difficulties were not the consequence of any obvious sectional or class antagonism, tidewater versus piedmont, aristocratic planters versus yeomen farmers. There was apparently no discontent with the political system that went deep into the social structure. But there does seem to have been something of a social crisis within the ruling group itself, which intensely aggravated the Virginians' antagonism to the imperial system. Contrary to the impression of confidence and stability that the Virginia planters have historically acquired, they seemed to have been in very uneasy circumstances in the years before the Revolution. The signs of the eventual nineteenth-century decline of the Virginia gentry were, in other words, already felt if not readily apparent.

The planters' ability to command the acquiescence of the people seems extraordinary compared to the unstable politics of the other colonies. But in the years before independence there were signs of increasing anxiety among the gentry over their representative role. The ambiguities in the relationship between the Burgesses and their constituents erupted into open debate in the 1750s. And men began voicing more and more concern over the mounting costs of elections and growing corruption in the soliciting of votes, especially by "those who have neither natural nor acquired parts to recommend them."[22] By the late sixties and early seventies the newspapers were filled

[21] Tate, "Coming of the Revolution in Virginia," 324–343.

[22] Robert E. and B. Katherine Brown, *Virginia, 1705–1786: Democracy or Aristocracy?* (East Lansing, Mich., 1964), 236; Alexander White to Richard Henry Lee, 1758, quoted in J. R. Pole, "Representation and Authority in Virginia from the Revolution to Reform," *The Journal of Southern History* XXIV (1958), 23.

with warnings against electoral influence, bribery, and vote seeking. The freeholders were stridently urged to "strike at the Root of this growing Evil; be influenced by Merit alone," and avoid electing "obscure and inferior persons."[23] It was as if ignoble ambition and demagoguery, one bitter pamphlet remarked, were a "Daemon lately come among us to disturb the peace and harmony, which had so long subsisted in this place."[24] In this context Robert Munford's famous play, *The Candidates,* written in 1770, does not so much confirm the planters' confidence as it betrays their uneasiness with electoral developments in the colony, "when coxcombs and jockies can impose themselves upon it for men of learning." Although disinterested virtue eventually wins out, Munford's satire reveals the kinds of threats the established planters faced from ambitious knaves and blockheads who were turning representatives into slaves of the people.[25]

By the eve of the Revolution the planters were voicing a growing sense of impending ruin, whose sources seemed in the minds of many to be linked more and more with the corrupting British connection and the Scottish factors, but for others frighteningly rooted in "our Pride, our Luxury, and Idleness."[26] The public and private writings of Virginians became obsessed with "corruption," "virtue," and "luxury." The increasing defections from the Church of England, even among ministers and vestrymen, and the remarkable growth of dissent in the years before the Revolution, "so much complained of

[23] Purdie and Dixon's *Virginia Gazette* (Williamsburg), Apr. 11, 1771; Rind's *Virginia Gazette,* Oct. 31, 1771. See Lester J. Cappon and Stella F. Duff, eds., *Virginia Gazette Index, 1736–1780* (Williamsburg, 1950), I, 351, for entries on the astounding increase in essays on corruption and cost of elections in the late 1760s and early 1770s.

[24] *The Defence of Injur'd Merit Unmasked; or, the Scurrilous Piece of Philander Dissected and Exposed to Public View. By a Friend to Merit, wherever found* (n.p., 1771), 10. Robert Carter chose to retire to private life in the early 1770s rather than adjust to the "new system of politicks" that had begun "to prevail generally." Quoted in Louis Morton, *Robert Carter of Nomini Hall: A Virginia Tobacco Planter of the Eighteenth Century* (Williamsburg, 1941), 52.

[25] Jay B. Hubbell and Douglass Adair, "Robert Munford's *The Candidates,*" *Wm. and Mary Qtly.,* 3d Ser., V (1948), 246, 238. The ambivalence in Munford's attitude toward the representative process is reflected in the different way historians have interpreted his play. Cf. *ibid.,* 223–225, with Brown, *Virginia,* 236–237. Munford's fear of "men who aim at power without merit" was more fully expressed in his later play, *The Patriots,* written in 1775 or 1776. Courtlandt Canby, "Robert Munford's *The Patriots,*" *Wm. and Mary Qtly.,* 3d Ser., VI (1949), 437–503, quotation from 450.

[26] [John Randolph], *Considerations on the Present State of Virginia* ([Williamsburg], 1774), in Earl G. Swem, ed., *Virginia and the Revolution: Two Pamphlets, 1774* (New York, 1919), 16; Purdie and Dixon's *Virginia Gazette,* Nov. 25, 1773.

in many parts of the colony," further suggests some sort of social stress. The strange religious conversions of Robert Carter may represent only the most dramatic example of what was taking place less frenziedly elsewhere among the gentry.[27] By the middle of the eighteenth century it was evident that many of the planters were living on the edge of bankruptcy, seriously overextended and spending beyond their means in an almost frantic effort to fulfill the aristocratic image they had created of themselves.[28] Perhaps the importance of the Robinson affair in the 1760s lies not in any constitutional changes that resulted but in the shattering effect the disclosures had on that virtuous image.[29] Some of the planters expressed openly their fears for the future, seeing the products of their lives being destroyed in the reckless gambling and drinking of their heirs, who, as Landon Carter put it, "play away and play it all away."[30]

The Revolution in Virginia, "produced by the wantonness of the Gentleman," as one planter suggested,[31] undoubtedly gained much of its force from this social crisis within the gentry. Certainly more was expected from the Revolution than simply a break from British imperialism, and it was not any crude avoidance of British debts.[32] The revolutionary reforms, like the abolition of entail and primogeniture, may have signified something other than mere symbolic legal adjustments to an existing reality. In addition to being an attempt to make the older tidewater plantations more economically competitive with lands farther west, the reforms may have represented a real effort to redirect what was believed to be a dangerous tendency in social and family development within the ruling gentry. The Virginians were not after all aristocrats who could afford having their entailed families' estates in the hands of weak or ineffectual eldest sons.

[27] Rind's *Virginia Gazette,* Sept. 8, 1774; Brown, *Virginia,* 252–254; Morton, *Robert Carter,* 231–250.

[28] See George Washington to George Mason, Apr. 5, 1769, in John C. Fitzpatrick, ed., *The Writings of George Washington* (Washington, 1931–44), II, 502; Carl Bridenbaugh, *Myths and Realities: Societies of the Colonial South* (New York, 1963), 5, 10, 14, 16; Emory G. Evans, "Planter Indebtedness and the Coming of the Revolution in Virginia," *Wm. and Mary Qtly.,* 3d Ser., XIX (1962), 518–519.

[29] Rind's *Virginia Gazette,* Aug. 15, 1766. See Carl Bridenbaugh, "Violence and Virtue in Virginia, 1766: or The Importance of the Trivial," Massachusetts Historical Society, *Proceedings,* LXXVI (1964), 3–29.

[30] Quoted in Bridenbaugh, *Myths and Realities,* 27. See also Morton, *Robert Carter,* 223–225.

[31] John A. Washington to R. H. Lee, June 20, 1778, quoted in Pole, "Representation and Authority in Virginia," 28.

[32] Evans, "Planter Indebtedness," 526–527.

Entail, as the preamble to the 1776 act abolishing it stated, had often done "injury to the morals of youth by rendering them independent of, and disobedient to, their parents."[33] There was too much likelihood, as the Nelson family sadly demonstrated, that a single wayward generation would virtually wipe out what had been so painstakingly built.[34] George Mason bespoke the anxieties of many Virginians when he warned the Philadelphia Convention in 1787 that "our own Children will in a short time be among the general mass."[35]

Precisely how the strains within Virginia society contributed to the creation of a revolutionary situation and in what way the planters expected independence and republicanism to alleviate their problems, of course, need to be fully explored. It seems clear, however, from the very nature of the ideas expressed that the sources of the Revolution in Virginia were much more subtle and complicated than a simple antagonism to the British government. Constitutional principles alone do not explain the Virginians' almost unanimous determination to revolt. And if the Revolution in the seemingly stable colony of Virginia possessed internal social roots, it is to be expected that the other colonies were experiencing their own forms of social strain that in a like manner sought mitigation through revolution and republicanism.

It is through the Whigs' ideas, then, that we may be led back to take up where the Progressive historians left off in their investigation of the internal social sources of the Revolution. By working through the ideas—by reading them imaginatively and relating them to the objective social world they both reflected and confronted—we may be able to eliminate the unrewarding distinction between conscious and unconscious motives, and eventually thereby to combine a Whig with a Tory, an idealist with a behaviorist, interpretation. For the ideas, the rhetoric, of the Americans were never obscuring but

[33] Julian P. Boyd and others, eds., *The Papers of Thomas Jefferson* (Princeton, 1950--), I, 560. Most of our knowledge of entail and primogeniture in Virginia stems from an unpublished doctoral dissertation, Clarence R. Keim, Influence of Primogeniture and Entail in the Development of Virginia, (University of Chicago, 1926). Keim's is a very careful and qualified study and conclusions from his evidence—other than the obvious fact that much land was held in fee simple—are by no means easy to make. See particularly pp. 56, 60–62, 110–114, 122, 195–196.

[34] Emory S. Evans, "The Rise and Decline of the Virginia Aristocracy in the Eighteenth Century: The Nelsons," in Darrett B. Rutman, ed., *The Old Dominion: Essays for Thomas Perkins Abernethy* (Charlottesville, 1964), 73–74.

[35] Max Farrand, ed., *The Records of the Federal Convention of 1787* (New Haven, 1911), I, 56; Bridenbaugh, *Myths and Realities,* 14, 16.

remarkably revealing of their deepest interests and passions. What they expressed may not have been for the most part factually true, but it was always psychologically true. In this sense their rhetoric was never detached from the social and political reality; and indeed it becomes the best entry into an understanding of that reality. Their repeated overstatements of reality, their incessant talk of "tyranny" when there seems to have been no real oppression, their obsession with "virtue," "luxury," and "corruption," their devotion to "liberty" and "equality"—all these notions were neither manipulated propaganda nor borrowed empty abstractions, but ideas with real personal and social significance for those who used them. Propaganda could never move men to revolution. No popular leader, as John Adams put it, has ever been able "to persuade a large people, for any length of time together, to think themselves wronged, injured, and oppressed, unless they really were, and saw and felt it to be so."[36] The ideas had relevance; the sense of oppression and injury, although often displaced onto the imperial system, was nonetheless real. It was indeed the meaningfulness of the connection between what the Americans said and what they felt that gave the ideas their propulsive force and their overwhelming persuasiveness.

It is precisely the remarkable revolutionary character of the Americans' ideas now being revealed by historians that best indicates that something profoundly unsettling was going on in the society, that raises the question, as it did for the Progressive historians, why the Americans should have expressed such thoughts. With their crude conception of propaganda the Progressive historians at least attempted to grapple with the problem. Since we cannot regard the ideas of the revolutionaries as simply propaganda, the question still remains to be answered. "When 'ideas' in full cry drive past," wrote Arthur F. Bentley in his classic behavioral study, *The Process of Government,* "the thing to do with them is to accept them as an indication that something is happening; and then search carefully to find out what it really is they stand for, what the factors of the social life are that are expressing themselves through the ideas."[37] Precisely because they sought to understand both the revolutionary

[36] John Adams, "Novanglus," in Charles F. Adams, ed., *The Works of John Adams* (Boston, 1851), IV, 14.
[37] Arthur F. Bentley, *The Process of Government: A Study of Social Pressures* (Chicago, 1908), 152.

ideas and American society, the behaviorist historians of the Progressive generation, for all of their crude conceptualizations, their obsession with "class" and hidden economic interests, and their treatment of ideas as propaganda, have still offered us an explanation of the revolutionary era so powerful and so comprehensive that no purely intellectual interpretation will ever replace it.

Suggestions for Additional Reading

Louis M. Hacker has argued the viewpoint presented at the opening of this volume even more pointedly in "The First American Revolution," *Columbia University Quarterly* 27, no. 3, pt. 1 (September 1935). A very similar view is expressed by Charles A. and Mary R. Beard in chapters 5 and 6 of *The Rise of American Civilization* (New York, 1934). Charles M. Andrews has summarized his view in "The American Revolution: An Interpretation," *American Historical Review* 31 (January 1926); more extensive treatment is given in his *The Colonial Background of the American Revolution* (New Haven, 1931), particularly in the final two essays. H. E. Egerton, *The Causes and Character of the American Revolution* (Oxford and New York, 1923), and W. Alison Phillips, "The Declaration of Independence," *Edinburgh Review* 244 (July 1926): 1–17, represent two significant interpretations by British scholars, while Arthur M. Schlesinger's "The American Revolution" in his *New Viewpoints in American History* (New York, 1922) presents a further view, in which considerable stress is laid on the role of the merchants. Bernard Bailyn's *Ideological Origins of the American Revolution* (Cambridge, Mass., 1967), an expansion of his important Introduction to his *Pamphlets of the American Revolution* (Cambridge, Mass., 1965), is the best known presentation of the viewpoint which emphasizes ideological more than social and economic factors.

In most cases, the works just mentioned offer interpretive or analytical, rather than narrative, treatment. For more general considerations of the period, the reader would do well to consult Carl Becker, *The Eve of the Revolution* (New York, 1921), in which Becker shows the unfolding constitutional crisis as it might have appeared to Benjamin Franklin as he watched from England; and Evarts Boutell Greene, *The Revolutionary Generation, 1763–1790* (The History of American Life, vol. 4, New York, 1943), in which the emphasis is on economic and social factors. A more popularized but interesting account, which represents the revolutionary period as one long series of American provocations against a long-suffering British king and government and paints American leaders in much less heroic guise than is usual, is given by British author Michael Pearson in *Those Damned Rebels* (New York, 1972). Sydney George Fisher, *The Struggle for American Independence* (2 vols., Philadelphia, 1908), and Edward Channing, *A History of the United States* (vol. 3, New York, 1912), are still among the best general summaries of the period.

Jackson Turner Main's work, *The Social Structure of Revolutionary America* (Princeton, N.J., 1966), is an excellent discussion of the subject described by its title. A good summary of the sectional and class divisions of colonial America is to be found in chapter 3 of Samuel Eliot Morison and Henry Steele Commager, *The Growth of the American Nation* (New York, 1937). Important works dealing generally with the revolutionary period and with the issues raised in this volume include John Richard Alden, *The American Revolution* (New York, 1954); Lawrence Henry Gipson, *The Coming of the Revolution* (New York, 1954); John C. Miller, *Origins of the American Revolution* (Stanford, Cal., 1959), the revised edition of a work originally published in 1943; and Richard H. Morris, *The American Revolution Reconsidered* (New York, 1968).

There are a number of studies which focus attention upon the influence of particular sections or classes. Among the most useful of these are James Truslow Adams, *Revolutionary New England, 1691–1776* (Boston, 1923), which is written with a distinct economic emphasis; Isaac Samuel Harrell, *Loyalism in Virginia* (Durham, N.C., 1926); and Arthur M. Schlesinger, *The Colonial Merchants and the American Revolution, 1763–1776* (New York, 1918), which lends considerable support to the economic interpretation. Elisha P. Douglass, *Rebels and Democrats: The Struggle for Equal Rights and Majority Rule during the American Revolution* (Chapel Hill, N.C., 1955), interprets the role of merchants and radicals somewhat differently than does Schlesinger.

A wealth of material concerning sectional and class conflicts (or their absence) in the colonies is to be found in the many works dealing with particular sections, colonies, or towns. Among the most notable of these are John Richard Alden, *The South in the Revolution* (Baton Rouge, La., 1957); Carl Bridenbaugh, *Cities in Revolt: Urban Life in America, 1743–1776* (New York, 1955); Robert E. Brown, *Middle-Class Democracy and the Revolution in Massachusetts* (Ithaca, N.Y., 1955), together with Brown's rebuttal and the original article by John Cary, "Statistical Method and the Brown Thesis on Colonial Democracy," *William and Mary Quarterly* 20 (April 1963): 251–276; Mack E. Thompson, "The Ward-Hopkins Controversy and the American Revolution in Rhode Island: An Interpretation," *William and Mary Quarterly* 16 (July 1959): 363–375; and Richard Walsh, *Charleston's Sons of Liberty: A Study of the Artisans, 1763–1789* (Columbia, S.C., 1959).

For more detailed analysis of the political and constitutional ideas of the Revolution, the reader should consult Charles H. McIlwain, *The American Revolution: A Constitutional Interpretation* (New York, 1923); Randolph Greenfield Adams, *Political Ideas of the American Revolution* (3d Ed., New York, 1958); and Claude H. Van Tyne, *The Causes of the War of Independence* (Boston, 1922). Carl Becker, *The Declaration of Independence* (New York, 1933), examines the significance and the sources of the ideas embodied in that document. A good account of the natural law background of American political thought of the time is to be found in Charles Frederic Mullett, *Fundamental Law and the American Revolution, 1760–1776* (New York, 1966), or Benjamin F. Wright, Jr., *American Interpretations of Natural Law* (Cambridge, Mass., 1931). Mullett also offers an analysis of the thought underlying British colonial policy in "English Imperial Thinking, 1764–1783," *Political Science Quarterly* 45 (December 1930). A significant work dealing with the whole context of British politics in which imperial ideas were formulated and developed is Charles R. Ritcheson, *British Politics and the American Revolution* (Norman, Okla., 1954); while Jack Richon Pole, *Political Representation in England and the Origins of the American Revolution* (New York, 1966), provides an excellent account of that most important segment of political ideas concerned with the problem of representation.

Philip G. Davidson, *Propaganda and the American Revolution* (Chapel Hill, N.C., 1941), offers an analysis of the ideas, symbols, and slogans of both revolutionists and Tories, and of the techniques and machinery used to win or to discourage support of the revolutionary cause. Two works of Arthur M. Schlesinger are also of interest in this connection: *Prelude to Independence: The Newspaper War on Britain, 1764–1776* (New York, 1958), and "Political Mobs and the American Revolution, 1765–1776," *Proceedings of the American Philosophical Society* 99 (August 1955): 244–250. Also of note here is Gordon S. Wood, "A Note on Mobs in the American Revolution," *William and Mary Quarterly* 23 (October 1966): 635–642. Military aspects of the conflict are considered in Allen French, *The First Year of the American Revolution* (New York, 1934); Eric Robson, *The American Revolution in Its Political and Military Aspects* (New York, 1955);

and John Shy, *The Road to Lexington: The Role of the British Army in the Coming of the Revolution* (Princeton, N.J., 1965).

Excellent collections of contemporary materials may be found in Bernard Bailyn, *Pamphlets of the American Revolution, 1750–1776* (2 vols., Cambridge, Mass., 1965); Henry Steele Commager, *Documents of American History* (New York, 1934); Henry Steele Commager and Richard B. Morris, *The Spirit of '76: The Story of the American Revolution as Told by the Participants* (Indianapolis, Ind., 1958); Bruce Ingham Granger, *Political Satire in the American Revolution* (Ithaca, N.Y., 1960); Albert Bushnell Hart, *American History Told by Contemporaries* (2 vols., New York, 1898); Samuel Eliot Morison, *Sources and Documents Illustrating the American Revolution, 1764–1788* (New York, 1929); Jack Richon Pole, *The Revolution in America, 1754–1788: Documents and Commentaries* (Stanford, Cal., 1970); and Benjamin F. Wright, Jr., *A Source Book of American Political Theory* (New York, 1929). An illuminating Report of the Boston Committee of Correspondence, written November 20, 1772, by Samuel Adams, is printed in part, together with Benjamin Franklin's Preface to the English edition of the Report, as *Old South Leaflet, No. 173* (Boston, n.d.).

The reader who wishes to compare the American Revolution with other great revolutions will find much to reward him in Crane Brinton, *The Anatomy of Revolution* (New York, 1938). For further historiographical arguments or compilations of them, he may consult Robert E. Brown, *Carl Becker on History and the American Revolution* (East Lansing, Mich., 1970); Jack P. Greene, ed., *The Reinterpretation of the American Revolution* (New York, 1968), especially Greene's Introduction, pp. 2–74; and Esmond Wright, ed., *Causes and Consequences of the American Revolution* (Chicago, 1966).

1 2 3 4 5 6 7 8 9 10